WORLEY'S IDENTITY DISCOVERY PROFILE (WIDP)

ANALYSIS OF THE 5 TEMPERAMENTS

MAXIMIZING INDIVIDUAL AND GROUP SUCCESS

WORLEY'S IDENTITY DISCOVERY PROFILE (WIDP)

ANALYSIS OF THE 5 TEMPERAMENTS

MAXIMIZING INDIVIDUAL AND GROUP SUCCESS

John Wayne Worley, Ph.D.

www.WIDP.org

Copyright © John Wayne Worley, Ph.D.

WIDP

WORLEY'S IDENTITY DISCOVERY PROFILE (WIDP)

ANALYSIS OF THE 5 TEMPERAMENTS

MAXIMIZING INDIVIDUAL AND GROUP SUCCESS©

Cover Image by IndieGraphics
Layout & design by Samuel Stevens in cooperation with StaceyCo.

Worley's Identity Discovery Profile WIDP, Inc.
Published by John Wayne Worley, Ph.D. 2023

For information:
Worley's Identity Discovery Profile WIDP, Inc.
www.WIDP.org
info@WIDP.org

DEDICATION

*My dear, precious High School "sweetheart" and wife for 62 years,
Barbara Ann Smith Worley (Barb), gets the accolades!
You are the most devoted and dedicated person in my life that
enabled me to complete this book and the huge project of WIDP.
I am grateful and will always be indebted to you. Without the time
needed to complete these projects and write this book on the
understanding of temperament and the value it will provide people,
this book and this system would not be here for them today.
They will be grateful to you just as I am! Everyone that is touched by
reading their temperament profile and reading this book
will find that their quality of life will improve.
Why? Because of the sacrifice of your time with me
so I could write and create this program for them.*

*Barb may you and our wonderful family (numbering 34 currently) be
blessed in every way by the production of this book and the WIDP
profile system. It's designed to help people learn how to get their needs
and desires fulfilled and be a more functional person in their life.*

*I thank God who gave me my unique temperament design and
intelligence that empowered and gifted me to be able to create WIDP
and write this book.*

*Thank you, God, for who I am!
Thank you, Barb, for your devotion to God and me!*

*Respectfully and with Endless love,
Your Soul Mate John*

FOREWORD

My father, Don Stevens, met "Dr. John" at a ministers' conference in the early-mid 90's. He noticed Dr. John at a booth, a man hard to miss, with a tall and confident demeanor. He visited his booth to see what he had to offer (Dad was always interested in learning what was out there). They hit it off immediately. Dad caught the vision and the power of WIDP, grabbed brochures, and when he went home, told my mother all about it. He desperately needed a tool that could help the people in the congregation. He had a couch in his office that was frequented by people who came to vent and get sound advice. A Preacher's job extends well beyond the pulpit.

Dad mentioned to Mom that he wanted to get certified in WIDP, but it would take a plane ticket, meals, seminar and software costs, etc. The total, he figured, would be just over $900, a price far out of reach. So, ever faithful, Dad said we'll just pray about it.

Years passed and Dad talked with Dr. John here and there, as they had become good friends and had much in common, from military service to both being ministers, counselors, and sharing a deep love for people.

Dr. John mentioned there was a seminar coming up late one year and Dad should attend. One day an odd return address was on a piece of mail, it was from a hospital he had been treated in over a decade prior. When he opened it, he saw a refund check, noted "for overpayment from a procedure" – in the amount of just over $900. He knew this was the sign to go.

So, Dad flew up (along with his nephew Dwayne), attended the seminar, and had wonderful conversations with Dr. John Wayne Worley right there in his home.

When it was time to depart, they arrived at the airport, Dr. John bid them farewell, Dad and Dwayne checked in, and they sat at a restaurant booth not far from their terminal, continuing to talk about the possibilities. They got so carried away in conversation and excitement about WIDP, they completely missed their flight!

This story was the first of many from the impact of WIDP. When he returned home, he gave the Profile to all 3 of us kids; myself and my two sisters. I was 12 years old at the time, and my Dad IMMEDIATELY changed the way he raised us. The revealing of our true needs altered how he dealt with each one of us, uniquely and intentionally. As I look back, I'm humbled by his choice to change his approach for our sake. Was he willing to do that before? I'm sure! He just didn't have the tools.

At that same time, Dad was pursuing becoming a Licensed Pastoral Counselor, and once obtained, he began using WIDP as his first step to any session. With that initial intake step, he was getting the critical information about them that he needed to know exactly how he should approach each person or couple that came through his doors. He soon found out that he only needed about 3 sessions with them before they were ready to launch out on their own with clear insight and direction.

I got the rare privilege to chat with him on many occasions, having a sincere love for people and God, we had a lot in common and Dad was quite knowledgeable (and qualified) to speak about either, often both!   He was always careful when talking about sessions he had, never mentioning names, or revealing private information. He simply wanted to discuss the general situation, talk about their Temperaments, and how he approached it. We would talk for *hours*.

I saw the potential of WIDP quite immediately, just as Dr. John, Dad, and Dwayne had even prior to '97.

After my military service, I had the unique privilege of working in downtown Houston with a top Oil & Gas company, amongst their Senior Leadership. I noticed over the next year that the problems in a multi-billion-dollar company were the exact same problems in a mom & pop shop, or even in close relationships. It was just people; and everyone was just trying to get their needs met. Even the most seasoned managers and most well-paid bosses know that business is powered by its people, but they just don't know exactly what to do to KNOW their people are receiving effective leadership that leads to top performance and top profit. The best people tools the world had to offer would give brief Ah-ha's in a team-building session, but come Monday morning, everything went back to business as usual. And worse, measuring the ROI on such tools was (and is) non-existent.

Fortunately, I was born with a heart (and Temperament) for just such a quest. I had spent my early adult years, my extra time in the military, my days in corporate America, and the several years that followed learning everything I could about people, about relationships, and about what was out there to help businesses function. I studied the most notable books, articles, research studies, and certainly had many conversations about these things with very qualified people.

One resolute truth had emerged in all that time of many possibilities and inventions – there was nothing that came close to WIDP and what it could do for people and for organizations.

So, in 2015, I launched my company to change that, with WIDP at the helm of my business model. The funny part was, I wasn't even certified in WIDP yet! I began speaking with Dr. John, through Dad, and even teamed up with a few potential clients. Finally in 2017, my dream came true, and I traveled to the beautiful Northeast to be trained by the man, himself, now responsible for 2 generations of Certified WIDP representatives. Meeting Dr. John and Barbara remains a cornerstone of my life. Since then, we have become quite close and have almost daily conversations, often talking about big visions, and continue to add to the arsenal of capabilities of WIDP.

Personally, since becoming certified, I chose to really put WIDP to the test, to see the extent of its accuracy. During individual result interpretations, management training, marriage retreats, couples' sessions, and more, I would ask questions that were formulated to be Temperament specific, and see if they would give a Temperament-specific answer, which would verify their results were correct; or, it could turn out to be quite embarrassing where they look at me funny for asking such a question. What I found after over 300 sessions was quite astonishing. Not only did WIDP hit the bullseye over and over from my viewpoint, they would comment on their own about how "spot-on" it was. Sometimes their answer would be so accurate I would just chuckle – WIDP for the clutch, once again. In 21 years of being aware of the tool and over 6 years of using it, it has proven to me with zero doubt that this is the tool people deserve. It is the fundamental reference point to finally reveal who you truly are. WIDP came through for me when I needed it. It can prove to you, too, that you are valuable. You are loved. You are unique. You are intentional.

It has been an honor and privilege to offer what little help I could to make this book, this tool, this program, and this gift for people the best it can be. WIDP is a world-changing tool. It is a tool ready to be equipped and used to benefit mankind.

I'm forever grateful for my Dad, for Dr. John, for Dwayne, for all that support my vision and dream, and for SO many people that have experienced for themselves the joy of finally knowing who they are because of WIDP.

With eternal gratitude,

Sam Stevens
Certified WIDP Affiliate Manager and outspoken WIDP Advocate

CONTENTS

Preface

You! That is why I wrote this book!

Because I care about you and your future, the quality of your life, and I choose to show you how valuable you are through this book.

As a clinical psychologist, I found a tremendous gap of understanding in the flaws of humanity and the challenging remedy of cognitive behavioral therapy and quality assessment instruments. After spending many years as a clinician, I became increasingly burdened with the single question: "Why aren't the systemic processes working?" The formal education, licensures, certifications, diplomas, and degrees, plus being certified on the most popular assessments instruments on the market, left me feeling like knowledge betrayed me. At the root seemed to be a flawed clinical process to begin assessing individuals by their personality, character, or even their behavior.

I found that **I could not have lasting confidence in modern assessments**, because they betray logic.

Here's what I witnessed:

I saw the same individuals, couples, and families returning time after time with the same problems and getting the same results — which amounted to short-term fixes. However, there were never any permanent positive results, primarily because none of the available "tools" addressed the fundamental, underlying problems that were causing these people pain. I spent thousands of dollars becoming certified on multiple character, personality, and behavioral instruments, and they all let me down in the end, providing no long-lasting solutions to life's complicated issues that clutter the mind, distort truth, and rob individuals of their quality of being emotionally, spiritually, and physically. I was frustrated, to say the least, that I could not provide more answers for them. I knew there was more to offer.

So, I created Worley's Identity Discovery Profile, also known as "WIDP". It is a 60-item questionnaire that only takes 7 - 10 minutes to complete and, from your answers, produces an immediate read-out of your results.

The training and application of WIDP has been utilized in multiple disciplines, including:
- Corporations, Executive Development, Pastoring, Leadership Development, Sales Management, Marketing, Upward Mobility, Change Agent Development, People Development, New Hire Assessing, and every area of Human Resource Management.
- Seminars presented on WIDP at the National Association of Sports Psychologists three years in a row.
- A Research project conducted at the Lowell Public School with a Class of 2nd Grade students (34), their teachers, teacher aids, Assistant Principal, and Principal.
- A High School Survey conducted at a Christian School Academy in New Hampshire.
- A Seminar in Lisbon, Portugal, for over 100 pastors from Portugal and Spain over five days, utilizing an interpreter.
- Workshops and presentations conducted throughout America.

- Wall Street - One of the former Twin Towers tycoons purchased WIDP Profiles and Software in a five-minute conversation!
- A Baseball Hall-of-Famer was a WIDP Affiliate Manager and had many WIDP Associates under his development.
- A Seminar for a church in St. Louis, MO with 39 elders who, along with every deacon, were interviewed individually.
- Conflict resolution for five board members of a finance corporation in Bedford, New Hampshire.
- Executive consulting for a real estate developer in New Hampshire who, after 7 years of trying, completed a 23-acre development in 18 months after WIDP training.
- Corporate consulting for a medical technology firm, developing their personnel infrastructure and identifying their top salespeople for recruitment using Temperament targeting.

For years, people who experienced the long-term benefits revealed by their new-found knowledge of WIDP challenged me to write a book about the tool because of the positive impact it had on their lives in every area.

As I considered whether to write such a book, I began to ask myself a series of questions. My thinking went something like this:

- Why should I undertake writing a book on a subject that is very misunderstood by most people, yet is a simple concept to understand?
    - You write the book because of the burning desire in your heart to help people out of their misery of doom and gloom. You write the book because you are compelled to attempt to free people from bondages that have held them captive for years, decades, even lifetimes. You write the book because you know it is needed because, otherwise, only the "tip of the iceberg" is offered by other resources claiming to be the best out there. People are in mental and emotional turmoil because they do not understand they are motivated by their specific Temperament needs. Yet, they also do not realize (as no one would) that the molding and shaping they went through by their upbringing and society may have been inappropriate and even unhealthy for them as a unique person. Thus, we have a society of dysfunctional, codependent behaviors (and beliefs) and mental health issues that require cognitive behavioral therapy (CBT) to bring balanced mental health back into their lives.

- How do you share with someone the idea that by understanding their Temperament their quality of life will change forever?
    - You take the time to teach them in a natural way that connects with their inner being, their thoughts about themselves, and their idea of themselves. You show them their goodness and uniqueness and that there will never be another person like them. Help them understand that they are extraordinary.

- Why write a book about Temperament?
    - Because for the most part, society does not understand what Temperament is or where it comes from — and to live successful lives they need to know what

Temperament is and how to function knowing that information. By writing a book about Temperament (WIDP), I can help more people understand than I could ever reach through one-on-one sessions or in a seminar setting. In psychology there are four terms that are used synonymously, but inappropriately: Temperament, Character, Personality, and Behavior.

- TEMPERAMENT refers to an individual's innate and biologically based patterns of behavior and emotional responses. Our belief is that Temperament is stable throughout one life and is often used to describe an individual's basic nature or disposition.
- CHARACTER refers to an individual's moral and ethical values, beliefs, and behaviors. It is often shaped by our culture, family of origin, societal norms, and can change over time as individuals mature and experience different life situations in different locations.
- PERSONALITY refers to an individual's overall pattern of thoughts, feelings, and behaviors that make up their unique identity. It is influenced by both nature and nurture and can change and develop over time.
- BEHAVIOR refers to an individual's actions or conduct in response to a given situation or stimuli. It is often influenced by both emotional and environmental issues.

To put it all together: While Temperament is stable throughout life and biologically determined at conception, character is shaped by our family of origin and environmental factors, personality is a combination of both nature and nurture, and behavior is the outward expression of an individual's Temperament, character, and personality in response to different situations.

So, I decided to write this book — a book about **TEMPERAMENT** — not character, personality, or behavior. As you read, take the time to grasp the concept of being the unique person that you are and your life will be transformed by **understanding your Temperament** by the end of this book!

WHO IS DR. WORLEY?
John W. Worley, Ph. D.
President and Founder of Worley's ID Profile

Dr. Worley, a Clinical Psychologist, has an earned Ph.D. in Marriage & Family Therapy from Evangelical Theological Seminary in Dixon, MO and a Master of Divinity (M.Div.) from Gordon Conwell Theological Seminary (GCTS). He is a Temperament Expert! He studied at the Institute of Holy Land Studies, Mount Zion, Jerusalem, Israel. Dr. Worley has thirty-nine years of experience in organizational and educational consulting, executive coaching, leadership development, seminar facilitations, and teaching.

Dr. Worley is a native of Ohio and has been a resident of Massachusetts since 1974. He and his wife Barbara Ann Worley have been married for over sixty-two years and have four daughters, three sons-in-law, seven granddaughters, one grandson and seven great-grandchildren at the time this book was written. He has been a leader in many capacities to include the following:

- Clinical Psychologist – Temperament Expert
- President and Founder of Worley's Identity Discovery Profile (WIDP), Inc.
- President and Founder of Christian Counselors Training International (C.C.T.I.)
- President and Clinical Director of Counseling in Groton
- Pastor and Co-founder of the Christian Church in Groton
- District Overseer of the New England District Christian Churches of North America (C.C.N.A.)
- President and Founder of Leadership Development Associates (L.D.A.)
- Currently a Corporate/Executive Coach (Developing People)
- Licensed Mental Health Clinical Counselor (MHCC) Commonwealth of Massachusetts
- Licensed Marriage and Family Therapist (M&FT) Commonwealth of Massachusetts
- Clinical Member of the American Association of Marriage and Family Therapists (AAMFT)
- Clinical Member of the Massachusetts Association of Marriage and Family Therapists (MaAMFT)
- Certified Sports Psychologist (CSP)
- Certified Taylor-Johnson Temperament Analysis (TJTA)
- Family Counseling & Enrichment, Individual, Marriage, Family, and Child Counseling
- Associate of Carlson Learning Company (a.k.a.; Performax and DiSC)
- Certified Behavioral Therapist from the Institute for Motivational Living (IML – Behavioral Certification)
- Diplomat of Clinical Forensic Counseling – American College of Certified Forensic Counseling with the designations of:
    - Forensic Assessment & Evaluation
    - Criminal Offender Counseling
    - Youthful Offender Counseling
    - Certified Domestic Violence Counselor
    - Certified Criminal Justice Counselor
- Diplomat Member National Board of Christian Clinical Therapists (NBCCT)
- Diplomat American Psychotherapy Association (APA)
- Diplomat Member of the Institute of Behavioral Science (IBS)

- Charter Member of the American Association of Christian Counselors (AACC)
- Advanced Teachers Certificate
- Ordained Minister and pastored for 10 years

Dr. Worley is a 15-year U.S. Army veteran wounded in Vietnam during the TET-1968 Offensive. He has many years of personal experience in dealing with problems that plague the military, corporations, educational institutions, professional counselors, ministries, families, and individuals. This personal experience, coupled with his extensive educational background, has earned him the reputation of being one of the best-qualified consultants and trainers in the trade today. Any individual or corporation who seeks reliable consulting or training will receive the best professional services available from Dr. Worley's "**Team WIDP**"!

As a Clinical Psychologist with thirty-nine years combined pastoral, consulting, and counseling experience, Dr. Worley has tried virtually every psychological, character, behavioral, Temperament, and personality questionnaire available. As a professional consultant, Dr. Worley feels obligated to his clients, individual or corporate, to meet their needs as quickly as possible.

Much time is spent during the initial interview process assessing corporations, individuals, Human Resource Departments, and managers before an effective plan is implemented. Dr. Worley was searching for a comprehensive profile that would help him assist corporations, educational institutions, professional counselors, ministries, families, and individuals to better understand themselves as individuals or to have a new understanding of their team members, co-workers, or potential new hires. The WIDP assessment requires completion of a simple questionnaire that measures their Temperament **needs** and **desires** in the Areas of **Social**, **Leadership**, and **Relationships**. Dr. Worley could not find any psychological, Temperament, behavioral, or personality profile anywhere that would accomplish the task of assessing these specific areas of an individual.

Dr. Worley tried the approaches of the various tests, profiles, instruments, assessments, and questionnaires, with their complex graphs, charts, demeaning individual labels, captivating adjectives, and besides being thousands of dollars more impoverished, received minimal benefits for his clients and for himself. Besides, who wants to administer and mine data from ten different assessments for usable information?

The frustrations that Dr. Worley encountered during the last three decades were that most assessments and profiles measure and focus on external behavior. The best response approach is cognitive behavioral therapy (CBT), understanding Temperament, the individual's internal needs and desires, for focused therapy where the true nature of behavior and motivation lives. When one is actively dealing with observable behavior that is of a contrary nature, emotional or intellectual, the necessary changes for improvement that need to be made within that person's behavior are evident. In these situations, behavioral modification is required and, in most cases, will produce acceptable results, although the behavioral change will only be temporary. Sub-par results are realized because **the root needs and desires** of the individual have not been dealt with appropriately or entirely. Therefore, adverse behavior and conflicts with co-workers and friends remain without permanent solutions. Instead, constant interruptions dealing with the manifestation of the adverse reaction continue to cost corporations, large or small, billions of dollars annually. Meanwhile, (an individual's) relationships continue to spiral into chaos.

When individuals produce unacceptable behavior because of their unmet needs, an objective behavioral profile is not adequate in identifying those problems. The physical pattern that defines one's personality based upon the present environmental focus of the individual answering the questions is defective because of the ecological focus based on behavior and not Temperament. The focus could be as a spouse, significant other, boss, friend, co-worker, employer, relative, or the local service station attendant. This discussion leads one away from the real issue(s) causing the personal turmoil. WIDP identifies the foundational <u>needs and desires</u> of an individual. With Temperament needs identified and fulfilled, the personality or behavior of the person becomes healthy and acceptable instead of being constantly in conflict with others (even within themselves!). Dr. Worley could not locate a profile that would meet the specifications of measuring a person's needs and desires based on that person's Temperament foundation.

It is important to realize that social interaction is influenced by the Temperaments of those involved in the conversation. Your emotional display is going to reflect your preferences based on your needs and desires according to your Temperament. So, you are going to react differently in a community setting than you do in a work setting or how you were at home, and so are the other people involved. We allow the people in our space to form our thoughts and opinions based on how we feel and what we perceive in that situation. Therefore, we may put on a "mask" and present what we want them to see, not what is really a reflection of who we are. Thus, you don't see the real person. Instead, you see their character, personality, or behavior. It is frustrating, to say the least.

After years of research and moving through a process of evaluating the most popular instruments
on the market; MBTI, DiSC, TJTA, PA, Keirsey, PUM, Strong's, Enneagram, and others, Dr. Worley decided to develop WIDP. This need for a more reliable, dependable assessment became apparent after years of counseling and consulting.

Dr. Worley feels that the most significant "people" issue existing today is the lack of understanding of fundamental <u>needs and desires</u> that are revealed only by understanding Temperament.

The objective of WIDP is not to measure intelligence or mental disorders, but to gauge needs and desires that are foundational to the individual profiled. There are many other excellent instruments for measuring intellect, psychological illness, and personality types. However, there lacked a questionnaire that got to the heart of the individual to identify their needs based on who they are foundationally.

Assisted by consultants, counseling professionals, and computer programmers, Dr. Worley asked the question,

"What would the ideal profile look like?"

Months later, Worley's Identity Discovery Profile (WIDP) was created!

Once you experience WIDP, you immediately see and feel the tremendous benefits. It is fast, easy, economical, and dependable. Corporations and individuals benefit equally. Due to measuring beneath surface behaviors and personality "masks", WIDP surpasses assessment instruments like:

- Myers Briggs Type Indicator (MBTI)
- Taylor Johnson Temperament Analysis (TJTA)
- Minnesota Multi-Phasic Personality Inventory (MMPI)
- Preventive Index
- Caliper
- Fundamental Individual Relational Orientation-Behavior (FIRO-B) (FIRO-BC)
- Personal Profile Survey (P.P.S.) (a.k.a. DiSC)
- Tim Lahaye's Temperament Assessment (with Florence Littauer)
- Enneagram
- Please Understand Me (PUM)
     …and others

WIDP is the most innovative Temperament assessment of the twenty-first century.

Try it today and see for yourself!

The WIDP Questionnaires are available in three languages: English, Spanish, and Portuguese, for Adult's and for Youth (Ages 6 —16). Visit **www.WIDP.org** to get your personal profile.

Chapter 1: What Is WIDP?

All around us we see chaos in relationships (ours and others'). We see social conflict, family dysfunction, corporate meltdowns, leadership failure, and in many cases, mental fatigue, and institutionalization. We look around us and realize there is something muddled in our world. And while we are trying to untangle the outer world, we find that the inner world is just as perplexing. WIDP was created to help uncomplicate both.

As human beings, we are seldom educated on *how* to be human. We all have needs to eat, to drink, and to sleep; basic physical biology. We know how vital air is to our lungs, yet we also curiously identify with someone who "feels like they're suffocating" in a relationship. A person could have trouble sleeping through the night yet could also sleep all night and still wake up tired. Identifying the differences between physical and emotional characteristics, WIDP interprets your emotional biological make-up, bringing powerful and personal "inside insight".

Your emotional biology drives the interactions and situations you live out every day. For example, emotional biology dictates why you gravitate to (or away from) people in society. These inborn qualities determine how you respond to situations in your career, how you make decisions, or even how you trust within your closest relationships. These qualities are attributes that do not change throughout your life. They are your emotional instincts teaching you about yourself, telling you how you breathe comfortably in your life, emotionally. They are what make you a very special, one-of-a-kind human being. There will never be another "you" in this world.

WIDP explains your specific emotional make-up contained within your genetic coding. It is this coding that determines your Temperaments. Through this knowledge of your Temperaments, as well as the Temperaments of others, you can participate in your life positively and confidently as the healthiest and most powerful "you" possible.

To understand a bit more the fundamental role Temperament plays in our daily lives, let's look at a fictional, yet common social scenario:

> It was a bright, beautiful Spring day when Frieda stepped out of her polished red Mustang into the sunshine. Tossing back her long, blonde hair, she waves at a small group sitting at a picnic table beneath a large oak tree.
>
> "Hiya, Sam!" she exclaimed, running over to the tall, middle-aged man in pressed khakis and a dark blue polo shirt. "How're the kids? - Oh, hi Jill, I didn't see you," noticing a short, plump brunette sitting on a lawn chair. "Hey, Pete!"
>
> "Kids are fine," Sam replied. "Um, Frieda, you *did* remember the grill, didn't you?"
>
> Frieda's face quickly went white, then blossomed red. "Ugh," she said, "I knew I forgot something. I mean, I brought the paper cups, napkins, and foil ... but, Sam, you can't expect me to remember everything."
>
> "Oh, great," Pete chimed in. "Sam, you should've known better than to leave it to her." He turned his back on the group and crossed his arms. "Now what're we supposed to

do?"

Sam resumed, "Frieda, at a cookout, the grill *is* everything." Sam turned to Jill, "Hon, you gather some wood for a fire while I get the matches and the chicken."

"Aw, c'mon Sammie," Jill whined. "Frieda forgot the grill - let her get the sticks. I don't want to eat chicken cooked on a smoky wood fire; it'll taste awful. Besides, there's nobody even here. Where is Dan and Sallie and Rob?"

"Dan's down by the creek fishing," said Pete. "Said to call him when the food's ready. Sallie and Rob aren't coming. They said these reunions always turn out disastrous."

"Guess they were right," mumbled Jill.

"I'm sorry, guys." Frieda clapped her hands together. "Look, this is simple - I'll drive back to town and get some friend chicken to-go! Then we won't have to worry about cooking! C'mon Pete, wanna take a ride?"

"And what about the chicken *we* brought?" Jill asked. "Besides, I hate fast food chicken. It's too greasy and salty."

"Wait," said Sam. "We can get a fire going if you'll all just help me gather some wood."

"Forget it, Sam," exclaimed Frieda. "C'mon Pete, let's go!"

"Whatever," said Pete.

"Sam, take me home," said Jill. "This is not what I had in mind at all."

"Me, neither" Sam said, shaking his head. "Frieda, when you pass by Dan, tell him *some* of us will be back in a little while."

End of Story!

What went wrong in this scenario? The short answer is: Everything!

While the above story is fictitious, the same type of scenario is played out millions of times each day across the world. People with different Temperaments are thrown together in a myriad of situations and just haven't learned to understand their own needs and desires, let alone how to recognize when their needs conflict with those of others. Yet, people are hoping and even expecting a great degree of harmony amongst very different individuals. It is frustrating, and unrealistic, isn't it?

How do we get to the point where we (1) understand our own needs and desires, (2) recognize other people's needs and desires, and (3) know how to approach our relationships for ultimate peace and harmony? This is where understanding the principles of Temperament will change your life. And *awareness* is the very first step.

Consider, again, the story above. While Temperament types were not mentioned specifically in this example, even a small "for instance" of Temperament information offers valuable, relatable insight.

Let's assume the one fishing, Dan, is the Temperament "Phlegmatic", a natural peacemaker (which is why he is far away from the conflict). Because Dan is a natural peacemaker, Dan happens to be the one person who could have helped resolve the situation. Ironically, the same characteristics that make Dan a peacemaker also drive the internal desire to avoid conflict altogether (conflict of any kind disrupts the peace Dan prefers in his life). If Dan were to understand his potential to serve as a mediator, he would remain conscious of his tendency to run away from the battle and instead capitalize on his natural strength of diplomacy. In this case, he had experienced so much previous conflict at prior group gatherings that he automatically disengaged the moment he arrived at the event and went fishing to avoid the conflict he knew would inevitably arise.

Temperament – An Introduction

Let's expound briefly on this new concept of Temperament. To start, Temperament is neither character nor personality. Instead, Temperament, character, and personality are three entirely different aspects of our inner self. The following descriptions show how Temperament influences character - and how nature shapes our personality (i.e., our behavior).

TEMPERAMENT	Our *Temperament* is determined while we are still in our mother's womb. Temperament is intrinsic to our being - that is, we were born with our genetic nature, and there is nothing we can do to change it. We can learn to recognize what our Temperament is, and we can learn to modify our behavior to get along with people who have differing attitudes, but Temperament is not changeable.
CHARACTER	Our *character* depends on (1) our Temperament and (2) our environment - that is, our family of origin and the influence of people as well as the experiences we encounter. Although we can learn to change our character, it is not easy. Once we learn to believe certain things and act on our beliefs, it's hard for us to turn.
PERSONALITY	Our *personality* is how we manifest ourselves to the world. In many ways, personality is a "self-selected mask"; it is what we choose to portray to a particular audience or person that we believe will best suit our present circumstance. Therefore, Temperament is often hard to accurately derive solely through observation because personality does not consistently nor accurately reveal the real person underneath the mask.

So, who is the real person?

Temperament vs. Personality

Many people mistake personality for Temperament and most modern psychological profiles focus on personality. For example, the DiSC Profile and the MBTI (Myers-Briggs) Profile focus on personality (they are personality assessments). As a result, the DiSC and the MBTI only reveal the objective (observable) side of a person's personality. But remember, personality does not necessarily represent the real person. Personality is a chosen mask an individual presents to the world and is what the person wishes to reveal about themselves at that moment. Five minutes later in conversation with a different person, the chosen mask changes again because of the nature of the discussion or the person with whom you are communicating has a different relational authority in your life (boss, mother, priest, friend, close friend, child, etc.). WIDP focuses on Temperament, which is not alterable or fluid like character and personality. A person's Temperament is stationary despite his or her environmental focus. Therefore, individuals who understand their Temperament can understand themselves and others more effectively. Each person is extraordinary and unique based on their natural Temperament makeup. God uniquely designs people at conception. Some prefer to call it genetic makeup or their "core, id, or ego." WIDP recognizes and prefers the term **Temperament**. Let's dive deeper into some of the differences between personality and Temperament.

An Overview of Personality

In the context of professional Psychology, personality training is designed to identify individual behavioral styles in a particular setting or environmental focus. In other words, the discipline (and the assessments therein) acknowledges that your personality changes depending on your current environment.

The Personal Profile Survey (PPS), also referred to as the DiSC, is designed to increase understanding, acceptance, and respect for individual differences in the work or social environment (they have increased the environments they assess through the years, but remain primarily focused on these two, generally speaking). Based on the DiSC model of behavior developed by William Moulton Marston and John Geier, this model identifies four distinct types of behavioral tendencies ("personalities") people use to meet their needs and desires. All people could use all four of these trends to some extent. However, individuals tend to use some behaviors more than others.

Here are brief definitions of DiSC's four behavioral tendencies:

D	Dominance	People with a high "D" behavioral tendency seek to meet their needs by controlling their environment through direct, forceful action, often overcoming opposition in hostile or antagonistic situations.
i	Influencing	People with a high "i" behavioral tendency seek to meet their needs by persuading others to work with them to accomplish results. They function efficiently in favorable, supportive environments.
S	Steadiness	People with a high "S" behavioral tendency seek to meet their needs by cooperating with others to carry out their respective tasks. They function efficiently in favorable, supportive environments.
C	Cautiousness	People with a high "C" behavioral tendency seek to meet their needs by working with existing circumstances to provide quality and accuracy. They strive to achieve their standards for results even in hostile environments.

Personality training deals with the person based on an environmental focus during evaluation. A person may respond one way as an employee, another as a spouse, another in a conflict situation, and still another in an intimate relationship with someone close, just to name a few environments.

As a result, using the DiSC assessment, you can end up with several different personality profiles for the same person. Nevertheless, each pattern requires the individual to fill out another questionnaire depending on which environment you'd like to evaluate next.

In the example above, a person can potentially exhibit multiple different personalities depending on how they are functioning in an environment:

- As an employee
- As a spouse
- At a family picnic
- In a conflicted relationship
- In an intimate relationship
- In a business meeting
- At a social gathering

Any environment yields a chosen personality to suit it.

The "mask" approach mentioned previously, in which a person only reveals what they want other people to see, is self-selected. As a result, the person only allows you to see certain facets of their personality. What you do not know is the individual's actual Temperament. Even with multiple personality assessments, you still can't know who the person is because of the fluctuating "mask" that is always changing based on what the person wants you to see or know about them. Therefore, you cannot accurately determine what is true or false about them. Everything is, quite literally, at "face value".

We can expect frustrations and misunderstandings in our relationships when we try to draw conclusions from tools that weren't designed to offer such conclusions. They were designed to tell you what people show and how it can change.

WIDP, a Temperament assessment, is designed to get to the true needs and desires of the person, offering a deep and lasting understanding of ourselves and others.

TEMPERAMENT

An Overview of Temperament

Assessing an individual's Temperament is an approach designed to identify their subjective side which is stable and unchanging and can only be determined through assessment, never by observation alone.

When you consider the synonyms for "Temperament," you will get the following: nature, character, personality, disposition, temper, spirit, outlook, and makeup. The thesaurus lists the terms as being interchangeable - they are not! Temperament is very specific and unique to your inner being.

Even modern authors in Temperament have categorized individuals as being made up of one primary and one secondary personality. Through research and observation, WIDP believes that humans are a much more complicated creation and therefore compartmentalizes the Temperament Profile of an individual into three Temperament **Areas**: **Social, Leadership, and Relationship** (Note, these are not defining outer environments, rather, they delineate areas within your emotional structure that house specific needs, vital to your mental health and stability). Individuals may have a different Temperament in each of the three Areas, or even a combination of Temperaments, which is called a **blended Temperament**, in one or more of the three Areas. Further, WIDP identifies each of the three Areas into two different **Regions**: **Demonstrated** behavior (behavior directed toward others) and **Desired** behavior (behavior desired from others).

The 5 Temperaments of WIDP

Introverted Sanguine		**Sanguine**
	Phlegmatic	
Melancholy		**Choleric**

Let's introduce the five Temperaments used within WIDP and a *brief* description of their traits:

(IS) INTROVERTED SANGUINE

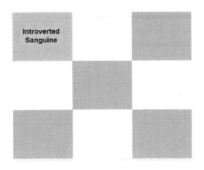

The INTROVERTED SANGUINE Temperament processes facts and then does not do anything with them unless they are asked to by others. This Temperament will also "bounce information off" of those they trust to see if the information and/or situation is correct from their perspective. The Introverted Sanguine is not dense in cognitive skills, just does not initiate action. They are very loyal followers, like to be included with others, and they appear as introverts. But when they are "invited in" by others, they respond as extroverts. When rejected, real or imagined, they will withdraw into isolation. Their motto: **"Will someone please recognize me?"**

(S) SANGUINE

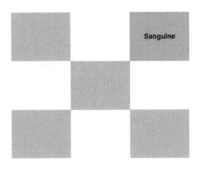

The SANGUINE Temperament processes information in simplified form and manner. For them, it is not that complicated. This attention span allows them the opportunity to act quickly and be off to other people and situations. The Sanguine is more people-oriented than task-oriented. They make excellent speakers and have a unique ability to rally people together and energize them onward. The Sanguine brings life to the forefront for the more logical and task-oriented Temperaments like the Choleric and the Melancholy. The Sanguine has excellent people skills and succeeds in any environment requiring interaction with individuals or groups of people. The Sanguine never gets enough socializing, recognition, and approval. Their motto: **"Let's play and have fun!"** For the Sanguine, anything with people is fun.

(P) PHLEGMATIC

The PHLEGMATIC Temperament will take their time and weigh out, dissect, and ponder a situation. After they sift through it, they are quite capable of making the necessary decisions, but don't expect a sudden change. Once their mind is made up, it is hard for them to change. This process will be less lengthy than that required for the Melancholy. The Phlegmatic is a team player and expects everyone to carry their weight. They make great diplomats. They function well as introverts or extroverts, having a higher tolerance for interaction than the Choleric and Melancholy but will retreat to their privacy once they reach their saturation point with people. Their motto: **"Everything in moderation."**

(M) MELANCHOLY

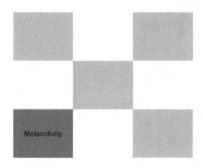

The MELANCHOLY Temperament is very intellectual and needs time and space to analyze the incoming facts. They will retreat into their private world and analyze the situation over and over. After this assimilation time, they are ready to make up their mind and usually have a clear understanding of the situation. Generally, they make excellent decisions. The Melancholy is extraordinarily introverted, preferring to be alone, and tolerates very little socialization unless the socialization involves something or someone with which they have an interest. They are self-sacrificing and very economically conscious. Criticizing the Melancholy is a sure way of creating direct conflict, as the Melancholy is a very "thin-skinned person." Their motto: **"Let's think about this."**

(C) CHOLERIC

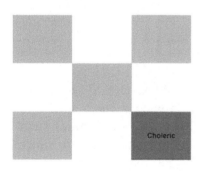

The CHOLERIC Temperament is quick to receive information and process it. They devour the facts and are swift to conclude. Quick decisions must not be confused with "jumping to conclusions", as they have processed the data that was given. This characteristic causes other Temperaments fear and frustration as the Choleric works at a much faster pace than others. The Choleric, if not careful, can overwhelm those around them. They are very powerful leaders and will almost always rise to the top. Their focus is constantly on the tasks at hand or the visions and goals they have set for themselves. Their people skills make them appear to be people-oriented. However, they are only people-oriented when needing people to assist them in completing their tasks. Once the work is complete, they neither want nor require socialization and become an introvert. Their motto: **"Lead, follow, or get out of the way."**

WIDP assesses 3 separate Temperament **Areas** (therefore, 3 separate sections within your WIDP results).

On the next few pages, we will overview each Area with brief explanations.

The 3 Temperament Areas of WIDP

SOCIAL　　　　　LEADERSHIP　　　　RELATIONSHIP

The <u>Social</u> Temperament determines: *"who is in or out of the relationship."*

The <u>Leadership</u> Temperament determines: *"who maintains the power and makes the decisions for the relationship."*

The <u>Relationship</u> Temperament determines: *"how emotionally close or distant the relationship."*

Let's look closer at each Area:

SOCIAL

The first Temperament Area in WIDP is called SOCIAL, denoting socialization. The Social Temperament is what dictates how one approaches and interacts with the world at large, in situations such as parties, career, outings, and other circumstances where other people are a consideration. The Social Area does not involve the thick, intense emotions of intimate relationships (these are in the Relationship Area, to be discussed in a moment). The Social Area deals with the surface relationships encountered in daily social situations. An individual's Temperament needs in the Social Area can range from involvement with many people to bonding with only a few selected individuals. Each Temperament treats interactions with people in different ways, but the Social Area also describes the cognitive or intellectual functions of their Social Temperament. Why do people process information in the way that they do? The Social Temperament is the answer to this question. (We touched on this in the previous section, more will be divulged in the chapters dedicated to each Temperament.)

The Social Profile outlines whether or not an individual seeks to have MANY or just a FEW relationships <u>socially</u> <u>and vocationally.</u>

LEADERSHIP

The second Temperament Area within WIDP is LEADERSHIP. Leadership deals precisely with what the title implies; how we lead or direct people in various situations and how we allow individuals and situations to direct or initiate towards us. An individual's Leadership Temperament dictates whether they will be a leader or a follower (in general) in life. The Leadership Area houses the "decision" part of that person, describing how individuals most comfortably make decisions and who will be dominant in relationships and interactions. Leadership Temperament needs can range from one completely directing within that relationship to one completely being directed by the other party in that relationship. Leadership must be understood in combination with either social/career orientation (Social) or with close personal friends and/or family members (Relationship).

LEADERSHIP PROFILE identifies the individual's capacity to provide leadership, make decisions and assume responsibilities

RELATIONSHIP

The third Temperament Area within WIDP is RELATIONSHIP. This area involves the deeper relationships individuals have in life as opposed to the general social situations covered by the Social Area. An individual's Relationship Temperament determines how individuals want emotional connection, affection type and frequency, and approval from others. Additionally, it details how an individual most comfortably "gives and gets" in their closest relationships: how they intentionally love and how they are most meaningfully loved/supported by those they hold dear. The Relationship Temperament Area deals with an individual's "heart stance" in a one-on-one capacity and is not a group function.

RELATIONSHIP PROFILE: identifies how emotionally OPEN OR CLOSED to deep relationships this individual may be.

OPEN - MANY CLOSE RELATIONSHIPS

CLOSED - FEW CLOSE RELATIONSHIPS

The Number Scale of WIDP

Before we go deeper into how each Area is broken down further within WIDP, let's discuss WIDP's numerical scale. While we will define introvert and extrovert as it applies to Temperament and WIDP in a later chapter, understanding how numbers within WIDP are to be interpreted is paramount.

Numbers within WIDP indicate Temperament.

Each Temperament has its own specific characteristics and are numerically represented to reflect how each Temperament uniquely (intrinsically) expresses and uniquely (intrinsically) desires. The combination of these two designates the Temperament.

Numbers do not have a "good" or "bad" value. These numbers help us understand how introverted or extroverted traits play out in our interactions.

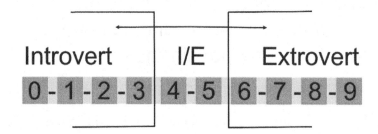

Numbers are used in each of our 3 profile Areas (Social, Leadership, and Relationship) and work in pairs (described in our next section covering Regions). A good way to think about numbers and their data is a "less" or "more" indicator. Here's how that might look:

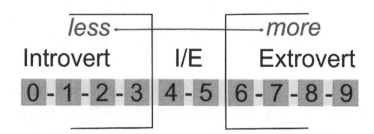

Important Note: As you go deeper into the book, recall this page frequently. Expect certain feelings (gratitude, disappointment, relief, anger) to begin to surface as you learn deep truths of who you are. This is natural and can be as liberating as you allow. Remember, your numbers are neither good nor bad, they are used to help visualize the level of natural expression to others or need from others within your Temperament. Equally beneficial is the awareness of those needs (represented by numbers) that are different or very different than your level of natural expression or need. This is discussed in detail in our next section: **The Two Regions of WIDP**.

The Two Regions of WIDP (The Chess Analogy)

We've covered the three Temperament Areas and briefly discussed WIDP's numerical scale. The 3 Temperament Areas are broken down further into two **Regions**, a most important concept for understanding Temperaments and their practicality in life's situations.

A chess analogy serves to help understand these invisible Regions:

Temperament is like playing a mixture game of chess where each person has six chessmen: the Pawn, Rook, Knight, Bishop, Queen, and King. They all have different moves they can make, and some are stronger than others. Each chessman has his traits and constraints, which determine how he will respond in various circumstances. In other words, the way a person will react will depend on the type of situation. And so, we have our own initiation (the offense, if you will) and our own responses (our defense). WIDP outlines this by breaking down each Area into two separate Regions that carry this Temperament principle.

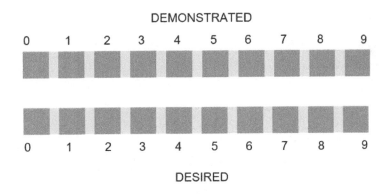

The first Region is how we **Demonstrate** (*towards others*) in that Temperament Area. The Leadership Area gives us an excellent example of this: the Demonstrated Region of the Leadership Area determines how individuals naturally control/direct others and how much of that directing one will exert. Those Temperaments with a high score in the Demonstrated Region of the Leadership Area will naturally direct and lead those people around them.

The **Desired** (*from others*) Region determines how much an individual will allow others to affect them in that Area of their Temperament. Again, Leadership gives us a good example: the Desired Region of Leadership determines how much individuals will allow others to make their decisions and control their behavior. Those Temperaments that would allow little outside control will have a low Desired score (they Desire less). If the person's Desired score is high within the Leadership Area, this would indicate the need to be directed and led by others.

Let's break them out visually (*these numbers are examples*):

Social Area (Social Temperament)

1. **Demonstrated** Socializing   (towards others)
2. **Desired** Socializing   (from others)

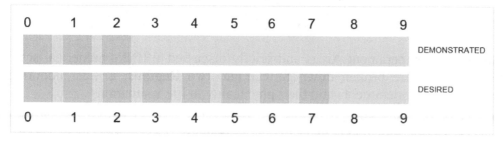

Leadership Area (Leadership Temperament)

3. **Demonstrated** Leadership   (towards others)
4. **Desired** Leadership   (from others)

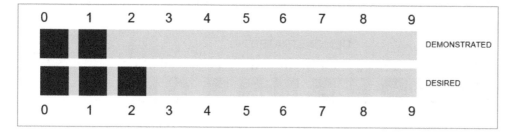

Relationship Area (Relationship Temperament)

5. **Demonstrated** Relationship   (towards others)
6. **Desired** Relationship   (from others

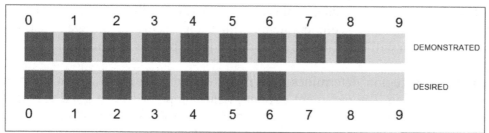

The Subcategories in WIDP

When reading your WIDP, you will notice that within each of the three Temperament Areas (Social, Leadership, Relationship) are subcategories which provide details to help you learn about your unique needs and how your Temperament plays out in that Area:

- Social Needs and Desires
- Leadership Needs and Desires
- Relationship Needs and Desires
- Criteria for Relationships
- Perception of Self
- Perception by Others
- Perception of Others
- Intellectual Orientation
- Emotional Orientation
- Work Orientation
- Motivation
- Rejection/Acceptance Profile
- Probable Strengths
- Potential Weaknesses

As we dive deeper into the 5 Temperaments, these subcategories serve as our guide to explain the unique Temperament traits.

In Summary

To summarize this chapter, we have discovered the following facets of Temperament:

There are five (5) **Temperaments**:

1. Introverted Sanguine
2. Sanguine
3. Phlegmatic
4. Melancholy
5. Choleric

These five Temperaments are assessed in three profiled **Areas**:

1. Social
2. Leadership
3. Relationship

Important Note: People can be any one (or blend) of the Temperaments in any of the three Areas of Social, Leadership, or Relationship. In other words, a person can be a combination of Temperaments depending upon which Area of WIDP they are studying. For example, an individual could be a Melancholy in Social, Choleric in Leadership, and Sanguine in Relationship.

The three Areas are further broken down into two behavior **Regions**:

1. Demonstrated behavior
2. Desired behavior

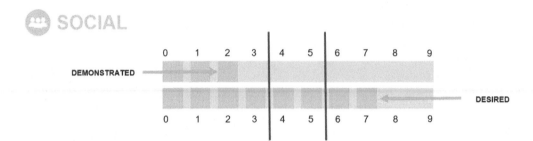

Demonstrated = TOWARD OTHERS
Desired = FROM OTHERS

In Chapter 3 and those that follow, we will explore the exciting nuances of the five different Temperament types and their Temperament characteristics, starting with the Introverted Sanguine (IS).

Before we do, let's set our mind's eye internally. Imagine three layers of a triangle. As you hold that picture, we'll journey into the invisible structure of your emotional biology.

Chapter 2: The Triangle

The Building Blocks

Temperament is your genetic coding at conception. You cannot determine a person's Temperament by observation alone.

The triangle concept below is one you should commit to learning and remembering, as it is one of the most critical issues in understanding Temperament as distinct from several other inner areas.

Let's look at the triangle as representing the whole makeup of an individual. As we progress, we will discuss the important internal structure of "The Building Blocks."

So, start with a simple empty triangle as the frame of the inner individual.

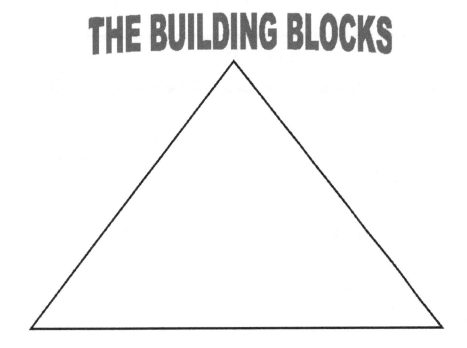

Point to remember: These words are NOT synonymous:

Behavior

Personality

Character

Temperament

As we lay the foundation, the broadest and fullest layer of the triangle, supporting everything above the base, is Temperament (WIDP).

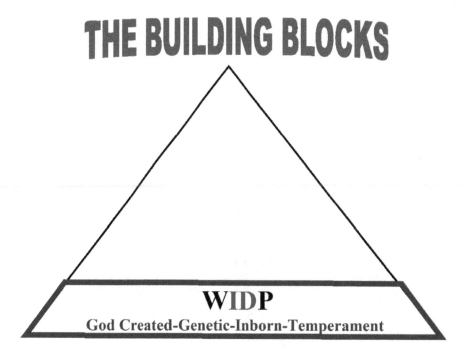

THE BUILDING BLOCKS

WIDP
God Created-Genetic-Inborn-Temperament

Your **Temperament** is who you are genetically, your "inborn" emotional biology, and this part of you, your Temperament, is fixed and does not change regardless of your character values, your personality, or your behavior.

Your Temperament is the real you.

Your Temperament is the "identity" that you became at conception. Temperament is your unique impression for life! It is the part of you that you cannot escape from, remove, alter, or oppose. Rather, it is your real identity to be aware of, embrace, and love.

WIDP is about discovering your Temperament, your real self underneath the "mask" of personality. Most people think they know who they are until completing WIDP. Reading your WIDP reveals you to yourself in a way that you have never experienced before and will continue to offer revelatory guidance and insight for the multitude of instances and situations of your life.

The Temperament approach (of WIDP) is even accurate to the point of being an "instruction manual" of who you are. Your WIDP is a diagram of all your features and functions. On your perfectly manufactured machine, there are no loose screws and no spare parts.

As we build our triangle further (and, consequently, as we move closer towards the surface of the individual), we can now begin to recognize the internal element and context of Character. Family of origin, environment, and culture assist in forming this part of your makeup, your Character, the middle section of our triangle.

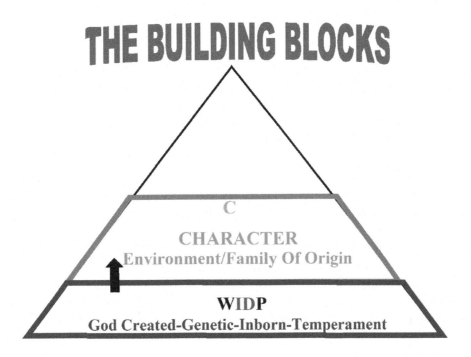

THE BUILDING BLOCKS

Character is defined as:

- The combination of qualities or features that distinguish one person, group, or thing from another.
- A distinguishing feature or attribute, as of an individual, group, or category.

Your environment and culture surrounding you will have an impact on character. This shaping begins to occur when our intellectual skills start to develop, somewhere between the ages of 18 - 24 months old, when we can process information and come to conclusions on the data we handle. From that age into the mid-to-late teens or early twenties, our character continues to be shaped.

Various facets of our life have molded our character:

- Our family
- Our environment
- Our neighbors
- Our friends
- Our teachers
- Our culture

Consider this - if you lived in North America and moved to Japan, your lifestyle would change dramatically, wouldn't it? Your character would take on a different presentation because of your new environment. You would experience "culture shock" at first, and then you would begin to adopt your new country's cultural "character"istics. Likewise, if you grow up in the country and move to the city, you will find your character affected in all sorts of ways based on your new environment. New surroundings influence character, and we "take on" the character of that environment.

Can we change our character by choice? Yes, we can, but it takes conscious effort to swim against the tides of family and the culture of where you lived, along with the many influences that directly affected your life. Think for a moment about who (and what) had a substantial positive impact and influence on you – do you not value or even seek to imitate those elements into your character as a better way of being?

Have you ever heard someone say, "You can tell who a person is from the character of their friends?" Your character is certainly influenced by the character, good or bad, of those you live with, socialize with, or choose as your closest friends.

People often derive an intellectual level of perception of others, where they believe something to be factual and conform those beliefs similarly within that perception. In religious circles it is quite common to simply learn (or ask) what church a person attends in a mental attempt to draw information and conclusions about their character or even lifestyle. However, just because other people think "this or that" about someone doesn't mean it is right about that person; it just so happens they may be that way at that moment in time.

What *reliable* conclusions can you derive about others?

How do you know those conclusions & perceptions are reliable?

Unfortunately, our understanding is very superficial when it comes to knowing who we are or who others truly are. The intellect of our observations has a hard time connecting logically to the innate part of us that has all those feelings and emotions that we cannot describe. We know we have them but are not aware of their origin. Oh, we have a good idea, or at least we think we do, but our character is still determined by what and how we were fashioned by our family of origin, environment, and the culture. So, we may go in and out of several different character definitions of ourselves during our formative years. However, sooner or later our role is defined. Moreover, unless there is a significant family of origin, environment, or cultural change, we will remain with those character traits while within the environment that fashioned them.

A close friend of mine was the 2nd of 6 children (4 boys, 2 girls). All the siblings grew up together within the same household, graduated from the same high school, and then went into the family business that their father had built. This man, some years later, decided to move about 2 hours away from his town of origin, saying, "I needed to be just close enough I could see them at any time, but just far enough that I would have my own life." He was ready to broaden his environment and define the culture that would positively impact himself and his own family, helping to shape his family's individual characters. He remarks that it was the single best decision he made. This is a healthy approach to acknowledging the things he could change and impact, such as the cultural origin of character, and within the unchanging truths of Temperament, creating a positive and cooperative environment that opened opportunities for freedom and rest within himself and for his world.

Most functional relationships are based on fulfilled needs and desires. True compatibility of two individuals is usually not understood without understanding Temperament. Two people can get along fine if they meet each other's Temperament needs and desires. However, without an understanding of each other's Temperament, a superficial bond of the relationship wears thin quickly, and then there is nothing left but an unfulfilled couple. So, they try finding happiness in many ways (in an effort to "get their needs met"). They may try gaining wealth, dabbling in different vocational aspirations, materialism, sex, having or focusing on children, alcohol, geographical relocation (to fix their problems), or hobbies of all kinds. Until an awareness and acknowledgement of Temperament, there will be a void of truly intimate partnership. Changing behavior, personality, or character is included in this willful attempt at success, commonly called "trying to love better" or even "fake it 'til you make it". Perhaps we try to find more things in common, attend marriage seminars, read books on how it's done, even connecting in prayer and asking God to strengthen you as a couple. These may help, but often are a temporary fix – while the root cause of disconnection and frustration resurfaces frequently.

Chasing the development of your character only leads to a dead end. Your character is not who you are – resting in being a "good person" based on character values is noble but does not root you in self. Understanding, first, the foundational context of Temperament needs and desires, places the other parts of you, like character, in their proper setting. This distinction and point of agreement between your Temperament and your character opens the door to also defining the most surface layer of our Building Blocks properly – your Personality.

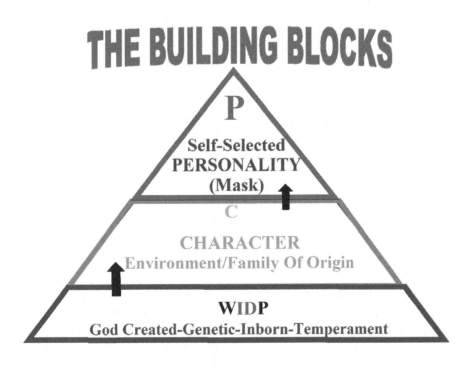

Personality is understood within WIDP as the self-selected "mask" one might put on in any given instance. (Notice it is nearest the surface of our inner self, on the triangle.)

The purpose of putting on a mask is so that you cannot see the person behind it. An interesting aside, all the Temperaments *except* the Sanguine "put on" a mask/personality. Other Temperaments only show you what they want you to see or want you to know about them. So, they put on a Personality mask appropriate for that situation, environment, or interaction.

For example, let's say an individual is looking for a job. It is common practice for people to write a different resume for each position they are interviewing so they can leverage themselves with that potential employer. They may research company history, products, size, net worth, and potential of upward mobility, and tweak their strengths and competencies toward projecting themselves as "just the right fit". It's no different in writing than in person, as they display the best and most cordial "mask/personality" for the hiring manager to perceive about them; a great "first impression". In effect, the company is not truly interviewing the person, but rather the "person"ality that is being portrayed. (Recall the earlier question: ***How do you know*** those conclusions & perceptions are reliable?)

You may be feeling a slight ethical dilemma within this thought of projecting a potentially false image (as if it's lying, in a sense), but let's encourage ourselves for now to objectively acknowledge this information as a broad example of a very real instance happening every day.

So, what happens next with the hiring company?

Let's say they conduct an in-person interview to match the written "mask/personality" (resume) and they decide to hire the individual. The company spends several thousands of dollars processing that person into their business and getting them acclimated to the new position, training them to understand the vision and specific goals of the enterprise. Everyone settles into their roles and in 60-90 days the company begins to realize that the person is not producing the quality nor the proficiency that is expected. Now, not only is the company saddled with having someone in the organization that is neither qualified nor competent for the position hired, but they also spent thousands to put them there! What do they do now, start over? Quite likely. Worse still, how do they correct their mistake and find a person who can actually deliver?

Hiring a "mask/personality" is a major problem in any industry and a costly risk for any company.

Even if the interview had covered previous training, experience, accomplishments, and focused on skills-based questions, they could still have significant problems. Why? The company did not take into consideration the individual's Temperament during the hiring process and compare those to the role's expectations and even the company's culture.

Many companies today acknowledge that more than a resume are needed and are using "Personality" instruments during the hiring process to try and close the gap. What they do not know is that if they are using MBTI (Myers-Brigs Type Instrument), the DiSC, the Professional Analysis, Kersey, FIRO-B, 16 PF, Enneagram, or others like them, they are using mask/personality instruments, which are only designed to tell you how that person may choose to project themselves in that environment. Well, the person was doing that anyway. These instruments are not designed to get beneath the surface of one's personality, which can change as often as the blowing wind.

Remember, just like dating, everyone puts on his or her best "mask/personality" initially. However, over time the actual person will come out and you will see changes in that individual's day-to-day performance and behavior.

Keeping our "mask" on is EXHAUSTING!

One of the fundamental concessions of Temperament is that the Temperament truths about you are self-proving. There are things about you that simply cannot be compromised or negotiated and internal reflection and acknowledgement about these unique aspects are vital.

- There is no smile-school training for someone who breathes freedom by enjoying seclusion and quiet.

- There is no Leadership seminar you can send someone who is a joyful helper that will change them into craving more sole responsibility.

- The "keys to the kingdom" of the heart isn't found by loving someone "more" or "harder" without knowing precisely how.

- There is no way to know who a person truly is through observation alone, as this may be a mask or may not be a mask.

- Who a person truly is can be confirmed (to themselves and to others) only through Temperament, and to find that out, one must be able to measure it accurately.

This brings us to the final portion of our triangle, the most visible (surface layer) part – our Behavior!

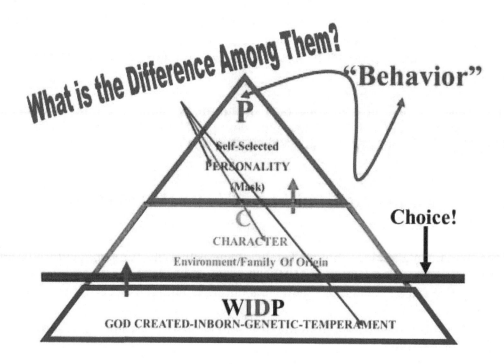

Behavior is the visible manifestation of your mask/personality and does not necessarily reveal the actual person, either.

Notice the purple line of "Choice" on our triangle. Every inner aspect above that line is chosen. Character is adopted qualities, personality a selected mask, and behavior determined by the shaping of the other two! Your character and personality breed your behavior – all are chosen.

Consider this analogy: Music is first understood by knowing its base structure. Know your notes individually. Study and practice well the chords and their progression. Root yourself in the fundamentals. It is from that foundation you can then "play" with music. Great Jazz players know how to move the feeling of a song while keeping the integrity of each piece.

In the same way, knowing The Building Blocks of your inner self provides you a base structure (Temperament) that then allows the freedom to choose how you ebb and flow in the other areas (character, personality, behavior). It is liberating to see your true form (found in Temperament) and know it is okay to be you! Then, choose your values, your ethics, your morals (all part of character). Go "hog-wild" choosing what face you put on today. These are all perfectly functioning aspects of your inner self and now you know which cannot be changed and which can. Go play in the world!

Summary

So, let's sum up!

The Building Blocks of your inner person consist of these layers:

Your Temperament is who you are genetically, or "inborn", and is fixed, it does not change regardless of your chosen character, self-selected personality, or displayed behavior. Your Temperament is all 6 parts of the real you. This makes up the foundation of your inner self.

Your character introduces deep parts of your value system you adopt by choice. It reflects the environment in which you have lived or are now living and is shaped by the people and culture within that environment.

Your personality is the mask you select based upon the situation. Since personality only reveals what you want others to see about you, it is not a reliable mechanism of understanding people as they are, rather only as they show.

Your behavior is a compilation of your character and personality "played out" in situations.

Much will be revealed to you as we talk about the individual Temperaments in the following chapters. You will feel it resonate inside of you as "Truth" to your soul. While we have spoken at a high level about what WIDP is, the information to come will not only be read but also felt. Listen to these feelings as your soul confirms who you are and what you need and deeply desire.

You are worth discovering!

For the educator, the WIDP eliminates the potential for reduced classroom behavior. For the counselor, it pinpoints motivators that regulate psychological patterns of clients.
Dr. Worley's training sessions are equally as valuable. They are casual, informative, and practical. I was most impressed by the diverse range of professionals that attended. Only by comparing the WIDP with other programs out there, can one truly appreciate its value!

Karen Dude, High School Teacher
New Hampshire Public Schools

Chapter 3: The Introverted Sanguine

What is an "Introvert"?

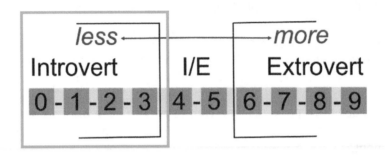

If you are an introvert, you are born with a Temperament that craves to be alone, delights in a few meaningful connections, thinks before speaking, and observes before approaching. If you are an introvert, you thrive in the inner sanctuary of the mind, heart, and spirit, but shrink in the external world of people, parties, noise, drama, and chaos. As an introvert, you are loyal, sensitive, perceptive, gentle, and reflective. You prefer to operate behind the scenes, preserve your precious energy, and influence the world in a quiet, but powerful way. Most of all you want to be left alone so you can think, dream, and regenerate. If this is how you think, feel, and behave, you're an introvert! Introverts are special, beautiful people.

Let's look at Bill, for example, who demonstrates/expresses as an introvert, but desires as an extrovert. Bill is an Introverted Sanguine. As such, he longs to take center stage. Though Bill could be the life of the party, he never will be. That's okay — he has many gifts and has a lot of exceptional principles. For instance, Bill is people-oriented, gentle, diligent, loving, compassionate, supportive, and loyal — not a bad list of qualities. The problems occur when Bill (the Introverted Sanguine) lets these positive attributes get out of balance and doesn't get his needs met. He becomes passive, inward, awkward, and withdrawn. He shrinks away from the people he needs because of his fear of rejection. And while that rejection is 99% false, Bill perceives it as absolute truth of rejection.

At work, Bill is a hard worker, devoted and very loyal. No matter what his boss asks, Bill exhibits a can-do attitude and will work long hours, always willing to go the extra mile. He resents it when his boss fails to recognize his contributions, but that only makes Bill more determined to do a better job next time. Bill does so much better when he gets regular "pats on the back" or "praises of his work" and that makes him want to do an even better job. Bill loves to be recognized and needs a lot of validation.

It takes a great deal of conscious effort for Bill to start a conversation (it feels almost impossible!). But if someone else takes the initiative and starts talking to him or invites him into a conversation, he readily responds. Of course, sooner or later Bill will grow tired of the conversation or lose interest in the subject matter; then he will give one excuse or another and slip back into inconspicuousness, watching the real players work the room. The reason he will move back into obscurity is that he was not getting the personal attention he desired.

Perceiving that as rejection, whether it is real or imagined, Bill will withdraw, waiting for the potential of another invitation. Unfortunately, Bill lives in a very lonely world and "thinks" that people do not like him. Of course, this is not true, it is just a misunderstanding on Bill's part of not being fully aware of his Temperament dynamics and needs.

In his close relationships, Bill is guarded, yet loyal and giving. He needs frequent reassurance from people close to him, yet he questions it when it is provided, still wondering if their reassurance is genuine or not. Bill is the kind of person that always puts the responsibility on the other person in the relationship to maintain the relationship. He feels confused in relationships because he doesn't know his real value to other people. When someone tells him something confident about himself, he will doubt the sincerity of their statement and expect them to prove it through their behavior towards him. However, once that honesty of action is shown (consistently), Bill becomes a trusted and loyal friend to the end.

The Introverted Sanguine — Demonstrated vs. Desired Behavior

The Introverted Sanguine, by nature, has a very intricate social orientation. As the chart shows, in the extreme they Demonstrate introverted behavior but Desire that others respond to them like an extrovert.

Their "Demonstrated Behavior" says

"Stay away from me!"

Their "Desired Behavior" says

"I hope they approach me, talk to me, and

invite me into their space!"

As you read the graphic above, using our "less" and "more" concept, note that the Introverted Sanguine naturally **Demonstrates** less towards others, yet **Desires** more demonstration from others. This may already begin to resonate with you if you identify with these traits. Do the graphic statements reflect how you feel (Desire) in situations?

Because of this dichotomy, the Introverted Sanguine can appear very snobbish, as if he doesn't care. He can seem aloof and act like an outsider. He will not initiate interaction with others and instead go off by himself as if he is not interested in interacting with them. Then, when nobody approaches him, he wonders why. The behavior he Demonstrates is interpreted by others as "leave me alone, I'm not interested in talking to you." And guess what? They leave him alone - which is the opposite of what he desires! Introverted Sanguines are naturally non-expressive but have a high need for others to initiate towards them. When others do, they feel seen, valued, loved, included, and appreciated. When others do not, it takes on a feeling of confirming what they fear most – that they are not worthy of those things.

An Introverted Sanguine wants and needs inclusion. He feels a significant lack of recognition and approval. This explains why it's hard for him to say "no" to someone without feeling guilt or shame. He desires inclusion and fears rejection, so excluding someone (saying no) feels like it invites rejection – the thing he fears. Saying no feels very unnatural. So, not wanting to be rejected, he says yes, then becomes weighed down trying to be the "do-gooder." The irony is he then finds it harder and harder to say no when asked to do even more! As a result, he always feels overwhelmed with his workload. Thus, one important lesson the Introverted Sanguine will benefit from learning is that it's okay to say no.

An Introverted Sanguine's self-esteem is typically low. If an Introverted Sanguine doesn't feel good about himself and feels he doesn't deserve recognition and approval, he will disengage emotionally and physically. Unfortunately, he will react to things, whether real or imagined, as though it is real. Because of how this works in his mind, that is the logical reasoning he may feel he doesn't have the "right" to refuse anyone. This results in being easily abused by more assertive Temperaments.

Imagine an Introverted Sanguine is invited to a social function like lunch or an evening with friends. He would appreciate being invited and is likely to attend. However, he will need to be asked again next time. An Introverted Sanguine needs inviting. His value is measured from situation to situation, and he consistently places the responsibility for validating him on the other person.

Recall that within WIDP there are three profile Areas (Social, Leadership, and Relationship).

Let's see what makes an **Introverted Sanguine** tick in the **Social** Area.

The Social Profile – Introverted Sanguine

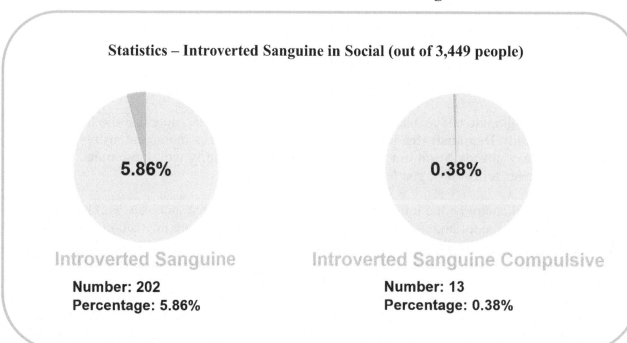

Statistics – Introverted Sanguine in Social (out of 3,449 people)

5.86%

0.38%

Introverted Sanguine

Introverted Sanguine Compulsive

Number: 202
Percentage: 5.86%

Number: 13
Percentage: 0.38%

A Note about the Social Profile

The Social Profile outlines your needs and desires for light friendships, work/career associations, and other casual relationships. By comparing the Social Area with your current life situation, you can understand conflict areas and achieve a comfortable level of interpersonal contact in the work or social environment.

Remember: Information within the Social Area should be applied only to the individual's casual social/career contacts. To determine the individual's needs and desires in close personal relationships, review the Relationship Area of the WIDP report.

Social Needs and Desires

The Introverted Sanguine demonstrates (expresses) as an introvert (which means they do not directly, naturally, or openly express) but is relationship-oriented (meaning a high need for acceptance and socialization with people). Introverted Sanguines tend to remain socially introverted until others initiate contact. When others welcome the Introverted Sanguine into an interaction, the Introverted Sanguine will respond as an extrovert.

This characteristic is called an "approach/avoidance conflict" which means the individual has a strong need and desire for socialization but is inhibited in the expression of their needs because of a fear of rejection. The Introverted Sanguine's requirement is to be accepted and included by people. The problem they face is that acceptance and inclusion depend on others to take the initiative in establishing and maintaining them.

Introvert Sanguines also need repeated assurances of approval in established friendships and connections and have a strong need for security in their lives. Although they are loving and kind in interactions where their needs are recognized and met, Introverted Sanguines may experience conflicts caused by their dependence on others and their non-expressiveness to meet their needs. Having many talents and excellent character qualities to contribute to interactions, they may frequently encounter difficulties caused by being non-assertive in a hostile world. As Introverted Sanguines gain self-understanding and confidence, they can begin to ensure their needs are recognized and met.

An Introverted Sanguine that is married to someone, for example, who is a Choleric in the Social Area, will experience a lot of internal conflict in that relationship. The Choleric in Social orientation will show a lot of attention to people with handshakes, hugs, and touches. They do this because they are making contacts that assist them in achieving a goal they have in mind. Therefore, they socialize easily and delight in making potentially helpful contacts. The Introverted Sanguine will see this openly expressive and initiating behavior and assume it is "to relate" to others, which could have the potential to meet their need of someone initiating "relating" activities. However, to the Choleric, the social contacts are strictly to assist in achieving goals, not specifically to relate or even socialize. Once the socializing is over and they go home, the Choleric will have forgotten with whom they have spoken unless they have made a mental note of how a person could assist them in achieving their goal. Meanwhile, the Introverted Sanguine would have had their feelings hurt because they want that interaction that was shared with strangers directed towards them, and they expect their spouse and friends to know they want to be approached, as if others were mind-readers. Introverted Sanguines could feel quite jealous of their spouse and spend a lot of their life in depression because of it. Unfortunately, the Introverted Sanguine is unable to confront the strong Choleric for fear of rejection and will continue to do a slow burn internally. This lack of communication (from the Introverted Sanguine) about their spouse's (the Choleric's) interaction with others causes constant anger and frustration in the relationship due to the unknown expectation. Both must understand each other's Temperament needs and desires, otherwise they will live in constant turmoil and conflict, potentially putting their relationship in unnecessary jeopardy.

Temperament Note: In the prior paragraph, did you imagine the Introverted Sanguine was the female, and the strong Choleric, the male? Temperament is not gender-specific, it is gene-specific.

Each person's Temperament was determined at birth, and does not change.
The combination of Temperaments across the 3 Areas is specific to each individual.

Criteria for Friendships. An Introverted Sanguine has a high need for inclusion in social relationships but does not express this need. As a result, he may remain socially isolated unless people reach out to him. He is very responsive when others initiate socialization and will become friendly and outgoing. He relates well to people who are close, supportive, and sensitive to him. Loving and committed when trust is established, he needs frequent reassurance that he is accepted and needed — even in long-standing friendships. Once he's "invited in" he can be quite active, colorful, and lively towards individuals or groups. It is like they become another person. But social inclusion for the Introverted Sanguine is like being freed from a prison of isolation.

Perception of self. An Introverted Sanguine tends to be self-protective because of his low self-esteem and poor self-image. He may perceive himself as worthless in comparison to others and readily takes the blame for problems even when he is not responsible. The Introverted Sanguine tends to project his negative self-image onto others and fears their rejection; in fact, his reluctance to initiate relationships may be a defense against possible hurt and rejection. This low self-esteem and fear of rejection create barriers to his ability to express his skills and foster his compassionate, people-oriented nature. Working toward a more positive self-concept will help him achieve his full potential in life.

Perception by Others. In social situations, an Introverted Sanguine often appears passive and quiet and will remain alone until personally invited to join the group. Often his behavior is indirect, and he may express an action that is the opposite of what he desires. While an Introverted Sanguine may appear uninterested in pursuing friendships, he is very responsive when included and encouraged by others. Gentle and kind, he is loving and self-sacrificing with people who have earned his trust. And, because he is non-assertive, he may be used or taken for granted by more aggressive people.

Perception of Others. An Introverted Sanguine feels a strong need to assist people and make them happy. Sensitive to their problems, he is very willing to serve and support them. He may have difficulty refusing their requests and can become exhausted trying to meet the claims and demands of others — all while neglecting his own needs. An Introverted Sanguine may expect others to know what he needs and wants; at the same time, he has a strong desire for other people to recognize his efforts. He tends to be suspicious of people and may distrust their motives until they earn his trust, or he believes they sincerely accept him. An Introverted Sanguine usually tries to maintain peace at any cost. As a result, he is very susceptible to peer pressure and may seek approval by following the crowd — even if the behavior conflicts with his values. He will often ask friends for advice and assistance in decision-making and may become dependent on those close to him. He might ask, "Are you coming to my promotion party (cook-out, housewarming, marriage, etc.)?" because he doesn't know whether you are coming or not, and it is important to him. But if you show up "on your own" he will think that you seem to like them and care about them.

Intellectual Orientation. An Introverted Sanguine possesses high intellectual capacities. His talents and abilities are hidden by his low self-esteem, preventing him from expressing his ideas and achieving his top potential. He wants support and assistance from others in assuming responsibilities and making decisions. When given a choice, an Introverted Sanguine prefers mutual accountability and decision-making. Introverted Sanguines are unable to make decisions and prefer that someone else makes their decisions for them. However, he wants to be part of the decision-making process. A quite unique thing takes place in the decision-making process within an Introverted Sanguine. Once someone has asks an Introverted Sanguine for his opinion, he does not care what the final determination is. He is satisfied that he has been considered. This is different than many others, but it is true for an Introverted Sanguine.

Emotional Orientation. Although the emotionally guarded Introverted Sanguine can be quite expressive in established relationships, he is reluctant to share negative emotions under any circumstances. Because of the inner conflict caused by his unmet needs, he may struggle with emotional difficulties such as fear, stress, guilt, feeling unloved, feeling unappreciated, etc. He requires assistance to assert himself and express his needs directly. As a result, even though he may experience much internalized anger and resentment, he avoids confrontation and rarely shows passion. He may feel frustrated when his aberrant behavior is not interpreted accurately by others or when he does not receive needed attention and approval.

A Note about Anger for the Introverted Sanguine

Introverted Sanguines are reluctant to acknowledge anger as anger and may describe it as "hurt feelings", but deep inside are filled with rage. One serious problem with this is that unresolved anger leads to more dangerous conditions that may manifest as moodiness, depression, and further isolation from people (which won't help them get their needs met). Introverted Sanguines can become vengeful toward those who hurt them. As they learn to express anger and deal with it appropriately, they will experience a marked increase in emotional stability and inner peace. An Introverted Sanguine needs to know that it is a natural part of his

Temperament to have internalized anger. It is not hurt feelings and may manifest as passive aggression. The key is for him to be able to learn to express his disappointments in life (anger) and not let people take advantage of him. He needs to know that it is alright for him to say "no" to people when people want him to say "yes" and it is alright to say "yes" when people want him to say "no." An Introverted Sanguine should not permit himself to be "run over" by the stronger Temperaments of the Choleric and the Melancholy. It is all right for him to say, "I do not like when you talk that way to me" or "Please don't treat me like I don't count, I count just as much as you do." When it comes to socializing and he wants to be involved, he can say "Hey, I would like to participate in the reunion committee, too" or "May I join the group for lunch?" Being aware that labeling anger as "hurt feelings" is a significant issue in his life, yet he can re-program with proper perspective, which will lend to a decreased risk in sabotaging himself (and his needs) and the relationships/connections with whom he hopes to be included.

Work Orientation. An Introverted Sanguine is a diligent and dependable worker. Careful and accurate, he maintains a steady pace as he works tirelessly to meet deadlines and achieve goals. Efficient and supportive of others, he works well as part of a team and readily volunteers his assistance. Relationship-oriented rather than task-oriented, he functions best in work situations that include opportunities to interact with people. He needs recognition and appreciation from others for his work and performs tasks accurately to gain approval. An Introverted Sanguine exhibits a high need for security in his career. Introverted Sanguines make great employees and are very loyal and trustworthy. He does need emotional encouragement occasionally to know that he is doing a good job and is necessary and valued. In the work setting, he needs to learn to speak the truth if he feels that he is being mistreated in any way by other co-workers or by his employer. Since he does not like confrontation, he is prone to permit himself to be abused and remain in the abuse without saying anything because he does not want to offend anyone.

Motivation. An Introverted Sanguine is stirred by the threat of punishment and may be highly responsive to emotional punishment such as guilt, rejection, and loss of recognition. An Introverted Sanguine can also be driven by the reward of approval and appreciation for accomplishments and is willing to modify his behavior to avoid negative consequences or to gain support. The most excellent motivator for an Introverted Sanguine is individual recognition, publicly or privately. He will beam when shown approval. As with other Introverted Sanguines, he would rather have proper support and recognition than a pay raise. They are the only Temperament that feels this way. The rest of the Temperaments would say "Show me the money!"

Rejection/Acceptance Profile. Much Introverted Sanguine behavior is born out of a severe fear of rejection and the need to avoid rejection and gain recognition. An Introverted Sanguine needs frequent reassurances of love and affection from those close to him. To others, his indirect manner may appear that he is rejecting others when he is, in fact, very accepting of people. Unfortunately for an Introverted Sanguine, he lives behind the "unwanted" mask of appearing as though he does not want others approaching him. His body language seems to indicate he does not want contact with people, so others do not approach him. As a result, an Introverted Sanguine perceives rejection, whether it is real or imagined, and acts on it as though it is real. This body language causes significant difficulty for an Introverted Sanguine. Realize, however, that an Introverted Sanguine is an entertaining person once he feels accepted.

He can improve his quality of life by an awareness and acceptance of his Temperament gifts, realizing that people do want to be around him and do like him.

The Leadership Profile — Introverted Sanguine

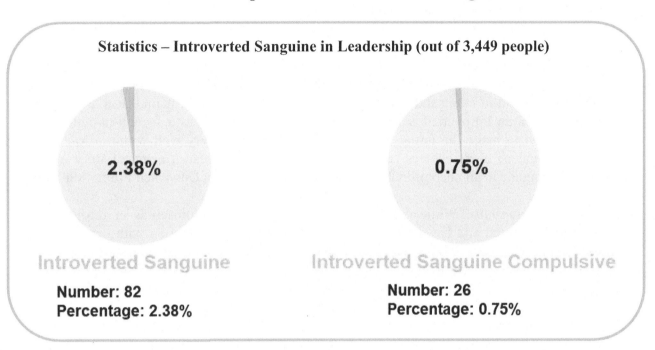

Statistics – Introverted Sanguine in Leadership (out of 3,449 people)

2.38%

Introverted Sanguine

Number: 82
Percentage: 2.38%

0.75%

Introverted Sanguine Compulsive

Number: 26
Percentage: 0.75%

A Note about the Leadership Profile

The Leadership Area within WIDP identifies the individual's ability to provide leadership, make decisions and assume responsibilities. This profile outlines the individual's needs and desires for independence, achievement, and recognition.

Because Leadership needs and desires are expressed through socializing with people, the Leadership Profile should not be evaluated alone. It should be interpreted with either the Social Profile or the Relationship Profile.

Evaluated together, the Leadership Profile and the Social Profile help determine the individual's career needs. By comparing the results with the individual's current employment situation, you can target conflict areas and help the individual maximize career skills.

Evaluated together, the Leadership Profile and the Relationship Profile help determine the individual's independence/dependence needs in close relationships. By comparing the results with the individual's current life situation, you can target conflict areas and help the individual enhance their closest relationships.

Leadership Needs and Desires

Leadership Needs and Desires. An Introverted Sanguine usually does not accept responsibilities or make decisions independently. Instead, he depends on others for assistance in directing his life while wanting little control over the lives and behaviors of others. Rarely expressing his dependency needs directly, he is most comfortable when people recognize and meet his needs. An Introverted Sanguine tends to lack confidence in his ability to successfully fulfill responsibilities or make decisions. As a result, he needs support and encouragement to achieve his goals, most often from a few close friends/coworkers to share his decision-making and responsibilities. However, an Introverted Sanguine can lead if he is in a number two position. The second-in-command always receives instructions from the main leader as to what to do. Therefore, an Introverted Sanguine can lead if he is driving as a second-in-command and not required to make the initial decision. He can function very well within a role that implements someone else's choices. At the end of this section, read a practical story of an Introverted Sanguine in an uncomfortable leadership position in "An Unwanted Promotion".

Criteria for Relationships. While an Introverted Sanguine expresses himself as an introvert, he is relationship-oriented and has a high need for acceptance and interaction with people. He tends to remain introverted until others initiate contact or welcome him into a relationship, after which he responds as an extrovert. An Introverted Sanguine exhibits an approach/avoidance conflict, that is, he has a strong need and desire for socialization but is unable to express his needs. Inhibited by a severe fear of rejection, he has a strong need to be accepted and included by people yet is dependent on those people to take the initiative in establishing and maintaining friendships. He needs frequent assurances of approval in established relationships, has a strong need for security in his life, and is loving and kind in relationships where his needs are recognized and met. He may experience different conflicts caused by his dependence on others and his inability to directly express his needs. Although he has many talents and excellent character qualities to contribute, he may frequently encounter difficulties caused by being non-assertive and feel powerless in a hostile world. As he gains self-understanding and confidence, he can begin to ensure that his needs can be articulated and met.

Perception of Self. An Introverted Sanguine tends to be self-protective because of his low self-esteem and poor self-image when it comes to assuming leadership. He may perceive himself as worthless in comparison to others and readily takes the blame for problems, even when he is not responsible.   He tends to project his negative self-image onto others and fears their rejection; his reluctance to initiate relationships may be a defense against possible hurt and rejection. His low self-esteem and fear of rejection are barriers to the expression of his abilities and his compassionate, people-oriented nature. Working toward a more positive self-concept will help him achieve his full potential in life and reduce the internal conflict he has with himself because he perceives himself as a nobody.

Perception by Others. Often appearing passive and quiet in social situations, an Introverted Sanguine will remain alone until he is personally invited to join the group. His behavior often is indirect; in fact, he may express an action that is the opposite of what he desires. For example, he may appear uninterested in pursuing friendships even though he will be very responsive when included and encouraged by others. He is compassionate when others initiate friendships and becomes friendly and outgoing. Gentle and kind; loving and self-sacrificing with people who have earned his trust, the Introverted Sanguine relates well to people who are supportive and sensitive to him. At the same time, he is non-assertive and may be used or taken for granted by more aggressive people. This non-assertiveness makes him vulnerable to the stronger Temperaments when it comes to providing leadership and managing people.

Perception of Others. An Introverted Sanguine has a strong need to assist people and make them happy. Sensitive to other people's problems, he is very willing to serve and support them. He may have difficulty refusing requests and can become exhausted trying to meet the requests and demands of others while neglecting his own needs. He has a strong desire for other people to recognize his efforts and may expect them to know what he needs and wants. An Introverted Sanguine is a great employee because of their loyalty and commitment. He will work around the clock to get the job done, but he does need validation for the great work he is doing. He tends to be suspicious of people until they earn his trust; even then, he may distrust other people's motives or have difficulty believing they sincerely accept him. An Introverted Sanguine usually tries to maintain peace at any cost. As a result, he is susceptible to peer pressure and may seek approval by following the crowd even if the behavior conflicts with his values. He checks with friends for advice and assistance in decision-making and may become dependent on those close to him.

Intellectual Orientation. Although an Introverted Sanguine has high mental capacities, his talents and abilities are hidden by his low self-esteem. Low self-esteem can prevent him from expressing his ideas and achieving his potential as a leader or managing people. He wants support and assistance from others in assuming responsibilities and making decisions.

Emotional Orientation. While an Introverted Sanguine can be emotionally guarded and reluctant to share negative emotions, he can be emotionally expressive in established relationships. Because of the inner conflict caused by his unmet needs, he may struggle with emotional difficulties such as fear, stress, guilt, feeling unloved, feeling unappreciated, and so on. An Introverted Sanguine needs assistance to assert himself and express his needs directly. Because an Introverted Sanguine avoids confrontation and rarely shows anger, he may experience much internalized rage and resentment. He may feel frustrated when his aberrant behavior is not interpreted accurately by others or when he does not receive needed attention and approval. At the same time, he is reluctant to acknowledge his anger and may describe his passion as "hurt feelings." Unresolved outrage may manifest as moodiness, depression, withdrawal, and further isolation from people. His temper can become vengeful toward those who hurt him. However, as an Introverted Sanguine learns to express anger and deal with it appropriately, he will experience a marked increase in emotional stability and inner peace.

Work Orientation. An Introverted Sanguine is a diligent, dependable worker, careful and accurate in his work. Efficient and committed, he works tirelessly to meet deadlines and achieve goals, maintaining a steady pace. Usually most comfortable in structured, non-leadership positions, he works well as part of a team and relies on supervisors for direction and encouragement. Quite supportive of others, he readily volunteers his assistance. Because he is relationship-oriented rather than task-oriented, he functions best in work situations that include opportunities to interact with people. He needs recognition and appreciation from others and performs tasks accurately to gain approval. An Introverted Sanguine has a strong need for security in his career.

Motivation. Motivated by the threat of punishment, an Introverted Sanguine may be highly responsive to emotional punishment such as guilt, rejection, and loss of recognition. He can also be motivated by the reward of approval and appreciation for accomplishments and is willing to modify his behavior to avoid negative consequences or to gain support.

Rejection/Acceptance Profile. An Introverted Sanguine has a severe fear of rejection and therefore directs much behavior toward avoiding rejection and gaining acceptance. He needs frequent reassurances of love and affection from those close to him. His indirect manner may appear to be rejecting others when, in reality, he is very accepting of people.

"The Unwanted Promotion"

Michael was Assistant to the Director of Purchasing for a large university. The Purchasing Department was responsible for a $40,000,000 annual budget. Michael was very active and functioned quite well for fifteen years. In this role, he did what he was instructed to do by the Director, mainly administrative tasks. Since Michael's primary responsibilities did not require him to make a lot of crucial decisions or manage a lot of people, Michael found himself successful and comfortable with his job.

Everything was going great, then Michael's boss, the Director of Purchasing, got relocated. Michael was automatically promoted to fill the vacant position of Director of Purchasing! Seeming like the most logical move that was right for the university, it was very wrong for Michael. Immediate stress, anxiety, and frustration became visible in Michael's life with the unwanted promotion. Michael's life and world turned upside-down. Along with managing twenty-seven staff members, he was also now chiefly responsible for the multi-million-dollar budget. After two agonizing years as Director of Purchasing, Michael was exploring the possibilities of early retirement due to the enormous daily pressure.

After struggling with the situation, Michael sought assistance from a business consultant. They administered the WIDP Profile to Michael and the results revealed that Michael was an Introverted Sanguine in Leadership! This means that Michael functions best as a true second-in-command. Since one of the characteristics of an Introverted Sanguine is a desire to not handle decisions by himself, it was no wonder he was stressed out as the Director!

With the insight provided by the WIDP results, Michael realized his areas of weakness as well as his strengths and they developed a strategy for coping with decision making and managing the staff members. The group divided into thirteen teams with two members each. One member is the buyer, and one is the seller. The two of them assist each other with decision-making issues. Each has their autonomous area of responsibility, thus eliminating the need for constant oversight. Only the decisions that they cannot make as a team are brought to Michael. The extra person, the twenty-seventh, is a floater and fills in where needed when someone goes on vacation or sick leave. The implementation of this model reduced the decisions Michael had to make by 85% and gained assistance from some of his key team members for the other 15%.

Michael's strategy worked for the next five years, and became eligible for retirement, but felt he'd like to stick around a few more years until his children graduated from college. Success for Michael and WIDP!

The Relationship Profile — Introverted Sanguine

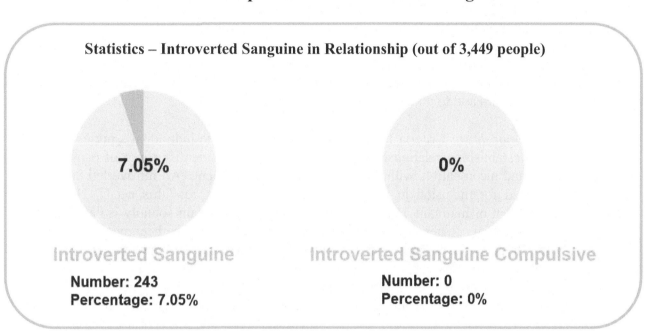

Statistics – Introverted Sanguine in Relationship (out of 3,449 people)

Introverted Sanguine	Introverted Sanguine Compulsive
7.05%	**0%**
Number: 243	Number: 0
Percentage: 7.05%	Percentage: 0%

A Note about the Relationship Profile

The third Area of WIDP, the Relationship Profile, identifies the individual's preferences for emotional involvement and shared affection on a one-to-one basis. For most people, the Relationship Profile is the dominant pattern that influences behavior in the Social and Leadership Areas.

By comparing the Relationship Profile with the individual's current life situation, you can target conflict areas and help the individual meet fundamental (heart) needs for a more well-rounded, healthy, and functional life across all relationships.

Relationship Needs and Desires

Although an Introverted Sanguine expresses himself as an introvert, he is relationship-oriented and has a high need for acceptance and interaction with people. He tends to remain introverted until others initiate contact, then responds as an extrovert when others welcome him into a relationship. He possesses a strong desire for close personal relationships and needs to receive high amounts of love and approval. An Introverted Sanguine suffers from an internal approach/avoidance conflict, that is, he has a strong need and desire for love and trust but is unable to express his needs. Inhibited by a severe fear of rejection, he needs to be accepted and included by people but is dependent on others to take the initiative in establishing and maintaining that relationship. He is loving and kind in relationships where his needs are recognized and met but still needs frequent assurances of approval in established relationships. An Introverted Sanguine may experience different conflicts caused by his dependence on others and his inability to express and meet his needs. Although he has many talents and excellent character qualities to contribute to relationships, he may frequently encounter difficulties caused by being non-assertive in a hostile world. As he gains self-understanding and confidence, he can begin to ensure that his needs are expressed and met. An Introverted Sanguine is exceptionally loyal to his significant other, his family, and his close friends. He is committed to the relationship and will endure a considerable amount of conflict to remain faithful to the relationship. However, he will expect to get his needs and desires met by his significant other, family members, and close friends. He is always there for you, and he needs you to be there for him and to understand his needs and desires.

Criteria for Relationships. Criteria for Relationships indicates the individual's preferences in developing and establishing relationships; this subcategory may identify types of people who are compatible and incompatible with the individual's Temperament. An Introverted Sanguine has a strong need for inclusion in interactions but does not express this need. He rarely attempts to establish or maintain a close relationship and may remain socially isolated unless people reach out to him. Responsive when others initiate interaction, he becomes friendly and outgoing and relates well to people who are close, supportive, and sensitive to him. Loving and committed once trust is established, he needs frequent reassurance that he is accepted and needed, even in long-standing relationships. Internally, an Introverted Sanguine responds like a dog wagging his tail when its master comes home. But it, the tail wagging, is all internal and not visibly seen by those close to him, family, or friends. He must feel comfortable and safe that you will not reject him first before he displays any emotion, touch, or communications that he is happy to see you. In reality, he is very excited and says things (internally) like "I'm so excited my woman is home, I have missed her so much" and "I hope she is happy to see me, too."

Perception of Self. An Introverted Sanguine tends to be self-protective because of his low self-esteem and poor self-image. He may perceive himself as worthless in comparison to others and readily takes the blame for problems even when he is not responsible. He tends to project his negative self-image onto others and fears their rejection. In fact, his reluctance to initiate relationships may be a defense against possible hurt and rejection. Low self-esteem and fear of rejection are barriers to the expression of his abilities and his compassionate, people-oriented nature. Working toward a more positive self-concept will help him achieve his full potential in life.

Perception by Others. Often appearing passive and withdrawn, an Introverted Sanguine remains alone until personally invited to participate. His behavior often is indirect, and he may express an action that is the opposite of what he desires. Although he may appear uninterested in being close to others, he is very responsive when included and encouraged. His nature is to be gentle and kind, and he is loving and self-sacrificing with people who have earned his trust. He is, by nature, non-assertive. As a result, he may be used or taken for granted by more aggressive people. When other Temperaments first see an Introverted Sanguine, they are quite taken back by their non-display of emotions and behavior. He seems to appear that he doesn't care whether you are even there. An Introverted Sanguine's stand-offish demeanor may cause other Temperaments to stay away from him, although that is the last thing he wants them to do.

Perception of Others. An Introverted Sanguine genuinely loves those who have earned his trust and may show his love by performing tasks rather than by open expressions of love. He has a strong need to assist people and make them happy, is sensitive to their problems, and is very willing to serve and support them. He may have difficulty refusing their requests and can become exhausted trying to meet the claims and demands of others while neglecting his own needs. He may expect others to know what he needs and wants and has a strong desire for recognition for his efforts. He tends to be suspicious of people until they earn his trust and may distrust their motives or have difficulty believing they sincerely accept him. An Introverted Sanguine usually tries to maintain peace at any cost. He is susceptible to peer pressure and may seek approval by following the crowd, even if the behavior conflicts with his values. He checks with friends for advice and assistance in decision making and may become dependent on those close to him.

Intellectual Orientation. Although an Introverted Sanguine possesses high mental capacities, his talents and abilities can be hidden by his low self-esteem, which prevents him from expressing his ideas and achieving his potential. Diligent and dependable in his work habits, he wants support and assistance from others in assuming responsibilities and making decisions.

Emotional Orientation. An Introverted Sanguine is emotionally guarded but can be emotionally expressive in established relationships and responds well to love and affection. He is reluctant to share negative emotions. Due to the inner conflict caused by frequently unmet needs, he may struggle with emotional difficulties such as fear, stress, guilt, feeling unloved, feeling unappreciated, etc. He needs assistance to assert and express his needs directly. Although he avoids confrontation and rarely shows anger, he may experience much internalized rage and resentment. He may feel frustrated when his erratic behavior is not interpreted accurately by others or when he does not receive needed attention and approval. An Introverted Sanguine is reluctant to acknowledge his anger and may describe his passion as "hurt feelings". He can become vengeful toward those who hurt him, and his unresolved anger may manifest as moodiness, depression, withdrawal, and further isolation from people. As he learns to express anger and deal with it appropriately, an Introverted Sanguine will experience a marked increase in emotional stability and inner peace.

Motivation. An Introverted Sanguine is motivated by the threat of punishment and may be highly responsive to emotional punishment such as guilt, rejection, and loss of recognition. At the same time, he is motivated by the reward of approval and appreciation for accomplishments. He is willing to modify his behavior to avoid negative consequences or to gain support.

Rejection/Acceptance Profile. An Introverted Sanguine possesses a severe fear of rejection and directs much behavior toward avoiding rejection and gaining acceptance. He needs frequent reassurances of love and affection from those close to him. His indirect manner may communicate rejection to his loved ones, yet he is actually very accepting of people and incredibly loving and faithful in secure relationships.

An Introverted Sanguine is a complex individual, possessing a considerable number of gifts and potential. We detailed specific needs and desires happening internally for an Introverted Sanguine, now let's simplify by looking at another section located within WIDP.

A Note about Strengths & Weaknesses

The *Probable* Strengths & *Potential* Weaknesses section is located at the end of each of the 3 WIDP Profile Areas. An individual's Temperament may be different in one or all Areas, thus the Strengths & Weaknesses will coincide with their uniquely identified Temperament in that respective Area. It is important to interpret the labels *probable* and *potential* correctly. The difference of which characteristic is experienced or observed depends on several factors.

Any individual whose Temperament needs are actively getting met has the greatest chance of exuding their strengths. For instance, after we eat a meal, we are much happier, as our hunger need has been satisfied. The same is true with Temperament needs. Someone whose Temperament needs are getting met will tend to be a balanced and healthy individual, able to proactively participate within their strengths for a positive impact in their life.

However, if certain Temperament needs have been frustrated, the potential for negative performance could be experienced and observed, leading to unbalanced behavior and emotional instability.

**Like a runny nose is a symptom,
<u>think of weaknesses as symptoms</u>
that indicate unmet Temperament needs.**

**Wiping our nose doesn't address the true problem.
Instead, identify and treat the root cause:**

Meet Temperament Needs!

Remember: No Temperament is automatically broken by design. Each Temperament is genetically wired with unique, specific needs that allow the individual to be mentally and emotionally healthy and functional within that context. Temperament makeup can be referred to as one's emotional biology.

Basic Strengths/Weaknesses of the Introverted Sanguine

Probable Strengths
- Relationship-oriented; is highly relational and responsive to people but must be personally invited into relationships.
- Kind, gentle, and loving to others.
- Diligent; is a very determined, dependable, and hard worker if praised, recognized, and appreciated.
- Compassionate; is highly sensitive to people's needs and problems.
- Supportive; has a natural servant's heart and is very willing to assist people.
- Loyal; is faithful to family and friends.

Potential Weaknesses
- Dependent/independent conflict; appears withdrawn like an introvert yet desires to be an extrovert.
- Low self-esteem; exhibits many insecurities and is often depressed and very sensitive to rejection from others; often feels like "nobody likes me".
- Non-assertive; likes for others to take the lead in the decision-making process; is reluctant to refuse requests from others.
- Isolated; is reluctant to initiate friendships but becomes depressed about being alone; often ends up alone because of their own non-assertiveness.
- Manipulative and controlling; will often use indirect behavior to get people to do what they want.
- Internalized anger; becomes anxious or depressed when he is not acknowledged; can become bitter and resentful for the same reason.

Decisions for the Introverted Sanguine

Recall the story of "The Unwanted Promotion". Decisions, in general, involve an acknowledgement of some level of responsibility for that choice, which is not natural for an Introverted Sanguine, as they desire to be directed (someone else bears the responsibility for the decision, they are just carrying out orders or giving their opinion). One key element about the decision-making process, however, is that the Introverted Sanguine *does want to be taken into consideration* as part of the decision-making process; to be included (a prime need), which means he also feels recognized as a valuable member. Once he gives his opinion/perspective, he is perfectly fine with the final decision being made by another. He will feel thrilled he has been considered and heard (Remember an Introverted Sanguine's theme: **"Will someone please recognize (see) me?"**)

Other Potential Weaknesses
of the Introverted Sanguine

Appearing Withdrawn	Bodily appearance looks like they do not want others to approach, but they do; have many interests and concerns, but do not express them.
Fear of Rejection	Perceive rejection whether real or imagined and act on it as though it is real.
Isolation	Can isolate from people and retreat away emotionally, and no one will ever know. They expect others to "read their mind" or guess their need to be acknowledged, accepted, and included.
Passive Aggression	They can become unreceptive in their career/vocational responsibilities and relationships if they feel jilted.
Non-assertiveness	They have difficulty initiating themselves into interactions/ situations with people.
Soft-spoken	Their soft or laid-back mannerisms may elicit potential exploitation.
Avoidance	Choose to avoid accountability and responsibility for decisions they have made, may be prone to point the finger at any other target to relieve the stress of sole responsibility.
Underdog	Not being strong in desire for leadership causes them to potentially end up in situations they do not want due to not advocating for themselves when needed.
Apprehensive	They can get very nervous when tensions rise, or things go wrong for them.
Depression	Can become downcast due to lack of recognition, leading to anger, then bitterness, and possible retribution. Often have trouble differentiating between what is real and imagined.
Offended	If not recognized for their quality of effort, they could become annoyed and bitter.
Calculated	Can be very cunning and begin scheming if feeling rejected or disliked.
Decisions	Making decisions is a challenging task since authoritative pronouncements are difficult for them. Do not naturally desire to

assume responsibility.

Evading Responsibility	Authenticates suggestions or advice (even from experts/professionals) by bouncing it off those whom they trust, may choose to do what their trustworthy contact says regardless of whether they agree or disagree themselves.
Life Directions	They welcome guidance on life's issues, and they like others to help them with decision-making.
Anxiety	If they do not receive the desired response or recognition, they will begin to manufacture bitterness and resentment, which leads to severe stress.
Pouting	Can be a grouch and go around moping with a scowl on their face showing their unhappiness.
Non-initiative	Have a tough time engaging a conversation with anyone due to their fear of rejection and not being accepted. Characterized by "low-voice, high-response".
Breakdown	They are susceptible to burning themselves out due to mental or physical exhaustion.
Lack of Boundaries	May tend to accommodate and over-serve others at their own expense.
Vengefulness	Anger builds over time, then can manifest into cold, calculated violence, sometimes passive aggression, to even the score they've been keeping.

Other Probable Strengths
of the Introverted Sanguine

Dependable Workers	You can give them a job, and it will get done on time; if overtime is needed to complete the task, they will be there.
Team Players	They enjoy knowing and following the rules and participate as required however they can assist; great team players.
Optimistic	Good attitude and pleasant to be around.
Presence	Their appearance is always neat, and they are very colorful and bright.
Loyalty	Trustworthiness is their strong suit and qualifies them for essential tasks. Performs tasks dutifully to show love for others and loyalty to employers.
Innocent	They maintain behavior and bearing of innocence.
Consistency	Key element for them to show based on high need for security as a friend, employee, or partner.
Accommodating	They will go out of their way to assist friends and co-workers.
Relational	Likes to go places and be around others that accept them without judgment; seek to be acknowledged and genuinely want connection.
Service	Drawn to serve, prefer to be acknowledged for their kind service.
Sincere	They are soft and tender.
People-oriented	They love people and being with people anywhere and anytime.
Acceptance	Accepts most people without interrogation.
Friendly	Has many friends and always has room for more.
Diligence	Prioritizes work and relationships, putting them at the center of life. Persistent with tasks if it will bring praise or acknowledgement and/or build deep relationships.
Punctual	Will be where they are supposed to be at the correct time.
Social	Enjoys community functions and being with energetic people.

Helpful Tips for the Introverted Sanguine

An Introverted Sanguine doesn't have to resign himself to allowing his potential weaknesses to rule him (and blaming weaknesses won't work, either), that's why weaknesses are only *potential*. Though many needs depend on others, there are things he can do to improve his life and assist himself in getting his needs met. The following several sections address multiple areas and some possible ways to increase healthy function of the internal and external life of an Introverted Sanguine.

General Do's and Don'ts

DO'S

- Seek a job role that can give you a sense of recognition
- Find someone who will hold you accountable
- Choose one time per week to clean/arrange
- Plan people on your calendar for each day
- Face reality, life isn't always a party
- Put things back in the same place
- Concentrate on truth and honesty
- Try to remember your obligations
- Be sensitive to others' needs
- Keep track of spending
- Listen more, talk less
- Finish what you start
- Aim for quiet dignity
- Make schedules
- Get organized
- Ask questions
- Be on time
- Make lists

DON'TS

- Be too aloof
- Shirk everything off
- Become debt-laden
- Control by manipulation
- Become socially distant
- Always be on the sideline
- Always make yourself scarce
- Walk into a room unemotional
- Interrupt or add to others' stories
- Over-commit yourself emotionally
- Overbuy to compensate loneliness
- Expect others to protect and care for you forever

Evaluating intentions and determining the "whys" of actions and speech are an excellent way to focus and align the mind and heart of an Introverted Sanguine. This will aid in proactively navigating situations and decrease prolonged internal exposure to depression and thoughts of worthlessness.

Helpful "why" questions:

- Why do I always feel I need to isolate myself from others?
- Why do I feel as though I'm not as good as other people?
- Why am I fearful of initiating toward others?
- Why do I always feel that they do not like me or want to be involved with me?
- Why do I always say "yes" when I don't want to?
- Why won't others initiate toward me?
- Why can't I initiate and ask others if I can join them in their activities?

To overcome passive shyness:

- Learn to initiate conversations with others.
- Approach others for what you want.
- Enter groups and ask to take part in their activities.

To avoid being a "hidden servant":

- Let your desire to serve others be made known
- Announce your interest to participate
- Invite yourself to groups or social activities

How to Recognize Whether Your Child Is an Introverted Sanguine

Strengths	Weaknesses	Emotional Needs
Baby		
Is quiet and cuddly, does not need a lot of attention	Acts uninterested, subdued, but very personable	Can be satisfied with minimal affection

Strengths	Weaknesses	Emotional Needs
Child		
Looks uninterested, very personable but silent, darting bodily movement to avoid contact, great responders	Will not initiate relationships, isolates, lives internally	Constant fear of rejection keeps them downcast

Remember:

If you are an Introverted Sanguine (in any Temperament Area), awareness is the single-greatest gift you can give yourself. This awareness is the beginning of freedom and a step towards advocating for your needs (to yourself), your worth (to yourself), and your infinite value (to yourself). Then, you can begin speaking up to others from this beautiful and stable foundation of self-security and self-worth.

"I have been an instructor on the MBTI for years. After fifteen (15) minutes of evaluating Worley's ID Profile, I recognized the superiority of WIDP over the MBTI. Corporate America will rapidly be replacing the MBTI, the DiSC, and other instruments with the WIDP when they experience the validity and reliability of WIDP. Every MBTI trainer and corporate user needs to consider WIDP!"

Carl Erickson, MBTI Trainer, The Beacon Group, Northbridge, MA

Chapter 4: The Sanguine

For as long as anyone can remember, Aurora has been full of energy. She bounces from one thing to the next like a rocket. She is always the life of the party and can carry on several conversations at once while helping people get drinks, find a place to put their coats, prepare snacks, you name it. She is always the first one at any social event — church, concerts, parties, etc. — and the last one to leave, often volunteering to help clean up or plan the next gathering. Sometimes she attends functions she hasn't even been invited to, telling herself that it was just an oversight that she wasn't on the list. As far as Aurora is concerned, the world is her oyster, and life is meant to be uncomplicated and fun (whether others like it or not)! Wherever she goes, she brings joy and laughter.

At work, Aurora loves her job and just about everyone she works with loves her. She can't wait to chat with her co-workers and frequently wanders the halls looking for someone to talk to about anything. No matter who needs help with a project; subordinates, peers, and superiors alike, Aurora is right there pitching in. She will always go the extra mile to make sure everyone is happy with her work, even staying late to finish the job. As a result, she endlessly juggles her work and family life trying to make sure things at home don't fall apart due to over-committing herself. Then, when her husband or children complain that she's not there for them, she feels defeated, but only momentarily. "Next time," she tells herself, "I'll work harder and faster, and everything will be perfect."

In her relationships, Aurora is loving, warm, and genuine. She searches for deep connections from anyone: friends, acquaintances, or even strangers. She doesn't quite understand when others aren't willing to open and share their heart and emotions, especially when asked. She loves showering people with attention and will drop whatever she is doing to go places and be with people. She loves to know exactly what people like and want and then fulfill that for them. Occasionally, she may find herself saying or doing things that go against the grain of her moral fabric. Of course, she mentally justifies it by saying it's only when she's around them, because she wouldn't want anyone to feel offended or displeased with her. She does it so *they* don't feel awkward.

Aurora is a Sanguine.

Unlike the Introverted Sanguine, she has no qualms about taking center stage anytime, anywhere. In fact, it's difficult to get the Sanguine *off* the stage! What makes a Sanguine so exciting is her positive qualities. She is outgoing, people-oriented, enthusiastic, expressive, talkative, and loving. Sometimes these amazing qualities are exactly what gets her into trouble! She is constantly talking with someone or actively doing something and may leave herself little time to recharge. Then, when she becomes fatigued, she is susceptible to losing her temper or acting in ways that she ordinarily wouldn't even consider (Sanguines – be aware of this!).

A Sanguine can seem very "up & down" emotionally. She may flare up and explode over the smallest issue. Then, twenty minutes later, she will forget what made her angry. She forgives easily and wants to be forgiven the same way. She might even ask herself, "What's the big deal, everything's okay now." Of course, that's not the way other people see it. Her anger can push other people away from her, which causes her additional stress, because **acceptance from others is a foundational need**.

Externalizing anger can affect a Sanguine physically, emotionally, and spiritually:

Physically. She may self-indulge by going on eating or drinking binges, compulsively shop, gamble her money away, etc. She also may neglect her body by not bathing or wearing dirty clothes and bite her nails in nervous anxiety. She could even hurt herself expressing her anger by punching walls and other objects, that is, if there was no one around to take the punches. All of these adopted destructive behaviors are how a Sanguine may deal with rejection, and often result in alienating from friends and loved ones.

Emotionally. A Sanguine may become as down, depressed, and moody (there are specific reasons for this, unique to the Sanguine). When she is down, no one can pull her up until she is ready to be pulled up. She may be so down that no one wants to be around her. Her emotions are like a pendulum swinging back and forth from a depressed mood to boosted with enthusiasm. When she becomes happy, she will go out and talk to anyone who will listen to her. Without awareness of others, she could tend to "wear out her welcome" with her remaining friends. Ashamed, she will retreat to isolation but find that she simply cannot be away from people for long spans of time.

Spiritually. When a Sanguine is downhearted, she has a hard time focusing on "higher" aspirations or even meaning. She may even know it would be good to take the high road, but be too exhausted from not resting or experiencing negativity. Conscience can become compromised for the present moment without regard to consequence. Being so relationally oriented, Sanguines need someone with "flesh and bones" with whom to talk, relate, and share presence. When a Sanguine is spiritually secure, the world around them is beautiful and right – a playground to have fun and be with friends and family.

The Sanguine — Demonstrated vs. Desired Behavior

A Sanguine is naturally outgoing, people-oriented, and enthusiastic. She is very talkative and lovingly responsive to people, full of sincerity. As the chart shows, a Sanguine both Demonstrates and Desires highly extroverted behavior. (This high Demonstration and Desire is known as the Sanguine's "swing".)

Their "Demonstrated Behavior" **says**

"Come on let's play and have fun!"

Their "Desired Behavior" **says**

"I want all of the PEOPLE, to connect with

me and let's enjoy life and have fun!"

Sanguines are "honest" in their expression. In other words, the level of expression equals the level of desire. <u>A Sanguine lives to connect with others in a meaningful way.</u>

The WIDP is valuable for a Sanguine: It solves the riddle of how they can better relate with others and how others can relate better with them – solid gold!

One of the greatest talents of a Sanguine is the ability to make others feel instantly accepted (and they really do accept them!). A Sanguine can seamlessly navigate through the emotional nuances of interpersonal interactions with anyone; family members, co-workers, or even people they are meeting for the first time.

The "Swing" of a Sanguine

The Sanguine Temperament is quite unique in nature. The chart on the previous page shows that a Sanguine naturally Demonstrates *towards others* more (as opposed to introverts that demonstrate towards others less), which explains why they are expressive and boisterous, natural initiators. Others may sit in awe watching a Sanguine work the room. They are the life of the party! This seems to be quite effortless for a Sanguine. Yet, a Sanguine also Desires more *from others*. This is the part of a Sanguine that others don't know and could cause significant strain in a Sanguine's life and relationships.

Imagine watching a Sanguine - great big smile, captivating personality, joy radiating from her. Now picture her walking up to you and extending her hand to greet you, "Hi, I'm Aurora!" This is her natural expression in full form, and she is genuinely excited to interact with you. With her hand extended to greet you, though, she has an internal dialogue happening at the same time, silently saying, "Please love me, please accept me, please like me." What presents itself as immediate acceptance of other people deeply longs to be accepted as well. (Which explains why they are so accepting of others.) This swing between confidence and dependence reflects her Demonstrated and Desired needs well. They need to initiate an open, warm, and deep connection, while needing others to participate by reciprocating an open, warm, and deep connection in return.

Sanguines are the only Temperament that "swings" between their Independent Demonstration and Dependent Desire simultaneously!

This "swing" is so apparent, you could even hear it swing back and forth in the same sentence:

"Hi, Jack, I'm glad to see you,	(*Independent Demonstration*)
I thought you may ignore me because of our argument,	(*Dependent Desire*)
but I'm glad you didn't!"	(*Independent Demonstration*)

Just as we dove deeper into who an Introverted Sanguine is in each of the 3 Temperament Areas, let's do the same for a **Sanguine**, starting in the **Social** Area.

The Social Profile – Sanguine

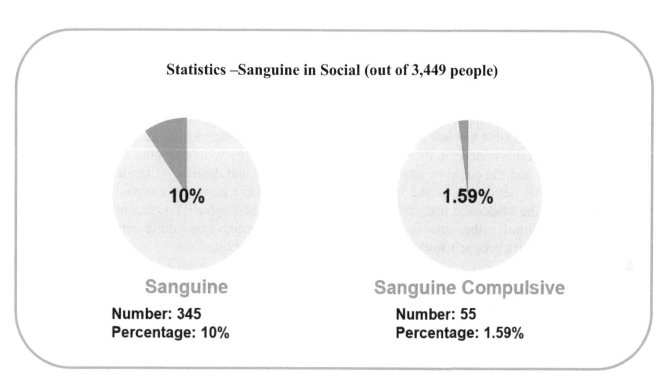

Statistics –Sanguine in Social (out of 3,449 people)

10%

Sanguine

Number: 345
Percentage: 10%

1.59%

Sanguine Compulsive

Number: 55
Percentage: 1.59%

Social Needs and Desires

A Sanguine possesses excellent social skills and is outgoing and friendly. She feels an intense need to be with people and may feel compulsively driven to socialize and interact with others. She has great difficulty being alone for extended periods and avoids individual activities. A Sanguine needs to give and receive affection, and uses touches, hugs, and other physical demonstrations of love towards others. She is highly energetic and prefers to maintain an active, fast-paced lifestyle. Always seeking attention and approval, she has a strong desire to be popular with everyone.

A Note About the Social Profile

The Social Area outlines your needs and desires for light friendships, work/career associations, and other casual relationships. By comparing the Social Profile with your current life situation, you can understand conflict areas and achieve a comfortable level of interpersonal contact in the work or social environment.

Remember: Information contained in the Social Profile should be applied only to the individual's casual social and career contacts (surface-level relationships). To determine the individual's needs and desires in close personal relationships, please consult the Relationship Profile.

Criteria for Friendships. A Sanguine is exceptionally enthusiastic about life and prefers to associate with those who share her need for energetic, fun-filled activities. She values people who share her excellent communication abilities and is attracted to people who express the immense love and approval she craves. While she usually avoids hostile or rejecting people, she is accepting of all types of people and may have an unlimited number of friends and acquaintances. A Sanguine frequently initiates friendships and organizes social events — and is usually the center of attention.

Perception of Self. Optimistic and enthusiastic about life, a Sanguine tends to focus on her successes and ignore her failures. She projects self-confidence but fears rejection and loss of approval in her struggle against low self-esteem and insecurities. She needs frequent reassurance that she is approved and accepted and uses her strong social skills and regular activity to defend against her fear of rejection. A Sanguine possesses a high need to project the "right" image to others and gain their approval. She may unconsciously assume different roles to please people and she could be unaware of her inner needs and desires. (I know a Sanguine that was asked by her date how she liked her eggs – she didn't know; in the past she had so focused on serving others she realized she had never been asked herself!) Often responding to environmental stimuli rather than inward convictions, a Sanguine stays quite active, and this constant contact with people affords little time for self-introspection.

Perception by Others. Friendly and open, even with strangers, a Sanguine exhibits contagious excitement about life and attracts many people by her warmth, empathy, and readily expressed approval of others. She possesses an innate ability to make people feel loved and valued. Usually the center of attention, she uses her excellent verbal communication skills and sense of humor to dominate conversations. She has a strong need to please and assist people and is willing to listen, do favors, and encourage anyone who needs her. Her high energy level and enthusiasm may be overwhelming to less extroverted people. At times, a Sanguine may unintentionally exaggerate and could appear demanding and manipulative due to her needs for reassurance and attention.

Perception of Others. A Sanguine genuinely likes and accepts people and is responsive to their needs, focusing on their positive qualities rather than their faults. She is sincere, identifying easily with the feelings of others. She gives many positive reassurances to people, freely expressing praise and compliments, even to strangers. A Sanguine needs frequent verbal feedback that her behavior is correct and is alert to verbal cues indicating acceptance or rejection by others. She can be susceptible to peer pressure and may go along with an individual or group even if the behavior conflicts with her values. She may allow herself to be depleted and exhausted by the demands of others.

Intellectual Orientation. Although a Sanguine possesses good mental abilities, she understands people better than ideas and concepts. She has a short attention span and is very responsive to outside stimuli. As a result, her environment may easily distract her. A Sanguine's decision-making can be impulsive and is based on emotions and people's needs rather than on possible consequences. A Sanguine does not have to put a lot of time into analyzing things or situations to decide. She prefers to keep decision-making an uncomplicated process. For her, life is better when it's simple and straightforward. She lives in the present, may not learn from past mistakes, and may postpone goal setting and planning for the future.

Emotional Orientation. A Sanguine is emotionally open and expressive with most people and can become "high" and excited by contact with others. Usually cheerful and optimistic, she laughs and cries easily and may appear emotionally volatile at times. She may be hot-tempered and expresses anger verbally, but she quickly forgives and forgets and rarely internalizes rage or holds a grudge. She feels jealous when attention is shown to someone else, and not her. If her needs for consideration and approval are frustrated, she may become bitter and hostile. Although she prefers recognition for good behavior, she can use negative behaviors (crying, pouting, and tantrums) to get attention or even adopt destructive habits. A Sanguine is rarely depressed and can improve her mood by a change of environment. She often expresses the desire to change, improve, or adopt different behaviors but she may lack the self-discipline to implement her good intentions. She may become anxious through forced inactivity or if she is required to spend much time apart from activities involving people.

Work Orientation. Relationship-oriented with an excellent ability to inspire and motivate people, a Sanguine has outstanding promotional capacity and excellent verbal skills. She excels in communication and interpersonal relationships but is easily bored with tasks, systems, and routine work. She can assume many responsibilities and be self-sacrificing for others. At the same time, she may have difficulty directing energies toward task completion and tends to be impractical and disorganized. She is an energizer and motivator as part of a team. A Sanguine possesses differing needs for independence and dependence when it comes to her vocation. She is influential in groups and valued by others for her ability to help people work together. She has a high energy level and needs constant activity. Always seeking recognition for her accomplishments, she needs frequent opportunities to interact with people in her employment setting. Note, however, that she may have difficulty working under authoritarian leadership or in a highly structured environment. She also may have trouble staying out of close relationships, and often she will make her leadership decisions based on the level of the relationship with that person. A Sanguine needs affirmation and is quick to have her friendlier co-workers positioned to work with her.

Motivation. Motivated by the need for approval, a Sanguine craves to be recognized and loved just for who she is, above all else. She has little desire to be rewarded with money or possessions. Her greatest motivation is having people like and approve of her. She is also motivated by her fear of losing recognition or approval and may adjust her behavior to meet people's expectations. These motivations drive her to succeed, but if her emotional decision-making and impulsivity do not match company culture and professional conduct expectations, these motivational avenues can cause significant complications in their role and career.

Rejection/Acceptance Profile. A Sanguine has an intense fear of rejection and needs extensive social interaction to meet her need for approval. She is unwilling to hurt others by rejecting them and conveys unconditional love and acceptance. She will even come to the defense of others if you talk negatively about them in their absence, offering alibis or corrections on your statements about them. She reacts as if you are talking about her, but she is defending the person's character/dignity that is being talked about. If anyone rejects her at any time, she quickly forms new friendships and moves on in life, dismissing the former connection. She may have hurt feelings and feel defeated for a period but promptly adjusts mentality to "begin anew" with a new connection.

REMEMBER

The prior paragraphs in this section talked <u>only</u> about a Sanguine in the Social Area. But it is possible that a person could be a different Temperament in the other Areas. This is <u>crucial</u> to remember about Temperament. Each Temperament has different specific needs that will "play out" in that Temperament Area. For example, a Sanguine in Social will display specific characteristics and motivations with their surface-level contacts (Social) and need specific things from those interactions and people. But what about a person who is Sanguine in the Social Area but an Introverted Sanguine in the Relationship Area? Their behavior and their needs would be <u>notably different</u> when they are around their closest people.

This awareness will dramatically improve the quality of life for individuals and for those around them, just by understanding how each person is uniquely designed.

Temperaments cannot be determined solely by observation; it <u>must be assessed</u>.

The Leadership Profile – Sanguine

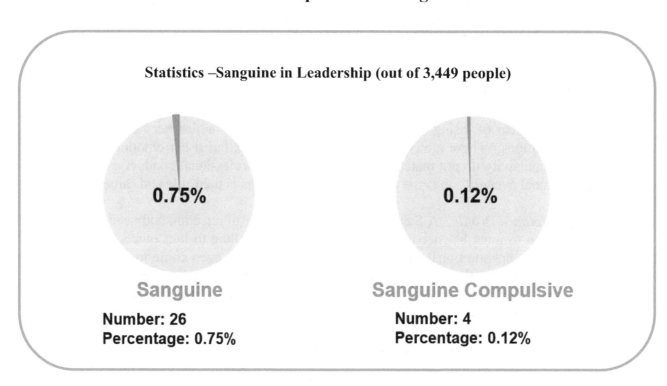

Statistics –Sanguine in Leadership (out of 3,449 people)

0.75%

0.12%

Sanguine

Sanguine Compulsive

Number: 26
Percentage: 0.75%

Number: 4
Percentage: 0.12%

A Note About the Leadership Profile

The Leadership Profile/Area identifies the individual's ability to provide leadership, make decisions, and assume responsibilities. This Area outlines the individual's needs and desires for independence, achievement, and recognition. Because Leadership needs and desires are expressed through interacting with people, the Leadership Profile should not be evaluated alone. It should be interpreted with either the Social Profile or the Relationship Profile.

Evaluated together, the **Leadership Profile** and the **Social Profile** help determine the individual's career needs. By comparing the results with the individual's current employment situation, you can target conflict areas and help the individual maximize career skills.

Evaluated together, the **Leadership Profile** and the **Relationship Profile** help determine the individual's independence/dependence needs in close relationships. By comparing the results with the individual's current life situation, you can target conflict areas and help the individual enhance relationships.

A Sanguine in Leadership is VERY RARE. If you have taken WIDP and are a Sanguine in Leadership, read this section carefully as this affects all aspects of your life. Understanding the "swing" that you naturally go through is foundational for all your needs getting met (and realistically meeting others' needs, which you WANT to do!) granting a healthy, functional, and fun life! You are unique and powerful!

If you know someone who has taken WIDP indicating a Sanguine in Leadership, recognize these characteristics and become aware of their unique needs!

A Story of a Sanguine's "Swing" in Leadership

I once met an individual who is a Sanguine in Leadership that experienced tremendous difficulty leading because of the internal independent vs. dependent needs: the Sanguine's "Swing". He spent 15 years at a talent organization and was never very successful. He would take the lead on an action and charge forward, but when a team member or peer would challenge him, all his initiative would dwindle, and he would "swing" into his dependent mode. When in the dependent mode he would sulk, pout, and disengage from responsibilities and people. After some time, he would swing back into his independent mode and take charge again. Emotionally swinging back-and-forth caused significant confusion to those serving under him. When this pendulum-like characteristic of his Temperament was explained to him, he immediately became angry and said: "Well I might as well ride the back of a garbage truck and throw trash cans around, so I don't lead anybody." Then he swung back to the independent side and said, "I can't think like that because I do like to lead." He was swinging in that very conversation! Being a Sanguine in Leadership could be challenging for them to handle since they are genuinely caring people. Choosing the right role and having an aware and encouraging manager in charge of that person are paramount to the success of a Sanguine Temperament in the Leadership Area, which would be nearly impossible to achieve without the insight of WIDP.

> # Remember – All Sanguines "Swing"!

Leadership Needs and Desires

A Sanguine possesses differing needs for independence and dependence. As a result, her behavior may vary as she tries to satisfy both extremes of needs. Her independence needs include a strong desire to please other people and seek their recognition and approval. She tries to attain this by assuming many responsibilities and decision-making tasks as well as function confidently and productively. If she does not receive the approval and recognition she desires, however, she may begin to feel deprived by unmet dependency needs and temporarily abandon her responsibilities, becoming self-indulgent with social activities, hobbies, or avoidant behaviors. Eventually, however, feelings of guilt and worthlessness will drive her back to independence, and she will assume responsibilities until the dependency needs again become overwhelming. As she gains an understanding of her needs and behavior patterns, these inconsistencies can change.

Criteria for Relationships. A Sanguine values individuals who share her excellent communication abilities. In her independent mode, she is drawn to people she can influence and motivate. In her dependent mode, she wants others to meet her needs and make decisions for her. So, relating will be largely decided by which mode she is currently in. And if you are in tune with her Temperament, then you will be able to acknowledge and appreciate her leadership and interactions.

Perception of Self. Optimistic and enthusiastic about life, a Sanguine tends to focus on her successes and ignore her failures. She projects self-confidence yet fears rejection and loss of approval. She struggles with low self-esteem and insecurities and needs frequent reassurance by those she reports to that she is doing well and is accepted, and she uses her strong social skills and regular activity to defend against her fear of rejection. "Frequent" could be daily or several times a week (there's no number) – as she begins to see that it's a safe environment by people who acknowledge her effort, support her and back her, and are aligned with her intentions to do well, this may decrease slightly, but will still be welcome each time it is given. The rule of thumb is that each time approval, acceptance, and support are given, it is welcome, air to her lungs! A Sanguine feels an intense need to project the right image to others to gain their approval. She may be unaware of her inner needs and desires and, as a result, unconsciously assume different roles to please people. She often responds to environmental stimuli rather than inward convictions and her craving for activity and contact with people allows her little time for self-introspection. Occasionally, she may express concern about her cycle of behaviors as she attempts to meet her conflicting needs for independence and dependence — especially when this cycle causes others to disapprove of her. At this point, she becomes despondent and non-productive and withdraws from relationships and responsibilities. Without awareness of what actions to take in her conflicting modes, she will continue the cycle of perceiving herself as unwanted and rejected, enduring tremendous emotional pain.

Perception by Others. Friendly and open, even with strangers, a Sanguine possesses a contagious excitement about life. She attracts many people with her warmth, empathy, and readily expressed approval toward them. Her innate ability to make people feel loved and valued, coupled with her excellent verbal communication skills and a sense of humor, make her the center of attention in most settings. She tends to dominate conversations and may unintentionally exaggerate ("fish stories" could have been the result of a Sanguine telling them!). She has a strong need to please and assist people and is willing to listen to, do favors for, and encourage anyone who needs her. A Sanguine has a servant's heart if she feels accepted and valued. She could feel that one of her assignments in life is to make people laugh and remain happy. If she feels that she has something funny to say and gets a laugh out of you the first time telling the story, she will say it a couple more times with just a little different slant to get another laugh out of you. Your laugh, to her, is a sign of acceptance, and she needs approval from everyone if she can get it. Her high energy level and enthusiasm may be overwhelming to less extroverted people — to the point of her appearing demanding and manipulative. Less expressive people may need to dismiss themselves to reduce the high-energy demonstration if she continues and is inattentive to verbal cues. Her friends and co-workers may be confused when she alternates between independence and dependence modes and have hard feelings when they must assume the responsibilities she abandons.

Perception of Others. A Sanguine genuinely likes people and is responsive to their needs. She conveys acceptance and focuses on their positive qualities rather than on their faults. Loving and compassionate, she identifies easily with the feelings of others and provides frequent positive reinforcement to people. She freely expresses praise and compliments, even to strangers. A Sanguine is keenly alert to verbal cues indicating acceptance or rejection by others and conforms her behavior to please them. If she determines that others are being insensitive, mean, or unfair to another person, present or absent, she may step in and defend the leader. Even if the leader is wrong, a Sanguine will find something good about the leader to share with the group to bring the tone back to positive. A Sanguine requires frequent verbal feedback that her behavior is "correct" and may cave into peer pressure; if challenged, she may conform to a group's values — even if the action conflicts with her values. This "collective values" type of behavior can become a serious issue of her violating her moral and ethical foundations to the point of jeopardizing her character. She may, also, allow herself to be depleted and exhausted by other people's demands.

Intellectual Orientation. A Sanguine possesses good mental abilities and understands people better than ideas or concepts. A Sanguine is often mentally adaptable, subconsciously processing/gauging communication and situations based more on how people feel than the idea or content another person is sharing. This could get frustrating for more linear, logical thinkers like the Melancholy Temperament. A Sanguine does not respond well to an academic or educational setting and may generally avoid them. Responsive to outside stimuli and often easily distracted by her environment, she has a short attention span. Her decision making can be impulsive, based on emotions and people's needs rather than on consequences. This, of course, will cause significant conflict for a Sanguine in Leadership. A Sanguine lives in the present, may not learn from past mistakes, and may postpone goal setting and planning. If these characteristics are not well balanced by either of the other Temperament Areas or by awareness of these tendencies, a Sanguine in a leadership role could feel constant stress and anxiety that will result in resignation or being dismissed from the role.

Emotional Orientation. Emotionally open and expressive with most people, a Sanguine laughs and cries easily and at times may appear emotionally volatile. But while she expresses anger verbally and may be hot-tempered, she quickly forgives and forgets and rarely internalizes rage or holds grudges. She may not understand why others insist on remaining angry over the issue. The way she sees it, they had a clash and now it is over and time to move on. What a Sanguine may not realize is that her Temperament is the only one that can "get over" an issue so quickly. Unfortunately, the other four Temperaments cannot adjust so soon, and therefore she feels rejected even when she has forgiven or agreed to be over the conflict. A Sanguine can become jealous of attention given to others, and if her needs for consideration and approval are frustrated, she may become bitter and hostile. If she feels undervalued, she may swing into the dependent mode, bearing heavy feelings of guilt and worthlessness. Interestingly, it is these negative feelings that will drive her back to her independence mode. While she prefers recognition for good behavior, she can use negative behaviors (crying, pouting, and tantrums) or adopt destructive habits to get attention. She often expresses the desire to improve her behavior but may lack the self-discipline to implement her good intentions. A Sanguine may become anxious through forced inactivity or if she is required to spend too much time alone. When going out is not pragmatic, engaging in activities involving people (listening to music, watching movies, talking on the phone, etc.) can effectively reduce the stress of silence. Modern technology has worked wonders for a Sanguine's people-presence needs.

Work Orientation. A Sanguine is highly relationship-oriented and possesses an excellent ability to inspire and motivate people. With her unique promotional capacity and excellent verbal skills, she excels in communication and interpersonal relationships and can function as an energetic leader and make good decisions. She is influential in groups, valued by others for her ability to help people work together. She has a high energy level and needs constant activity. And although she can assume many responsibilities and be self-sacrificing for others, she tends to be impractical and disorganized, is easily bored with tasks, systems, and routine work, and may have difficulty completing tasks. A Sanguine needs frequent opportunities to interact with people in her employment setting as well as frequent acknowledgement of her accomplishments. If she is criticized or deprived of attention, she may abandon all her projects and temporarily become dependent. She also may have difficulty working under authoritarian leadership or in a highly structured environment. Sanguines make excellent "up front" people and have excellent social skills that make them successful in selling, marketing, and motivating people. One great and unique talent of a Sanguine is navigating a situation where there is a group of people, and they don't know any of them but can "work the room" effortlessly. Sanguines have an uncanny way of making anyone they encounter feel comfortable and accepted, immediately.

Motivation. Highly motivated by the need for approval, a Sanguine seeks to be recognized and loved first and foremost for who she is, having little desire to be rewarded with money or possessions. She is also motivated by her fear of losing recognition or approval and quickly adapts her behavior to meet people's expectations. In leadership positions, this fear of losing approval could cause her significant problems; allowing "relating" with employees to sabotage work outcomes or deadlines.

Rejection/Acceptance Profile. A Sanguine fears rejection and needs extensive social interaction to meet the deep needs for acceptance and approval (extensive because it is not guaranteed every interaction will reap acceptance and approval, even at her best). Unwilling to hurt others by rejecting them, she will convey unconditional love and acceptance. Although she remains independent and productive when her efforts produce support and appreciation from people, rejection or criticism by others may trigger her dependent behavior. Rejection causes her to withdraw and become despondent.

The Relationship Profile – Sanguine

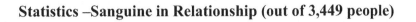

Statistics –Sanguine in Relationship (out of 3,449 people)

0.75%

0.12%

Sanguine

Number: 26
Percentage: 0.75%

Sanguine Compulsive

Number: 4
Percentage: 0.12%

A Note about the Relationship Profile

The third Area of WIDP, the Relationship Profile, identifies the individual's preferences for emotional involvement and shared affection on a one-to-one basis. For most people, the Relationship Profile is the dominant pattern that influences behavior in the Social and Leadership Areas.

By comparing the Relationship Profile with the individual's current life situation, you can target conflict areas and help the individual meet fundamental (heart) needs for a more well-rounded, healthy, and functional life.

Relationship Needs and Desires

A Sanguine in Relationship lives to connect with people openly and deeply. The chief priority of every interaction is the intention of maintaining deep connections with those closest to her heart. Outgoing and friendly, a Sanguine possesses excellent communication, and genuinely loves people. She has a strong need and desire to engage in activities involving people and may feel compulsively driven to socialize and interact with others. A Sanguine can become so involved in developing relationships that she will wear herself out physically and then "crash", sleeping well into the next day recovering from the interactions, the "social marathon", she chose to engage in. As a small child, Sanguines may be the ones who fall asleep in their chair, or food, at a meal. A Sanguine has difficulty being alone for extended periods and often actively avoids individual activities. When someone reciprocates closeness through open sharing of feelings or thoughts of the heart, she will readily respond. She has a strong need to give and receive affection and may use many touches, hugs, and other physical expressions of love towards others. Enjoying a naturally high energy level, she prefers to maintain an active, fast-paced lifestyle. She may even level-out or become calmer within environments that contain a lot of movement. Environments of disorder may not negatively affect a Sanguine, as they are quite adaptable. And, with a great need for attention and approval and an intense craving to be popular with everybody, she needs frequent reassurances of love from her close relationships.

Criteria for Relationships. Enthusiastic about life and accepting of all types of people, a Sanguine values individuals who share her excellent communication abilities and prefers those who share her need for energetic, fun-filled activities. A Sanguine is usually the center of attention at organized events and may have unlimited numbers of friends and acquaintances. The popularity of a Sanguine can become an area of potential conflict, as other Temperaments that are involved with a Sanguine could become jealous of her many friendships. A Sanguine is so transparent and open in her interactions that she could seem flirtatious, manipulative, and deceiving to the other Temperaments. While it may seem a Sanguine is being promiscuous, she is just being who she is – friendly and open. A Sanguine expresses to the same extent that she desires, meaning she has an "honest" expression. What you see is what you get. Due to her transparent, genuine nature as one who speaks her truth, most people may not understand why she (or anyone) would be so real. A Sanguine is attracted to supporting individuals who express the unconditional love and approval she craves and usually avoids hostile or rejecting people. Often, she will dismiss herself in the presence of negativity if she cannot turn the tone to fun and happiness. Negativity and sarcasm will drain a Sanguine's desire to interact with that person or within that environment, and she will move on to someone else or someplace else.

A Sanguine in Relationship has a strong need to know she is valued for who she is. When this is maintained (daily), she is a stable, loving person for deep, long-term relationships.

Perception of Self. Sustaining a naturally optimistic outlook on life, a Sanguine tends to focus on her successes and ignore her failures. She projects self-confidence but struggles with low self-esteem and insecurities and needs frequent reassurance that she is approved and accepted. To counter her fears of rejection and loss of approval, she uses her strong social skills to remain active while projecting the "right image" to others. One consequence of her constant activity and people contact is that she has little time for self-introspection and may be unaware of her inner needs and desires. She may allow herself to be exhausted by the demands of others while she tries to meet her need for attention and approval from them.

Perception by Others. Friendly and open, even with strangers, a Sanguine exudes a contagious excitement about life and attracts many people by her warmth, empathy, and readily expressed approval toward them. She has an innate ability to make people feel loved and valued. Possessing excellent verbal communication skills as well as a keen sense of humor, she is usually the center of attention and tends to dominate conversations, sometimes unintentionally exaggerating. She has a strong need to please and assist people and is always willing to listen to, do favors for, and encourage anyone who needs her. At the same time, her high energy level and enthusiasm may be overwhelming to less extroverted people, as she can seem manipulative and demanding. Her high need for love and approval may cause tension in close relationships. She may also be perceived as excessive and exaggerated in many areas of her life.

If a Sanguine were to take time to write an e-mail to someone close to them, here's how it might sound:

Melaney,

Okay I miss you, I know going back to school is awesome but not as awesome as here! My boss finally decided to get rid of the hideous paintings at the entrance that everyone sees when they get off the elevator and asked what I thought he should get and I told him obviously something more colorful, and he did! Maybe he'll paint next, Lord knows that wall couldn't get sadder.

Get this, turns out Julie fell and broke her nose! She said the ambulance was driving like she had cut her whole leg off, then she gets to the hospital and tells me that her doctor is a stud. Apparently, they didn't take her to any hospital within 100 miles from here. Ugh, I know y'all keep saying enjoy being single, but I was NOT born to be single.

I don't remember if I told you but Billy took a turn for the worse and didn't make it. I went to the funeral to make sure his sister was okay. She's the one I told you is a few years older than me and is stylish. Even at a funeral that chick can put an outfit together. They had a bigger family than I thought - Billy has 3 brothers not 2, Joe and Phillip were there, and the other brother drove in, I can't remember his name but he was nice.

Okay I'm back, sorry, Karen called and we talked forever and now I'm writing again. You better know how much I love you. I don't know how you keep a journal every day! My hands barely handle typing much less writing!

Okay last thing - remember how we were talking about Christina's wedding stuff in October? So I went shopping (yes, again) and found a dress that is light and airy, and I could wear capris under it for after the wedding and there's no way to tell! You HAVE to see it! You know how I dance so might as well be ready. With lots of deodorant!

We need to catch up!!! Miss you, you're the best!!

Angela

Perception of Others. A Sanguine genuinely likes people and is responsive to their needs. She conveys acceptance to others, focusing on their positive qualities rather than their faults. Highly compassionate, she identifies easily with the feelings of others. She gives constant positive reinforcement to people and freely expresses praise and compliments, even to strangers. Alert to verbal cues indicating acceptance or rejection by others; she will alter her behavior to please them. Although she needs frequent verbal feedback that her responses are correct and reassurances that she is loved, she can be susceptible to peer pressure and may conform to a group's values — even if their behavior conflicts with her values.

Intellectual Orientation. Possessing good mental abilities, a Sanguine understands people better than ideas and concepts. She has a short attention span, is responsive to outside stimuli, and may be easily distracted by her environment, often postponing goal setting and planning for the future. Her decision making can be impulsive, based on emotions and people's needs rather than on consequences. A Sanguine lives in the present and may not learn from her past mistakes, thus repeating the same ones. Since "no one is perfect" it isn't a big deal to her, and she will move forward with optimism. Her repeated negative behavior could catch up with her and cause broken relationships and problems at work. By finding constructive, healthy ways to address the legitimate needs causing the negative behavior, she will reap quality relational interactions. Self-reflection of relational impact will grab a Sanguine's attention faster than logic or reason ever will.

Emotional Orientation. Emotionally open and expressive with most people, a Sanguine laughs and cries easily and may appear emotionally volatile at times. She honestly expresses her inner needs and emotions and expects others to be emotionally open with her, requiring deep emotional sharing in close relationships. She is usually cheerful and optimistic but may be hot-tempered, expressing anger verbally. A Sanguine rarely internalizes rage or holds grudges but quickly forgives and forgets. At the same time, she may become bitter and hostile if her needs for attention and approval are frustrated or if feeling jealous of the attention given to others. Rarely depressed, a Sanguine can improve her mood by merely changing her environment. She can become "high" and excited by contacts with people and may become anxious through forced inactivity or if she is required to spend much time alone. While she needs recognition for good behavior, she can use negative behaviors (crying, pouting, and tantrums) to get attention. A Sanguine often expresses the desire to improve her practices but may lack the self-discipline to implement her good intentions.

Motivation. Highly motivated by her need for approval, a Sanguine seeks to be recognized and loved for who she is. When she has a conflict within her closest relationships, the best thing the other person can do is to tell her they love her regardless of the offense and to hug and hold her. Once she feels they're genuine towards her by seeing her for her best self, she will emotionally move right back into a good mood. This intentional initiation of emotional acceptance "levels" her from the emotional charge or perceived threat of relational loss. While she has little desire to be rewarded with money or possessions, she is motivated by her fear of losing recognition or approval from close relationships and quickly adapts her behavior to meet people's expectations.

Rejection/Acceptance Profile. A Sanguine fears rejection and needs extensive social interaction and daily assurances of love from her close relationships to meet her need for approval. A Sanguine can never get too much love and attention from her closest relationships. If her needs are frustrated, she usually tries harder to win approval; if she feels rejected, she will quickly form new relationships. Unwilling to hurt others by dismissing them, she conveys unconditional love and acceptance.

A Note about Strengths & Weaknesses

The *Probable* Strengths & *Potential* Weaknesses section is located at the end of each of the 3 WIDP Profile Areas. An individual's Temperament may be different in one or all Areas, thus the Strengths & Weaknesses will coincide with their uniquely identified Temperament in that respective Area. It is important to interpret the labels *probable* and *potential* correctly. The difference of which characteristic is experienced or observed depends on several factors.

Any individual whose Temperament needs are actively getting met has the greatest chance of exuding their strengths. For instance, after we eat a meal, we are much happier, as our hunger need has been satisfied. The same is true with Temperament needs. Someone whose Temperament needs are getting met will tend to be a balanced and healthy individual, able to proactively participate within their strengths for a positive impact in their life.

However, if certain Temperament needs have been frustrated, the potential for negative performance could be experienced and observed, leading to unbalanced behavior and emotional instability.

> **Like a runny nose is a symptom,**
> **think of weaknesses as symptoms**
> **that indicate unmet Temperament needs.**
>
> ↓
>
> **Wiping our nose doesn't address the true problem.**
> **Instead, identify and treat the root cause:**
>
> **Meet Temperament Needs!**

Remember: No Temperament is automatically broken by design. Each Temperament is genetically wired with unique, specific needs that allow the individual to be mentally and emotionally healthy and functional within that context. Temperament makeup can be referred to as one's emotional biology.

Basic Strengths/Weaknesses of the Sanguine

Probable Strengths
- Compassionate — is sensitive, gentle, kind, warm, and friendly; has a great need to give and receive love and attention; cries and forgives easily; makes people feel accepted and likes to give and receive hugs and handshakes.
- Outgoing — is the life of the party, warm, friendly; loves to cheer people on and make them laugh; is the most emotional and extroverted of the Temperaments.
- Skilled communicator — uses very descriptive and colorful language; is an excellent conversationalist and a great encourager.
- Creative — is talented in developing new projects; loves the arts, music, entertainment, and hospitality industries.
- Optimistic — lives one day at a time; is enthusiastic and brings life and humor to the other Temperaments.
- Transparent — "what you see is what you get"; is open and honest with thoughts and feelings and tries to help others do the same.

Potential Weaknesses
- Undisciplined — is disorganized and has a short attention span (unless tasks are people oriented).
- Emotionally volatile — experiences mood swings; when upset can be verbally caustic or use indirect behavior to manipulate or control others.
- Impractical — inability to function as an extrovert or focus their compassion, spontaneity to people, and a great need to give and receive affection and approval can cause them to become impractical or disruptive.
- Egotistical — needs to be the center of attention; use of negative behaviors to gain attention; can become annoying by dominating conversations; tends to exaggerate; colorful with adjectives and explanations.
- Unfocused — usually not academically or administratively oriented; don't like to concentrate for extended periods of time on "things"; prefers "people" oriented tasks.
- Insecure — has a severe fear of rejection; tends to care about others too deeply, which causes a lot of pain and overreactions.
- Complex — struggles with competing needs for dependence/independence.

Decisions for the Sanguine

A Sanguine does not worry like the other Temperaments. Her present-moment wiring naturally drives her toward simplifying what seems to others as complex. Otherwise, it could introduce unnecessary time, strain, and even the potential for negative thinking into the flow of their life, thoughts, and interrupt their chief intention - making close connections with people! This quality could be very useful to Temperaments that may refer to themselves as "overthinkers". Sanguines do not complicate the issues of life and are not swayed solely by data or facts. **For a Sanguine, decisions are assessed based on the emotional and relational impact. In other words, decisions are relationally based, not solely data based.** If the impact to the relationship/interaction is neutral, she may not care what the final decision is!

Other Probable Strengths
of the Sanguine

Animated	Full of life, expressive with hand, arm, and facial gestures
Playful	Fun should be budgeted into every day
Sociable	Gets a "high" from being with people, sees social life as an opportunity to be liked and build potential connection rather than as a challenge or business opportunity
Convincing	Can win you over to anything through the sheer charm of her personality
Refreshing	Can lift a room just by walking in it; renews and energizes, making others literally feel better
Spirited	Full of life and excitement
Present-Minded	Lives in the moment, every day is a new day
Promoter	Urges or compels others to go along with or join an activity
Spontaneous	Prefers all of life to be impulsive, not restricted by plans or weighed down by negativity; often fluid and adaptable, including with emotional relating
Optimistic	Sunny disposition who naturally sees and exudes the light and bright side of life, even in dire circumstances
Funny	A sparkling sense of humor that can make virtually any story into a hilarious event
Energizer	A talent only Sanguines possess, can give unlimited energy to those around them through their natural disposition
Inspiring	Encourages others to work, join, or be involved and makes the whole thing fun
Demonstrative	Openly expresses emotion, especially affection, and doesn't hesitate to touch others while speaking to them
Sincere	Naturally genuine and able to spot genuineness in others; expresses needs genuinely, gives sincere compliments, and means them

Mixes Easily	Ready to meet and interact, including with strangers; loves people and seeks opportunities to know more about them
Talker	Frequently talking, tells funny stories to entertain the room, fills silence to make others comfortable
Popular	Life of the party, much desired as a party guest and helps carry the crowd along
Relational	Prioritizes relationships over "things", actively maintains emotional aspects of relationship, keen on, and attentive to, the needs of others

Other Potential Weaknesses
of the Sanguine

Brassy	Showy, flashy, comes on strong, very loud
Undisciplined	Lack of structure/order permeates almost every area of her life
Repetitious	Retells stories and incidents to entertain you without realizing she has already told the story several times before, is always needing something to say (anxious in silence of any kind)
Forgetful	Lack of memory, which is usually tied to a lack of discipline and not bothering to mentally record things that aren't fun
Interrupts	A person who is more of a talker than a listener, who starts speaking without even realizing someone else is already talking
Unpredictable	May be ecstatic one moment and down the next, or willing to help but then disappears, or promises to come but forgets to show up
Haphazard	Has no consistent way of doing things, often preferring it that way
Permissive	Allows others (including children) to do as they please to keep from being disliked
Angered	One who has a flash-bang temper that expresses itself in tantrum style, but then over and forgotten very quickly
Naïve	Simple and child-like perspective, lacking sophistication or comprehension of what the deeper levels of life are
Wants Credit	Thrives on approval from others; as an entertainer this person feeds on the applause, laughter, and acceptance of an audience ("All the world's a stage…")
Disorganized	Lack of ability to ever get life in order
Inconsistent	Erratic (inconsistent) and contradictory, with actions and emotions not based on logic
Messy	Living in a state of disorder, unable to find things
Show-Off	Needs to be the center of attention, wants to be watched
Loud	A person whose laugh or voice can be heard above others in the room

Scatter-Brained	Lacks the power of concentration, or attention, flighty
Restless	Likes constant new activity because it isn't fun to do the same things all the time
Changeable	A child-like, short attention span that needs a lot of change and variety to keep from getting bored

Helpful Tips for the Sanguine

By now, you should have a pretty good idea of what makes a Sanguine tick: people and fun! Even though a Sanguine is outgoing, upbeat, and confident, she can suffer from a turbulent array of insecurities that, when needs and desires are left unmet, can make her behave in ways that are destructive. Sanguines express more, naturally. Therefore, both positive and negative behaviors will be expressed depending on needs getting met.

If you are a Sanguine, here are some things to be aware of that will help:

1. You are upbeat, open, and friendly. It is okay to be genuine with others and is one of your greatest natural traits. As a Sanguine, you have an inborn, compelling need to be with people. You can lift an entire room just by walking in it, a great blessing to other Temperaments. So, learn to become sensitive to those around you. Know that not all people are people-oriented; some people are task-oriented and cannot relate to you, or achievement-oriented and may resent you hogging the spotlight. In your social/vocational relationships, you are regenerated by being with people; individuals with different Temperaments may be restored by silent, daily time alone or by focusing on their goals or projects. Learning this will help you become more sensitive to other people's needs and not just focus on your own. "Relating" is different for all 5 Temperaments. It's also helpful to know that when you cannot be with other people, talking on the phone, listening to the radio, watching television, or even reading a good story will lessen the stress of being alone.

2. You will tend to take on the morals of the crowd. It is okay to adopt the morals of the group you are with — if the mob has good morals! To keep from being rejected, you will find yourself suddenly saying and doing things you do not want to say and do, so it is essential that you associate with people of good morals and ensure you know your boundaries and honor them. As a Sanguine, you are very emotional, and your emotions will tend to run from high to low and then low to high. You are either happy as a lark or as depressed as a person stranded alone on an island. To balance yourself, know your needs in the highs and the lows so you can recognize which needs are getting met and which are not. You must remember that you do not have to say and do things you know are wrong to avoid rejection or even to "make" people happy. Awareness of needs and healthy self-worth along with proper boundaries will dictate your level of success.

3. You are talkative. Expressing through words (including thinking through your thoughts out loud) is natural and valid. Realize you cannot always be the center of attention and filibuster every interaction. Share the spotlight. Other Temperaments can only take so much high energy and "lime-lighting" and, if overwhelmed, they will look for ways to step away from you which likely means they will avoid you in the future. This is the opposite of what you need and want. You are good at paying attention to relational cues – hone this by being keenly aware of signals that indicate when others are interested to receive and do not overload them with "the Sanguine show". As you go, watch for body language that says, "I've had enough." Then, quietly disengage or dismiss yourself politely and let someone else have the floor for a while to distribute the attention off you. An easy technique to balance energy in the interaction is to ask about them; it does wonders for relationships and, since you love deep talks, it could spark a deep connection and conversation! When at your job, try not to distract others from doing their work. You tend to want to tell every little thing that happens to you to anyone that is around — whether they listen or not. Learn self-discipline and remember that there is a time and a place for socializing.

4. You get angry. It is okay to get angry, but it is *not* okay to be hot-tempered and fly into a rage. Remember, expressing feels natural, but is not always wise when it's "in the raw". Learn to recognize when your blood pressure skyrockets, or when fears begin to flood your mind. In those moments – pause and breathe. By understanding your Temperament, you can interact and function responsibly in your anger in a way that maintains healthy relationships and interactions with others.

General Do's and Don'ts

DO'S

- Seek a job role that can give you a sense of recognition
- Find someone who will hold you accountable
- Choose one time per week to clean/arrange
- Plan people on your calendar for each day
- Face reality, life isn't always a party
- Put things back in the same place
- Concentrate on truth and honesty
- Try to remember your obligations
- Be sensitive to other's needs
- Keep track of spending
- Listen more, talk less
- Finish what you start
- Aim for quiet dignity
- Make schedules
- Get organized
- Ask questions
- Be on time
- Make lists

DON'TS

- Become debt-laden
- Laugh everything off
- Become a party animal
- Speak before you think
- Walk into a room talking
- Control by charm and wit
- Ignore your bank account
- Be too loud or belligerent
- Always try to be "on stage"
- Burn bridges with your words
- Neglect setting firm boundaries
- Silence yourself about your needs
- Expect others to protect you forever
- Overcommit yourself to too many projects
- Let fear cause you to sabotage relationships
- Interrupt, add to, or try to "one up" others' stories

How to Recognize Whether Your Child Is A Sanguine

Strengths	Weaknesses	Emotional Needs
Baby		
Is bright and wide-eyed; acts curious; gurgles and coos; wants company; shows off, is responsive	Knows he/she is cute; screams for attention	Very frequent care and affection

Strengths	Weaknesses	Emotional Needs
Child		
Is daring and eager; acts innocent; is inventive, imaginative, cheerful, and enthusiastic; is fun-loving; chatters constantly; bounces back; energized by people	Does not follow through, is disorganized, and easily distracted; has a short interest span; experiences emotional ups and downs; wants credit for everything he/she does; tells fibs; is forgetful	Very frequent attention; approval; affection

Strengths	Weaknesses	Emotional Needs
Teen		
Cheerleader; charms others; daring; joins clubs; is popular, the life of the party; is creative; wants to please; apologizes often	Deceptive; gives creative excuses; is easily led astray; craves attention; needs peer approval; won't study; acts immature; gossips; avoids dull tasks and routines; can't handle criticism; doesn't pay attention to details; has lofty goals	Very frequent attention; approval; affection; acceptance; the presence of people and fun activity

Helpful questions to keep a Sanguine sharp:

- What are some ways I could improve my follow-through with commitments I make?
- What are some phrases I could use to initiate with others?
- What ways could I secure my inner value and worth that doesn't involve verbal reassurance from people?
- What is one boundary that I should not compromise (for my own sake)?

To engage with others more effectively in conversation/communication:

- If not asked about you first, ask about them.
- Take an active listening class/course and practice true hearing to increase quality of your engagement.
- Take a pause when a person finishes a thought, this may offer time for them to say something else rather than you chime in with your thoughts immediately.
- Watch for mannerisms or signs of boredom and, if present, wrap up your thought, ask about them, or kindly dismiss yourself.
- Do your best to exaggerate less – your statements may be better received.
- Condense your comments and, once you've stated your thoughts, yield the floor, or ask, "What do you think?" to help the conversation along.
- Give others the chance to speak for themselves, don't "pounce" in to tell a better version or one-up another's story – catch yourself from saying "Oh, that's nothing, listen to THIS…"

Proactive Remembering (to avoid "forgetfulness"):

- Pay attention to names
- Don't repeat so often
- Write things down
- Don't forget the children
- Use systems to assist with task management
- Do easy chores when you think of them

Remember:

If you are a Sanguine (in any Temperament Area), awareness of your Sanguine "Swing" is a game-changer for yourself and your relationships. While expressing your needs and recognizing periods of (valid) dependency on others, pay attention to the level of willingness to acknowledge your independent and dependent needs by others. Keeping company with positive support, along with your own stable self-worth and value, can afford a more balanced "swing" and offer energy, fun, and joy to yourself and your world.

"Wow! No more worrying who to hire! WIDP hit the nail right on the head. It told me precisely who the right person was to fill the job. It worked. What a cost saver. What a time saver. Never again will I go through the anguish of not being sure. WIDP has made a believer out of me."

Martin Anderholm, President,
Anderholm Press, Inc., Orange, MA

Chapter 5: The Phlegmatic

David has always been able to get along with everyone. He is confident, well spoken, and an excellent conversationalist. David is patient, kind, and an excellent listener who empathizes with other people's problems. At parties and social events, he carries on just as quickly with the dominant, outgoing types as he does the quiet "wallflowers". When a conversation remains even and level, David will participate. However, David can sense even a hint of potential conflict. In these cases, he will use his dry wit and sarcastic sense of humor to bring things back to calmness. Some people, however, don't want calm, and this is unsettling for David. If his efforts to bring balance prove unsuccessful, he will dismiss himself from the conversation and, if necessary, from the entire social event.

David loves peace and does not invite conflict nor drama, making him naturally enjoyable company. David, like other Phlegmatics that share his level expression, is light and humorous. He likes to tell a good story (and loves a surprising twist) and he has a great sense of humor. In a nutshell, David is the kind of person everyone likes to have around.

At work, David keeps his nose to the grindstone most of the time. Meticulous and systematic, he produces quality work, consistently. He is not what you would call a "take-charge" guy and usually prefers to reach consensus rather than make decisions on his own. While he may have contributed to process improvement to increase efficiency in the office, he prefers not to be forced to adopt other new changes. Change itself can be difficult for David and he would appreciate time to think through and adapt to any new change, receiving plenty of advanced notice. Change, to David, equates to unplanned imbalance to his routine, which can quickly drain his energy and motivation.

For a Phlegmatic, balancing physical, mental, and emotional energy is the key for functional health in every life area.

In his relationships, David is very committed and trustworthy. Although he rarely goes overboard when expressing his emotions — that is, he does not "come on strong" or "shower" anyone with affection, he does give (and needs to receive) moderate amounts of love from his close relationships. While David may have many acquaintances and casual friends, he has few close friends. It isn't that David does not like people or can't find friends – it is because of his limited energy. A Phlegmatic carefully selects close friends based upon whether those friends contribute to maintaining peace and moderation, which results in balanced energy levels and balanced life activity for him. A non-demanding friend is a welcome friend for David because he can get his needs met without exerting energy that has already been budgeted for other things. David chooses his level of involvement based upon the energy demand and sustainability. Energy affects everything David does, and he will quickly shed parts of his life that drain him to restore his precious energy reserve.

To a Phlegmatic, if balance is the ship, moderation is the propellor. The Phlegmatic Temperament is the only Temperament that does not have extremes/compulsivity.

A Phlegmatic will exert extra energy
to ensure they won't have to exert extra energy!

A Phlegmatic is not excessively outgoing, but he also would not isolate himself from people and social activities for extended periods of time. He will "moderately" express himself socially (if Phlegmatic in the Social Area), and then he will "moderately" disengage from individuals and social events and head for his quiet place.

Recall from the previous chapter the "Sanguine Swing". A Sanguine has a high natural expression and high desire for others to be expressive towards her, both of which are the natural needs of the Temperament. Similarly, a Phlegmatic, which has both a moderate expression and a desire for others to be moderately expressive towards him, naturally needs to have both in his life – thus, moderate modes of demonstration and of desire ensure life is moderated/balanced. A Sanguine Swing is triggered by her level of acceptance/rejection, yet a Phlegmatic is the most naturally stable of all Temperaments. His root need isn't acceptance, it's conserving energy (balance)! Therefore, when a Phlegmatic has been secluded for a time, he will desire moderate people interaction. When he has his fill of interaction with others, he secludes himself to maintain balance. The "mode" a Phlegmatic is in depends on his level of energy at the time.

A Note about Anger for a Phlegmatic

In general, David is not quick to anger, nor does he express anger often. When he does become angry, he tends to minimize it, so he does not have to exert energy to deal with it. If pushed to the limit by someone trying to motivate him to do something he does not want to do, he will dig in his heels and will not budge. David uses his dry sense of humor or witty remarks (sarcasm) to derail conflict and "block" the demands of others. David may feel like everyday life is draining, so it makes sense that he must be strategic each day to only deal with whatever is necessary – and nothing more. This includes dealing with anger, which tops the list of draining activities.

How does anger affect David internally and what can be done about it? Let's look at what David may experience physically, emotionally, and spiritually when feeling angry.

Physically. David will expend energy to diplomatically negotiate a peaceful solution or to motivate someone else to handle the situation. Frustration may cause him to overeat as a way of dealing with the pressures that others try to exert on him. He would rather sit and eat than expend precious energy to resolve the root cause of demand or imbalance. Of course, this is an unhealthy response. Instead, David needs downtime to rest and recuperate from the anger to rejuvenate physical strength. Recovery could take several days depending on the level of physical strength and energy lost. Poor care of physical elements will render less energy at the start of each day to handle even the necessary elements of daily living such as parenting and house maintenance.

Emotionally. David has a unique ability to maintain internal composure - his "feathers are not easily ruffled", so he generally expresses few emotions, including expressing anger. When David does get angry, it internally intensifies because this emotion (and situation) forces him into a corner, and that makes him angrier. David may downplay it as being "upset", which belittles the situation that made him angry, morphing the single emotion into a ripple-effect state of depression. If David then seeks medical assistance for his depression and begins taking depressive medication(s), it exacerbates the situation by causing him to function outside of the normal range of emotions, clouding his true feelings even further. What a cascade! Discussing what is causing anger from a "needs-based" (Temperament) standpoint of balance and energy is healthier for David long-term.

Spiritually. Balance and moderation, to David, is often found in re-centering – whether from a faith-based perspective of peace or through natural/holistic methods of reconnecting with the energies of nature. David may tend to sleep to restore his energy, which helps physically, but finds himself spiritually exhausted even after waking. Anger tends to upset the spiritual balance that requires focus and time to restore. If David were to choose to seek modes of spiritual equilibrium as a daily lifestyle best practice, he could regather his spiritual balance regardless of whether anger was present that day.

Because Phlegmatic anger can maintain an objective mentality that affords him the talent to negotiate, this Temperament is the least prone to experience stress because of anger (due to possessing balance intrinsically). During a period of recovering from anger, David could seem to be displaying characteristics of depression. He should allow himself a reasonable amount of time for this recovery; it may take a couple of days or a couple of weeks. In the meantime, he will likely try to avoid the person that introduced the conflict (because he certainly didn't!) for fear of another bout of emotional expression causing him more distress. If you are a friend of a Phlegmatic, helping to maintain peaceful conditions gives a stable foundation of anger/energy recovery.

The Phlegmatic — Demonstrated vs. Desired Behavior

The Phlegmatic is a very even-keeled individual, very pleasant to be around. Notice how the numerical illustration below reflects this balance - moderate in both *Demonstrated behavior towards others* and *Desired behavior from others*. In other words, a Phlegmatic is neither highly introverted nor highly extroverted and desires to (1) give moderate amounts to others and (2) receive moderate amounts from others in the respective Temperament Area. Let's dive into this naturally balanced Temperament, beginning with details in the **Social** Area.

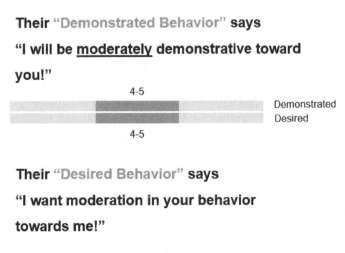

Their "Demonstrated Behavior" **says**

"I will be <u>moderately</u> demonstrative toward you!"

4-5

Demonstrated
Desired

4-5

Their "Desired Behavior" **says**

"I want moderation in your behavior towards me!"

The Social Profile – Phlegmatic

Statistics – Phlegmatic in Social (out of 3,449 people)

3.86%

N/A

Phlegmatic

Number: 133
Percentage: 3.86%

Phlegmatic Compulsive

Number: N/A
Percentage: N/A

A Note About the Social Profile

The Social Area outlines your needs and desires for light friendships, work/career associations, and other casual relationships. By comparing the Social Profile with your current life situation, you can understand conflict areas and achieve a comfortable level of interpersonal contact in the work or social environment.

Remember: Information contained in the Social Profile should be applied only to the individual's casual social and career contacts (surface-level relationships). To determine the individual's needs and desires in close personal relationships, please consult the Relationship Profile.

Social Needs and Desires

A Phlegmatic has a strong need to maintain a peaceful, non-demanding lifestyle and is comfortable with or without social interaction. He adapts quickly to being alone or with moderate interaction with others, possessing excellent social skills and a keen ability to interact well with all types of people. Content with whatever situation he encounters, he tends to accept the status quo in life. He is conservative in his attachments and realistic with expectations. Because of his low energy reserve, he prefers to expend available energy on tasks rather than large amounts of interaction. He needs a quiet lifestyle and structured daily routine and directs much of his behavior toward avoiding fatigue and maintaining balance in all life areas.
Criteria for Friendships. Friendly and sociable, a Phlegmatic genuinely likes people and is free from urgent needs, fear of rejection, low self-esteem, and other barriers to relationships.

Because people tend to drain his energy, he avoids extensive social interaction and chooses to be involved as a spectator in life more than an active participant. While he depends on others to initiate and maintain social interactions and friendships, he readily participates when invited and is faithful and committed to friends and coworkers.

Perception of Self. Confident and self-contained, a Phlegmatic possesses good self-esteem and a healthy self-image. He is usually satisfied with his abilities and accomplishments and remains secure in believing his own opinions and perspectives are correct, due to his uncanny ability to see all sides of a situation. He maintains a practical approach to life and people and is calm and complacent. Despite his ideas and abilities, however, his need to protect his energy reserve may cause him to be an underachiever, prioritizing balance in place of goals and overinvolvement.

Perception by Others. A Phlegmatic appears calm and stable, even under pressure. Others usually perceive him as friendly, understanding, easy to be around, and one who finds humor in most situations. He can hold an audience in stitches and never crack a smile. His ability to relate well to people, including hostile or difficult personalities, makes him a diplomatic negotiator who brings objectivity and peace into troubled situations. While he is skilled in helping people resolve conflict, he avoids personal involvement in any conflict situation. He is naturally non-assertive and non-confrontational and may use his excellent verbal skills, especially sarcastic humor, to help avoid conflict and preserve energy.

Perception of Others. A Phlegmatic is an empathetic listener, compassionate and understanding of others. He is usually very patient, willing to assist and encourage other people. He is accepting of people and views others positively, remaining tolerant of their faults and mistakes. He avoids over-involvement in the lives and activities of others and maintains some distance even in close relationships. He may become critical of those who attempt to change or control him. Instead, he needs to receive recognition and appreciation for his efforts. Usually does not argue or try to persuade, rather he waits for others to come around to the reality of his reasonable, well-rounded perspective.

Intellectual Orientation. Possessing high mental abilities, a Phlegmatic carefully gathers facts and considers options before deciding; he rarely changes his mind once he has formed an opinion. Remember, a Phlegmatic needs time to adjust to any change. You cannot just "spring" an idea on him and expect him to endorse whatever the plan may be. It is essential to give him time to process the idea of change before he makes the transition. Even then, you may experience resistance depending on the energy impact this change demands directly from him. Objective, practical, highly self-disciplined, consistent, and dependable, a Phlegmatic quickly identifies problems and inequities and inspires others to develop solutions. He has strong principles of correctness and accuracy.

Emotional Orientation. Emotionally stable, a Phlegmatic usually remains cheerful and calm, avoiding extremes of emotional expression and using a sense of humor to keep things conflict-free. He is not prone to moodiness or depression and, while he experiences strong emotions, he does not express them easily. He rarely becomes angry or suffers "hurt feelings" and usually avoids confrontation, attempting to maintain peace in every situation. He may become anxious or fearful when faced with change, when people make excessive demands on him, or when placed in conflict situations — even if he is not directly involved. The stress of any kind robs him of energy. He can replenish energy by taking "power naps" when his reserve is low. If only for ten or fifteen minutes, it helps get him back on track emotionally.

Work Orientation. A Phlegmatic is task-oriented rather than people-oriented. He is organized, and quite good at his job, thorough in his approach to tasks, accurate and precise in his work, and a perfectionist about details. He handles routine or tedious assignments efficiently, maintains a slow, steady work pace, and consistently produces excellent results. He is disciplined and efficient and draws his excellent self-concept from successful job performance. While his ideal career involves tasks, not people, he relates well to people for short time periods and is willing to accommodate coworkers. He adapts well to those in authority and can be a capable leader, although he may not often seek leadership roles, preferring to work independently or as part of a team so he can manage his energy more effectively. He needs reassurance from others before assuming responsibilities and is unlikely to take risks. He functions best in a stable, controlled work environment, where his relaxed style brings a stabilizing harmony to teams composed of varied work styles. He may procrastinate when faced with decision-making and can be stubborn and resistant to change, even if the changes will bring improvement. Because he is so meticulous about his performance and spends a considerable amount of energy adhering to strict requirements, he may be exhausted by the end of the day. If working 9 to 5, he will punch in at 8:59 and out at precisely 5 o'clock. Overtime is not in his vocabulary unless everyone is working overtime with him. He is the kind of employee that will stay in the same job for 30 — 40 years doing the same thing every day and look forward to his gold watch and retirement.

Motivation. A Phlegmatic is self-motivated but needs to be convinced intellectually before acting. He has a strong desire to avoid conflict or change and is seldom motivated by outside influences to change. He may change his behavior to avoid conflict (punishment) or achieve peace (reward). One reasonable way to describe a Phlegmatic is that he is deliberate and has only one pace – the pace that he determines.

Rejection/Acceptance Profile. A Phlegmatic does not fear rejection or need acceptance, and rarely uses dismissal against others. He does not take rejection personally and possesses an excellent ability to make people feel accepted. Put bluntly, what you think of him does not determine his inner value.

The Leadership Profile — Phlegmatic

It's important to note that within WIDP, **Leadership** is understood within the context of:

1) <u>Directing</u> decisions and responsibilities. [Demonstrated]

and

2) <u>Receiving direction</u> for decisions and responsibilities. [Desired]

To restate it more practically, the higher the number in the Demonstrated Region (6-7-8-9), the more that Temperament will direct and guide others through decisions and responsibilities at work and at home. The higher the number in the Desired Region (6-7-8-9), the more that Temperament will want to be directed and guided through decisions and responsibilities.

The Leadership Profile – Phlegmatic

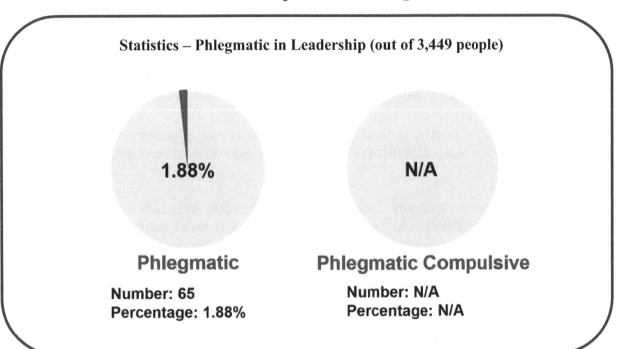

Statistics – Phlegmatic in Leadership (out of 3,449 people)

1.88% — **N/A**

Phlegmatic — **Phlegmatic Compulsive**

Number: 65 — Number: N/A
Percentage: 1.88% — Percentage: N/A

A Note About the Leadership Profile

The Leadership Profile/Area identifies the individual's ability to provide leadership, make decisions, and assume responsibilities. This Area outlines the individual's needs and desires for independence, achievement, and recognition. Because Leadership needs and desires are expressed through interacting with people, the Leadership Profile should not be evaluated alone. It should be interpreted with either the Social Profile or the Relationship Profile.

Evaluated together, the **Leadership Profile** and the **Social Profile** help determine the individual's career needs. By comparing the results with the individual's current employment situation, you can target conflict areas and help the individual maximize career skills.

Evaluated together, the **Leadership Profile** and the **Relationship Profile** help determine the individual's independence/dependence needs in close relationships. By comparing the results with the individual's current life situation, you can target conflict areas and help the individual enhance relationships.

Leadership Needs and Desires

A Phlegmatic in Leadership expresses and desires a moderate amount of direction and guidance concerning decisions and responsibilities. As a result, he allows others to have reasonable authority over his life. There are very cool ways this plays out and, of course, specific reasons why this is so. A Phlegmatic, in fact, possesses excellent decision making skills and the ability to assume responsibilities, yet benefits most from shared tasks as opposed to carrying the burden alone.

You are not likely to find too many Phlegmatics leading companies. If you do, he or she would be top chair on a Board, or similar structure. What is more common is a Phlegmatic leader that is blended with another Temperament, such as a Phlegmatic Choleric (PC) or a Melancholy Phlegmatic (MP), to name a few possibilities. The Phlegmatic Temperament is the only Temperament that can blend with the other four Temperaments. We won't dive into blended Temperaments here, but briefly, in these cases, leadership is one of diplomacy, not of force, strength, or power. An individual that falls into these categories could be respectfully referred to as a "Soft Leader."

Criteria for Friendships. Friendly and sociable, a Phlegmatic genuinely likes people. He possesses excellent social skills and can interact well with all types of individuals. He is free from urgent needs, fear of rejection, low self-esteem, and other barriers to relationships. Because people tend to drain his energy, he avoids extensive socialization. He is faithful and committed to friends and coworkers. He needs friends to encourage his plans and decisions. Often, he is intuitively scanning for factors that are draining in people or situations, always aware of his energy level. When he has reached his saturation level of people interaction, he will retreat to a place of peace to recharge.

Perception of Self. Confident and self-contained with a positive self-image, a Phlegmatic is satisfied with his abilities and accomplishments and secure in believing his opinions and viewpoints are correct. To help alleviate concerns about criticism or failure, he seeks to share responsibility. Despite his ideas and abilities, his need to protect his energy reserve trumps overachievement in life, unconcerned with reaching full potential unless it is harnessed in a way that keeps life stable and predictable. Calm and complacent, he maintains a practical approach to life and people.

Perception by Others. Stable even under pressure, a Phlegmatic is usually perceived as friendly and understanding. He can find humor in most situations and possesses the ability to relate well, balancing out introverts and extroverts alike. Because he can perceive all sides of a situation, he can bring objectivity and peace to troubled situations. He may appear indecisive because of his tendency to procrastinate. Others will find him pleased when everyone is pulling their weight, which helps him to maintain a more consistent energy balance.

Perception of Others. A Phlegmatic is patient, compassionate, and understanding of others. He is an empathetic listener and sets realistic expectations. He views other people positively and accepts them for who they are, is tolerant of their faults and mistakes, and is willing to assist and encourage. At the same time, he avoids over-involvement in the lives and activities of others and maintains some distance even in close relationships. He needs recognition and appreciation for his efforts but does not call attention to his achievements. A Phlegmatic may become critical of those who attempt to change or control him and may find certain people incapable of accessing their "common sense", which is easy for a Phlegmatic but requires a lot more thought by the other four Temperaments.

Intellectual Orientation. A Phlegmatic will not be seeking out Leadership positions although he does possess high mental abilities. Objective, practical, and highly self-disciplined, he is excellent at identifying problems and inequities but low on energy to be the workhorse of carrying out the solutions. He carefully gathers facts and considers options before deciding. Although he seeks input and support from others and often inspires others to develop solutions, he does not necessarily change his mind if people disagree with his decision. Often, you will find he just waits for others to either come around to his perspective, or he will allow things to "play out" to show his predictions are valid and perspective should be heeded.

Emotional Orientation. A Phlegmatic is emotionally stable, is not prone to moodiness or depression, and usually remains cheerful and calm. He avoids extremes of emotional expression and uses his sense of humor as a defense. Although he experiences strong emotions, he does not express them easily and does not become angry as much as he can help it, as anger drains his energy quickly. He actively avoids confrontation and tries to maintain peace in every situation. He may become anxious or fearful when faced with change and when people place excessive demands on him, as well as in conflict situations. If he is forced to face a situation, he can make decisions and promises that will get them out of the situation but does not necessarily address the problem. The cost of energy is the measuring stick of every action and interaction.

Work Orientation. Task-oriented rather than people-oriented, a Phlegmatic is well organized in his approach to tasks. Disciplined and efficient, he is accurate and precise in his work and is a perfectionist with details. He is very dependable and can be relied upon to be at work and always be on time. He can handle routine or tedious assignments efficiently and maintains a slow, steady work pace that consistently produces excellent results. Because he draws his self-concept from successful job performance, his ideal career involves tasks, not people. He possesses the ability to relate very well to people for short time periods, is a team player, and adapts well to those in authority. Conservative in his approach and unlikely to take risks, a Phlegmatic functions best in a stable, controlled, and predictable work environment. His laid-back style brings harmony to his work environment and provides stability to teams composed of diverse work styles. He may procrastinate when faced with decision-making and can be resistant to change, even if the changes will bring improvement. Because he spends a considerable amount of energy adhering to strict requirements and ensuring that he performs well, he may be exhausted by the end of the day and needs to clock in and clock out exactly on time. Rewarding him with a raise, bonus, or extra days off would be welcome as any of these contribute to helping him maintain balance and conserve energy in all life areas.

Motivation. The motivation for a Phlegmatic to intentionally assume leadership roles is not all that common. He prefers to function as part of a team and will carry out the regular responsibilities, but it isn't in his best interests to seek out extra work or responsibilities. A Phlegmatic is self-motivated but, because of his strong desire to avoid conflict or change, he needs to be convinced intellectually before acting. He is seldom motivated by outside influences to change, often only changing his behavior to avoid conflict (punishment) or achieve peace (reward). The most exceptional reward/motivation for a Phlegmatic is money and working in a relaxed environment with no overtime.

Rejection/Acceptance Profile. A Phlegmatic can make people feel accepted and does not fear rejection nor need acceptance. He does not take rejection personally and does not often choose to dismiss others coldly or aggressively. Where the other four Temperaments can be "needy" in specific ways, he may pride himself in pulling his own weight so as not to be a burden, expecting others to give the same courtesy.

The Board of Phlegmatics

The Director of a non-profit organization needed assistance from a consulting firm to figure out a quick solution concerning a piece of property the group currently had under their control. The property had three buildings, was debt free, and valued at $500,000. Under the property agreement, the organization could keep the property so long as personnel occupied the premises. The personnel presently occupying the property were part of their group but had allied with another team that had visions of taking over the land and the buildings. So, the five-person Board had to decide, within three days, whether to hold this property to secure it legally.

The Director approached the consulting firm as an aggressive, focused, take-charge person who was able to make quick, intuitive decisions and go forward. He did not waver in conflict and was very direct and bold in his communications. However, the other four members of the leadership group were Phlegmatics. They were all very dependable, steady, task-oriented, and middle-of-the-road-type people. These members rarely make quick changes to anything and prefer changes to happen slowly, over an extended period, with everyone agreeing to the modification. The mindset is: "If it worked for this long, why change it now?" Without consensus on a solution, any issue could be postponed indefinitely.

The Director, having been alerted of the potential loss of the property to another organization via an anonymous phone call, organized a response plan consisting of arranging personnel from his organization to occupy the property and organizing a locksmith to put new locks on the buildings the following morning. With these response plans drafted, he only lacked approval from the other four members of the Board. In an emergency meeting, all the Phlegmatic members did not want to engage in conflict with or even question the integrity of the person who was currently occupying the property. They had difficulty believing the other organization would actively move to take the property and, so, the members chose not to permit the expense of changing locks on the buildings even as a safeguard. Remember, a Phlegmatic does not like to waste money and saw this as an unnecessary expense.

What happened? The other organization did take control, changed the locks, and walked off with $500,000 worth of property. Why?

There are essentially two rights that happened: The Phlegmatics were right in their stand against the Director who wanted to jump in, take over, and control the situation, which is why a Board is in place; to help gain consensus on situations involving the organization. This Board was an element of a more substantial parent organization, which also happened to be run by a Phlegmatic, and the pulse of the leadership was content to run as a status quo organization. The Director, who offered a reasonable aggressive response for an aggressive move by another organization, was simply out of place in a Phlegmatic-heavy board. As a result, the Director chose to resign and, candidly, the Phlegmatics rejoiced.

Do you think this was a success for Phlegmatics or did they lose $500,000 unnecessarily?

The Relationship Profile – Phlegmatic

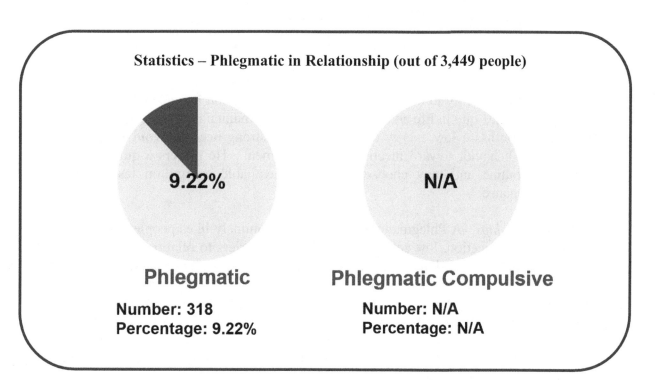

Statistics – Phlegmatic in Relationship (out of 3,449 people)

9.22%

N/A

Phlegmatic

Number: 318
Percentage: 9.22%

Phlegmatic Compulsive

Number: N/A
Percentage: N/A

A Note about the Relationship Profile

The third Area of WIDP, the Relationship Profile, identifies the individual's preferences for emotional involvement and shared affection on a one-to-one basis. For most people, the Relationship Profile is the dominant pattern that influences behavior in the Social and Leadership Areas.

By comparing the Relationship Profile with the individual's current life situation, you can target conflict areas and help the individual meet fundamental (heart) needs for a more well-rounded life and healthy, functional relationships.

Relationship Needs and Desires

Conservative in his attachments and expectations of people, a Phlegmatic is usually content with a few close relationships. Within those connections, he needs to express and receive moderate amounts of love and affection. He has balanced needs for communicating realistic gestures of respect to others and does not require repeated assurances of love to maintain these connections.

In his close relationships, he may expect the other person to expend more effort than he does to maintain the relationship and initiate expressions of love because of his energy – his ideal mode does not want to spend what power he has performing ongoing maintenance of his relationship.

Possessing an excellent ability to be content with whatever situation he encounters, a Phlegmatic tends to accept the status quo in life and has a strong need to maintain a peaceful, non-demanding lifestyle. Because he has a low energy reserve, he has a strong need to avoid fatigue and may direct much of his behavior toward meeting this requirement. He prefers a quiet lifestyle and structured daily routine and may choose to use his available energy on tasks rather than relationship maintenance.

Criteria for Relationships. A Phlegmatic is friendly and genuinely likes people. He is free from urgent needs, fear of rejection, low self-esteem, and other barriers to relationships. At the same time, because people tend to drain his energy (including those they are close to), he needs a predictable routine in his life and avoids extensive displays or demands of affection and reassurance (maintenance). He prefers quiet time at home instead of participation in people events and maintains an attitude of non-involvement in life, usually preferring to be an observer. In the beginning of relationships, he rarely initiates interactions or friendships, depending on others to start and maintain relationships with him. However, he readily participates when invited and is faithful and committed to friends and loved ones.

Perception of self. Confident and self-contained, a Phlegmatic is satisfied with his abilities and accomplishments, secure in believing his own opinions and viewpoints are correct. He maintains a practical approach to life and people. Calm, complacent, and rarely introspective, he has healthy self-esteem and a positive self-image. He has confidence he is loved and accepted by those close to him. Despite his ideas and abilities, he needs to protect his energy reserve. He will always try to create and remain in an environment that is hassle-free from stress, anxiety, commotion, and frequent demands.

A Phlegmatic will likely feel very comfortable with the lifestyle that he carves out for himself.

Perception by Others. A Phlegmatic is calm and stable, even under pressure, and usually perceived as friendly and understanding. He relates well to most people, including hostile or difficult personalities, often bringing objectivity and peace into troubled situations. As a result, he is a natural diplomat and negotiator, skilled in helping people resolve conflicts by seeing all sides of a situation to find the win/win. Non-assertive and non-confrontational, he usually avoids personal involvement in any conflict situation. Able to find humor in most cases, a Phlegmatic uses his excellent verbal skills, especially sarcastic fun, as a defense. Loved ones may feel neglected at times, wanting more attention and expressions of love than a Phlegmatic can give on a frequent basis, due to energy constraints.

Perception of Others. Patient, compassionate, understanding, and usually accepting of others, a Phlegmatic is an empathetic listener willing to assist and encourage. He views others positively and is tolerant of their faults and mistakes. At the same time, he needs recognition and appreciation for his efforts and avoids over-involvement in the lives and activities of others, maintaining some distance even in close relationships. He may become critical of those who attempt to change or control him. He will avoid people who are argumentative or display disruptive behavior. A Phlegmatic notices the driven and focused characteristics of a Choleric or Melancholy within group settings but limits his exposure to this aggressive approach to life or work to ensure he isn't given responsibilities beyond his preferential, balanced load.

Intellectual Orientation. A Phlegmatic is conservative in his approach to life, unlikely to take risks. He possesses high mental abilities, carefully gathering facts and considering options before deciding. Although he may procrastinate when faced with decision-making and prefers shared responsibility, he rarely changes his mind once he has formed an opinion. Objective, practical, and highly self-disciplined, a Phlegmatic is well organized, accurate, and precise in his work. He is excellent at identifying problems and inequities and inspiring others to develop solutions. A Phlegmatic positions himself so he can delegate or suggest to others how to correct the issues he has identified. Obviously, this approach creates quite a stumbling block within close relationships.

Emotional Orientation. Emotionally stable and usually cheerful and calm, a Phlegmatic avoids extremes of emotional expression. He is not prone to moodiness or depression and uses his sense of humor and sarcasm as a defense. In some situations, he will become the "clown" in a group of friends to deflect criticism or conflict. He experiences strong emotions but does not express them easily, even in close relationships, and has difficulty verbalizing his love for others. A Phlegmatic rarely becomes angry or experiences "hurt feelings." He avoids confrontation and tries to maintain peace in every situation. He may become anxious or fearful when faced with change or when close relationships place excessive demands on him. He feels anxiety in conflict situations, even if he is not directly involved. A Phlegmatic does have a breaking point emotionally and can explode if pushed too far, which will deplete his energy immediately. The best thing for him at that point is to sleep; a very beneficial energy restoration technique.

Motivation. While the Phlegmatic is self-motivated, he possesses a strong desire to avoid conflict and change and needs to be convinced intellectually before acting, even involving close relationships. He can be stubborn and resistant to change, even if the change would bring improvement within close relationships. This resistance can be a stumbling block of development for some connections. He is seldom motivated by outside influences to change and may modify his behavior to avoid conflict (punishment) or achieve peace (reward). The most important thing to remember is that he needs time to process a change regardless of the subject. He takes this time to digest and come to his own conclusions about whether the change is right for him. Rather than not knowing how long it will take to receive a response, it is appropriate for others to request a response time frame from him. His timeframe proposal will be an honest and reasonable amount for him to process and provide thoughts on the change.

Rejection/Acceptance Profile. A Phlegmatic usually does not fear rejection, take rejection personally, or need acceptance by others. He easily makes other people feel accepted and rarely uses dismissal against others. Although he does not deliberately reject loved ones, they may perceive his lack of involvement as rejection. His closest relationships are wise to remember it is about balanced energy expense and not necessarily that he does not like you or is not interested.

A Note about Strengths & Weaknesses

The *Probable Strengths & Potential Weaknesses* section is located at the end of each of the 3 WIDP Profile Areas. An individual's Temperament may be different in one or all Areas, thus the Strengths & Weaknesses will coincide with their uniquely identified Temperament in that respective Area. It is important to interpret the labels *probable* and *potential* correctly. The difference of which characteristic is experienced or observed depends on several factors.

Any individual whose Temperament needs are actively getting met has the greatest chance of exuding their strengths. For instance, after we eat a meal, we are much happier, as our hunger need has been satisfied. The same is true with Temperament needs. Someone whose Temperament needs are getting met will tend to be a balanced and healthy individual, able to proactively participate within their strengths for a positive impact in their life.

However, if certain Temperament needs have been frustrated, the potential for negative performance could be experienced and observed, leading to unbalanced behavior and emotional instability.

> **Like a runny nose is a symptom,**
> <u>**think of weaknesses as symptoms**</u>
> **that indicate unmet Temperament needs.**
>
> ↓
>
> **Wiping our nose doesn't address the true problem.**
> **Instead, identify and treat the root cause:**
>
> **Meet Temperament Needs!**

Remember: No Temperament is automatically broken by design. Each Temperament is genetically wired with unique, specific needs that allow the individual to be mentally and emotionally healthy and functional within that context. Temperament makeup can be referred to as one's emotional biology.

Basic Strengths/Weaknesses of the Phlegmatic

Probable Strengths
- Calm, quiet, and stable — is "easy going," cheerful, and rarely agitated by people or situations
- Sociable and friendly — the most likable of the Temperaments; is sympathetic and kind to people
- Objective and fair — is a born diplomat; a natural peacemaker in conflicts
- Dependable and consistent — remains faithful to people and responsibilities; is not prone to sudden change
- Humorous — enjoys a good joke; sees the lighter side of life
- Practical — is highly organized and efficient; pragmatic in his approach to tasks and life in general

Potential Weaknesses
- Slow-paced — appears to lack motivation; rarely does more than is expected
- Procrastinates — tends to ignore responsibilities more than the other Temperaments
- Self-centered — protects himself from pain and avoids involvement whenever possible
- Stubborn — refuses to change his mind; is highly resistant to change
- Fearful and indecisive — avoids situations that require confrontation, action, or involvement
- Frugal — can make him come across as cheap
- Sarcastic — uses cynicism and dry humor as a defense

Decisions for the Phlegmatic

A Phlegmatic avoids and fears to make decisions as it may require his involvement. His energy management requires that he not create more work for himself, which typically translates as choosing involvement as an observer, not an active participant. When he sees something that needs to be done, he will tell someone else and expect them to do it.

For a Phlegmatic, decisions are based on energy impact. He only has a certain amount of energy each day and must carefully balance this reserve.

He must be afforded the opportunity to assess a situation and likely will choose for himself what best will maintain his energy balance. In some circumstances, he will entertain planning far enough ahead of a required energy expense so that he can ensure all other areas are properly balanced for this change/event.

Other Probable Strengths
of the Phlegmatic

Steady	Level in nature, not shaken by external impacts
Patient	Can place themselves in others' shoes to gain understanding of behavior and situations
Stress-free	Opportunistic in the ability to find efficiencies and solutions that create a predictable and stable work and home environment, lending to peace and satisfaction
Balanced	Innate talent of seeing through a lens of life to ensure all perspectives have been considered, can find gaps intuitively
Comfortable	Satisfied with themselves and gives a calming presence for others that promotes evenness
Focused	No matter how mundane or complex, methodically paces through the task, to completion
Dry	Wonderfully enjoyable sense of humor turning normal phrases and events into delightfully unexpected remarks
Dependable	You can count on them due to their realistic outlook, if unrealistic, they will tell you
Efficient	Recognizes the path of least resistance since they innately want that in all areas of life
Perfect Parent	Models the epitome of balance that regulates and stabilizes children and teens who are seeking the same regulation of life and emotional areas for themselves, handles areas of concern with care and understanding
Salespeople	Due to not being pushy or belligerent, others respect their listening and reasoning skills when applying the product or service to their specific needs
Teammate	Work and home interactions and relationships strive to share the weight of responsibility and do not take a dictatorial, nor careless approach to responsibilities
Diplomatic	Ensures all sides entertain and agree on a win/win through peaceful negotiation

Easy	Enjoyable, flagrant in pursuing peaceful conversations and demand-free environments so all can relax
Analytical	Ready to offer perspective, especially when it is valued and all the information is brought forth for their perusal
Self-Sufficient	Moderates and stabilizes within self, doesn't need external validation of value, trusts themselves
Wise	Because of the gift of perspective, can often share thoughts that cover the ground others may have not considered because they couldn't see that side of things
Non-offensive	Delivery often professional, well-mannered, and offers easy-to-swallow advice and feedback

Other Potential Weaknesses
of the Phlegmatic

Watcher	Involvement is strategic, even to the point that if they believe they won't be heard, will let things fail, even if cost is substantial
Status Quo	Meets requirements, then stops
Unenthusiastic	Could be quite difficult to get a read on due to small range of outward expression
Fearful	Causes prolonged delay in decisions and even movement into necessary areas of action
Avoids Extra Burdens	Even within family activities, does not invite work upon themselves, which give the impression they do not care or don't want to contribute to events needing involvement
Deflection	Will seek to de-rail any potential conflict, anger, or demands
Emotionless	If drained about a thought or situation, will approach with cold, apathetic demeanor, like flipping a switch internally
Critical	Takes the inventory of the world; people and situations, could be prone to gossip about inequities of behavior or perceived intelligence with others who share their perspective or could potentially relieve their situation
Resists Change	Will hold firm ground to the way things are unless they convince themselves it will benefit their energy conversation
Teases Extroverts	Are annoyed at those who display "over"-expression, preferring those who "under"-express so that less energy is used to level the impact
Judgmental	Could use gift of perspective against others' situational condition
Discouraging	If a constant "wet blanket" on perspectives, ideas, or thoughts due to unyielding disposition, may back-fire by demotivating the drivers
Frugal	When not moderated, portrays as stingy or penny-pinching seen as unwilling to "pony-up"

Unworried	May choose apathy over involvement when issues are presented, due to not having energy to address it; a "go-with-the-flow", "it is what it is", "it'll work itself out" approach when others may need assistance in handling issues
Selfish	Approaches interactions with expectation that others will initiate and maintain it, including close relationships, leading to difficulty in deep intimacy and shared victories
Holds Grudges	May present a well-remembered "laundry list" of historical facts to minimize viewpoints when demands or criticality surfaces from others
Self-Righteous	Everyone else is wrong; pronounces judgments liberally in like-minded company
Veiled	Hides real feelings and emotions for many reasons, mostly to not get angry
Tired	May find it hard to accept they were created with an energy balance indicator, even to the point they begin to hate their design

Helpful Tips for the Phlegmatic

Often, a Phlegmatic interacting with the other four Temperament types may leave him puzzled. A phrase often heard from a Phlegmatic is "Well, it's common sense!" Be aware that because of your incredible innate gift of perspective and proclivity for problem-solving, what sticks out to you is not so apparent to other Temperaments. As such, help for a Phlegmatic isn't to improve themselves, but rather to affirm it is okay to be who you are and to embrace these gifts with others in mind. Your needs are equally unique and important.

IT IS OKAY

The following are some things about which a Phlegmatic should not feel guilty:

It is OKAY to be slow-paced. You tire quickly and you know there are certain things you must do. You do not have to feel guilty about a limited energy reserve. Pay attention to your people saturation level and learn when to seek interaction and when to retreat interactions and people activities. Recognize and accept that others balance out by being around your balance, thus they will find a sense of peace and calm in your presence, often dumping out their life and problems because you "actually listen". While observing requires very little energy, people interaction drains. When it's time to preserve energy, kindly dismiss yourself. If you are going to be attending an event or function that will take a lot of energy, budget and plan for that ahead of time, including time to recover and recharge. Additionally, do not make big decisions after 12 pm, wait until you are fresh the following morning.

It is OKAY to have a "dry" sense of humor. This humor can be hilarious when used in the right context and lifts the spirits of those around you. Offering this humor helps keep life light for the other Temperaments. This type of humor is quick and witty. Recognize the difference between humor and sarcasm used to deflect tension. Sarcasm often has a cutting or biting undertone, which can be a utility of keeping others at a distance, so they do not drain you. Be aware of healthy ways to meet your needs of limited, balanced involvement with people and practice gentle methods with Temperaments who simply have different needs than you.

It is OKAY to be an observer. Phlegmatic observation is a jewel. The importance of a Phlegmatic remaining an observer to situations cannot be overstated. Balance is found when he gets to decide his level of involvement because he knows himself and his limitations best. A Phlegmatic can meet his own needs as well as accomplish what must be done in healthy ways. Recognizing that energy is not a debilitating factor of your Temperament can yield a better perspective on how to properly manage it. Just as you must cook and eat to maintain proper physical health and balance, you also must put forth energy towards decisions, responsibilities, interactions, and relationships in life areas. Find those people and things in life that you actively notice do not drain you (some may even GIVE you energy). Remember, you need moderation in all areas. So, find your tribe, work that is predictable, activities you enjoy, and make time to rest.

It is OKAY to be frugal. Money is a great utility for peace of mind. It's obvious that it takes money to live. It is wise to budget and control spending. A Phlegmatic tends to be over-frugal (penny-pinchers) when some life area is unstable or unpredictable. The tense holding of his funds gives a sense of security because he will otherwise have to expend large amounts of energy in the future to get more money, and that could be exhausting. Frugality also must be balanced. For example, others may take notice of your lack of financial participation during "pay-up" time at lunch or outings. An unexpected family need could arise, even a small one. Everyone notices that you work hard, certainly deserving what you earn. So how do you maintain wise frugality without portraying an up-turned nose of entitlement? One way could be to simply budget for generosity. Set aside an amount from your paycheck specifically for buying someone a cup of coffee or a gift. Notice that in keeping strong, stable finances alongside a lifestyle that considers others, even in the small things, people witness a beautiful example of money management they can adopt for themselves.

General Do's and Don'ts

DO'S

- Finish three projects you have started and set dates for others
- If necessary, seek help for possible solutions and choose one
- Communicate your feelings so that people can relate to you
- Practice the etiquette of "rejoicing with those who rejoice"
- Maintain proper nutrition and exercise to help gain energy
- Show others you are actively hearing and that you care
- Focus on your strengths instead of weaknesses
- Write down problems that need a decision
- Find your true interests and pursue them
- Learn some phrases to encourage others
- Speak up and enter the conversation
- Involve yourself in the lives of others
- Move into action with enthusiasm
- Love yourself for who you are
- Model a winner's attitude
- Be willing to take a risk
- Say what you mean
- Trust your abilities

DON'TS

- Hold grudges
- Resist all change
- Harbor fearfulness
- Use sarcasm against people
- Be a wet blanket on others' ideas
- Get too wrapped up in possessions
- Be right in fact but wrong in method
- Always say "I do not care" to decisions
- Deflect negative emotions from others
- Let resentment build, in comes out as sarcasm
- Procrastinate and expect others to do your work
- Take the world's inventory when with other Phlegmatics
- Expect a relationship to be maintained by the other person
- Take advantage of others' loose pockets for coffee and lunches

How to Recognize Whether Your Child Is A Phlegmatic

Strengths	Weaknesses	Emotional Needs
Baby		
Easy going, undemanding, happy, adjustable, good with other children, not easily angered.	Slow, can be shy or indifferent	Moderate attention, praise, loving and gentle motivation

Strengths	Weaknesses	Emotional Needs
Child		
Watches others, easily amused, little trouble, loveable, agreeable	Selfish, teasing, avoids work, fearful, quietly stubborn, lazy, retreats to television	Peace and relaxation, attention, praise, self-worth, loving motivation, and sleep

Strengths	Weaknesses	Emotional Needs
Teen		
Pleasing personality, witty, good listener, mediates problems, hides emotions, leads when pushed, casual attitude, good with helping other students with their emotional problems, good at saving money, others flock to them for counsel, make excellent team members	Indecisive, unenthusiastic, too compromising, unmotivated, sarcastic, uninvolved, procrastinates, will of iron, avoids conflict, decisions, extra work or responsibility, chores, keeps their room in order, avoids tension/quarrels	Peace and relaxation, attention, praise, self-worth, loving motivation, good night's sleep, conflict-free environments

Become Aware of Your Natural Strengths and Learn to Use Them Wisely

Natural Strength	Strength Carried to Extreme	Avoidable Result
Low-key emotions	Hides emotions	Blocks out all feeling
Easygoing and adaptable	Lets others decide	Can't make any decisions
Cooperative and pleasant	Compromises standards	Easily becomes a pawn
Mellow	Becomes lazy and laid back	Refuses to budge

Humor in the Workplace

Rush! Produce! Collaborate! Compete! Sometimes a day at the office feels like a Mad Hatter Tea Party: "No time, no room, clean plates, move down!" When the pace overwhelms you, tame the whirlwind with humor!

Why does humor work?

A good sense of humor lets you deal with others' imperfections and gives you the ability to take yourself lightly and your job seriously. Laughter and fun help to bring out the lighter side of workday situations. People deal with stress differently. The passive approach to stress portrays a calm and collected demeanor but leaves you churning on the inside. The expressive approach to stress can lead to other obvious problems. The humor approach acts like the valve on the top of a pressure cooker – it relieves the steam. Appropriate use of humor not only helps to relieve stress, it develops harmony with peers, and creates goodwill. Moreover, it's free!

Practice makes perfect!

Like everything else we are good at, education and practice account for the skillful use of humor. However, remember you are at work, and joking could be divisive. Never use humor at the expense of another person and offensive humor, whether cultural or sexual, in the workplace, creates stress and ill will. Practice making humor meaningful and fresh. You're likely already quite good at it – flex it as a strategic value add to an enjoyable work experience with others.

Remember:

As a final note to you, a Phlegmatic, remember that your very nature is the template of balance. All of life moves towards this homeostasis but struggles to get there because life also gets in the way. You, however, naturally view the world through a lens of moderation above all else. While your perspective is powerful, your greatest gift to others could simply be your daily living; one modeling balanced emotions, seeking peaceful interactions, maintaining reasonable boundaries, and offering realistic expectations. It could be that others simply did not have exposure to healthy behavior from family and friends throughout their life. Meeting you, then, is refreshing for the soul. Never underestimate the power of your lifestyle.

As a professional clinical psychologist, I have used many psychological instruments in the last 40 years. I have not seen such a powerful apparatus that is so quick and easy yet provides so much critical data on my clients. Worley's ID Profile is indeed the tool of the 21st Century. I will be recommending WIDP to my professional clinical associates nationwide.
Raymond Daniels, Ph.D., President,
Institute of Behavioral Sciences, Derry, NH

Chapter 6: The Melancholy

WIDP Is Not A Box

Before we dive in, it's worth noting that the Melancholy Temperament almost always pushes back when they feel like they are being "put in a box". It's normal, perhaps even expected, to feel this way at first. I, Dr. Worley, am a (Social) Melancholy, and I share this feeling. Calling out your true needs can prompt both validating and triggering thoughts and emotions.

So, what does it mean to be a Melancholy?
It means you have specific needs for specific reasons.

The same is said for each of the five Temperaments – specific needs for specific reasons. WIDP, as a psychometric instrument, means it has gone through reliability and validity testing that, simply put, verifies the instrument "measures what it intends to measure". WIDP is a Temperament assessment, built to measure needs at the foundation of your mental/emotional design. It offers insight and awareness into your invisible, intrinsic nature. Your WIDP results feed that information back to you so you can digest the findings. A useful way to do that is to group needs that are related to the same mode of designed function.

Those are the five Temperaments.

When you fill out the profile questionnaire, so long as you are honest, you are telling WIDP what you genuinely prefer and desire. Therefore, WIDP is a self-proving tool in that as you read information about you, it not only resonates on the plane of logical, conscious thinking (mind/emotions) but also resonates deeply within your life being (spirit). Becoming aware of your true Temperament(s) yields relief and validation of what you likely have been feeling and needing all your life but may not have been receiving from the world-at-large. Examine yourself closely and as you read about what you truly need, feel how your profile relieves and validates you on each of these planes.

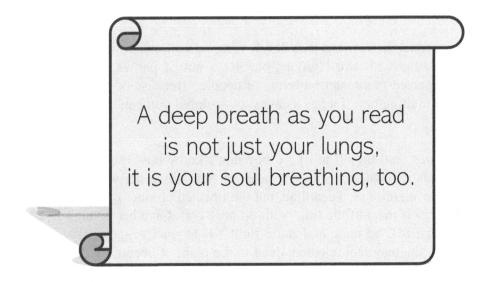

A deep breath as you read
is not just your lungs,
it is your soul breathing, too.

What is an "Introvert"?

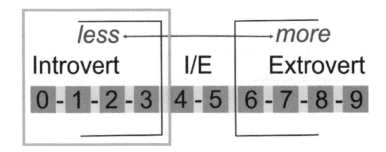

As a Melancholy, you need "less", which we can call introverted needs. You are born with a Temperament that craves to be alone, delights in a few meaningful connections, thinks before speaking, and observes before approaching. You thrive in the inner sanctuary of the mind, heart, and spirit, but shrink in the external world of people, parties, noise, drama, and chaos. As an introvert, you are loyal, sensitive, perceptive, gentle, and reflective. You prefer to operate behind the scenes and influence the world in a quiet, but powerful way. Most of all, you want to be left alone so you can think, dream, and regenerate. If you can relate to these preferences, you are an introvert! Introverts are special, beautiful people.

The Melancholy Temperament

Jill is very gifted, creative, and works hard to make the most of her talents. She is extraordinarily analytical and will work tirelessly to understand every facet of a problem before creating the solution. The ironic thing about Jill is, like a Sanguine, her positive qualities are also what tends to get her into trouble. Often, she is so faithful, diligent, and self- sacrificing that she ends up neglecting her own needs. Then, when criticized, or if her hard work isn't noticed or appreciated, she feels rejected. So, she ends up getting hurt on both sides of the equation. This is quite common for someone who is naturally non-expressive and often just wants to be left alone to her work.

Ask Jill's friends and acquaintances, and they'll tell you she's a loner who spends most of her time at home. She is okay with small groups but not a fan of parties, concerts, and other venues where she is expected to interact with lots of people. Because of her loyalty, she may even appreciate friends inviting her, if it has a caveat of "come if you can", as she hates to back out of a commitment.

Ask Jill's work associates, and they'll tell you they don't know how they'd manage without her. Everything she does is flawless. She may take her time doing her work and ask a lot of questions, occasionally even missing a deadline, but the finished product is well worth the wait. She likes to work by herself most of the time with no pressure. Give her enough freedom and time to get the job done, it'll be done and done right. If anyone suggests that her work is incorrect or incomplete, she may feel rejected, even to the point of becoming depressed. Even when people praise her effort, Jill is rarely satisfied with the results and feels she could have done a better job. This "perfectionism" is what renders high-quality deliverables.

I know a chiropractor whose professional pace is so intense that she only endorses the color beige. She doesn't have time to even THINK about other colors. Everything she has is beige; beige exterior home, beige clothes, beige paint in every room of her house, beige carpeting, beige furniture, beige car, down to and including her professional dress. This person is Melancholy in all three of the Temperament Areas – Social, Leadership, and Relationship. Talk about being driven!

Ask Jill's close friends and loved ones, and they'll tell you that no one is more faithful or committed. She will bend over backwards for her people, to the point of exhaustion, and complete everything she starts, no matter how long it takes and regardless of the cost in time & energy. Jill is very frugal with her money and rarely, if ever, spends frivolously or takes financial risks. Economic security is high on her list of priorities.

Jill's closest friends also know that even though she often appears exceptionally confident, she is very fearful of criticism, which is one of the main reasons she prefers to be alone or with one or two others. "Competency" is key to understanding the theme of her work ethic. She will work until she has become a subject matter expert, no matter the subject. From fixing a gourmet dinner to remodeling her home, whatever she chooses to take on as a task, she will always desire competency first. She will research and practice until she has satisfied her expected level of performance. It is possible she will be so focused that she will isolate herself from everyone, including her immediate family, so that she can dedicate herself to the task. She "burns the midnight oil" staying at work late to get the project completed. She must come across as a competent and qualified individual. Look at her desk or office and you will likely find her qualifications framed and on display to show everyone that she knows her stuff.

Melancholy needs are unique, special, and important, just like the other four Temperaments. And, like the other Temperaments, a Melancholy has *Probable Strengths* and *Potential Weaknesses*. Depending on how well her Temperament needs are getting met will determine what is being experienced internally. A Melancholy is, by nature, less expressive and does not thrust herself into other people's lives. As a result, a Melancholy can experience frustration from having legitimate needs, but not actively speaking up for herself to get those needs met.

Here's a basic taste of what can be experienced in these life areas for a Melancholy:

Physically: A Melancholy can hurt herself from pushing too hard at physical activities such as weightlifting, rock climbing, even house projects, etc., in her pursuit of perfection. She may suffer from severe headaches, be prone to irritable bowel syndrome (IBS) and back pain, and can suffer from dramatic, rapid weight loss if she undertakes projects that exceed her physical capacity. She has an inward drive of proving to herself and others how much she can do - and it is this noble quality of advancing toward greatness that prompts overexertion and physical injury. On the other hand, it is likely a Melancholy who brings home the Gold Medal at the Olympics. Watch a Melancholy in action as an ice skater, diver, runner, or any other Olympic contender and you're watching competence, precision, and perfection in action!

Emotionally: A Melancholy is quick to isolate and disengage from people if she is feeling criticized or judged, then becomes moody and angry. When she must be around people, like for work, she can be cold and indifferent to individuals within that environment. It's not that she does not like people, it's that being around people requires interaction and that interferes with her need to think and analyze. Due to internal struggles from being criticized, she may hurt others by becoming too self-centered, cynical, and critical in return. In a positive light, the Melancholy Temperament makes up the most significant percentage of faithful, loyal friends and significant others. You can depend on a Melancholy to be there for you through thick and thin.

Spiritually: A Melancholy can hurt herself and others by convincing herself God is not providing/is not loyal regarding her troubles. She blames God for allowing the conflicts and problems that have happened to her in the past or sensitive issues currently happening. This potentially consumes her with anger, and she will dismiss God from her life to do things on her own. Because of her overwhelming anger, she may feel like God has left her. Note that while her cup is full of anger about God, there is no room for unconditional love or forgiveness for herself or others. She may stay in this state for a period of time, unable to get over it, and unaware of how to break the unending downward thought spiral.

It is essential that a Melancholy learns how to appropriately FORGIVE and FORGET, opening the potential of healing for self and relationships/friendships.

Melancholy — Demonstrated vs. Desired Behavior

Their "Demonstrated Behavior" **says**

"I will not be demonstrative toward you!"

Their "Desired Behavior" **says**

"I do not want you demonstrating your

behavior toward me!"

A Melancholy is naturally introverted, introspective, and extremely sensitive. Although she is very compassionate and faithful to whom she allows to be close to her, she usually chooses to remain isolated and alone. As the chart shows above, she both demonstrates and desires introverted behavior; demonstrating <u>less</u> towards others and desiring <u>less</u> demonstrations/expression from others. This is her true nature and most comfortable preference of relating to others, all due to her specific needs. Recall the triangle from the beginning of the book. Behavior is a result of Temperament, and thus, a result of Temperament needs getting met or not getting met. We'll get into these specific Melancholy needs as we look deeper into each Temperament Area.

As a bonus for a Melancholy reading this, to whet the appetite of data analyzation, you'll see that an extra statistic has been added to the graphics for each Area. We've captured, out of 3,449 profiles, how many total Melancholies in number and in percentage are in each Temperament Area. It's important to realize as a Melancholy and that you are likely surrounded by fellow Melancholies who need the same as you do. What a relief! A Melancholy is certainly one to be celebrated.

Now, let's gain some knowledge and awareness of a Melancholy in the Social Area.

The Social Profile – Melancholy

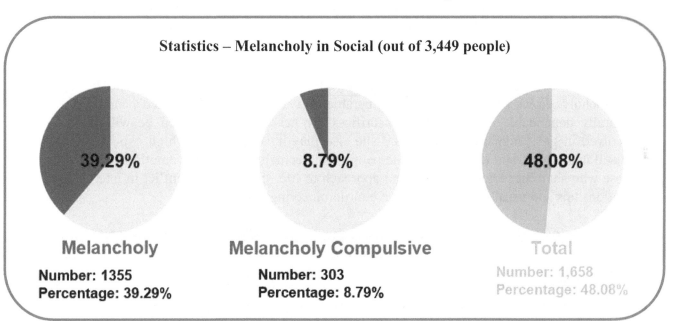

Statistics – Melancholy in Social (out of 3,449 people)

Melancholy	Melancholy Compulsive	Total
39.29%	**8.79%**	**48.08%**
Number: 1355	Number: 303	Number: 1,658
Percentage: 39.29%	Percentage: 8.79%	Percentage: 48.08%

A Note About the Social Profile

The Social Profile outlines your needs and desires for light friendships, work/career associations, and other casual relationships. By comparing the Social Profile with your current life situation, you can understand conflict areas and achieve a comfortable level of interpersonal contact in the work or social environment.

Recognize that the term "anti-social" implies a fictitious normal of social relating and that one is swaying from this generality. This baseless expectation does not capture the context of motivation of true human relating or connecting. Human connection is imminent and programmed into our being. Instead, **"How much and what type of interaction is needed for healthy balance for this individual?"** The Social Profile answers this question for each Temperament.

Remember: The Social Profile should be applied only to your casual social/career contacts. To determine your needs and desires in close personal relationships, please consult the Relationship Profile.

Social Needs and Desires. A Melancholy has a high need for privacy and usually prefers to be alone. As a result, she rarely initiates friendships, socializes with fewer people, and tends to avoid social events. Although she needs acceptance and approval from others, she prefers not to be approached by others, and her fear of rejection prevents her from becoming involved with people. She may find herself frustrated trying to understand people, especially when behavior is illogical, but she does appreciate tasks and may, in fact, view life as a series of jobs to perform. A Melancholy has a strong family orientation and considers her home a sanctuary from the world. She is far more comfortable relating one-on-one or in small groups than in large gatherings and needs daily time alone to counter the stress of interacting with people. A Melancholy's need for privacy dictates her lifestyle of non-involvement with people and she enjoys spending her time thinking out issues. Of course, the little socialization that a Melancholy does participate in may justify, in her own mind, that she is indeed a person that "socializes." She must remain aware of her true needs in order to identify the proper balance of privacy and interaction.

Criteria for Friendships. Loyal and committed to the few people she chooses as friends, a Melancholy allows herself to become vulnerable only with carefully selected people. She is naturally dependable, quick to make sacrifices for her friends and even be willing to get involved in great humanitarian causes. She also may have impossibly high expectations for herself and others, and tends to evaluate people intellectually rather than emotionally, favoring those who share her logical and rational approach to life. She avoids conflict in interpersonal relationships and usually avoids aggressive or domineering people.

Perception of Self. Although a Melancholy is intellectually gifted in many areas, she is hindered by low self-esteem and fear of rejection. She is often introspective, but with a heavy narrative of self-criticism where she may endlessly analyze her behavior and her own perceived faults. She focuses on her thoughts rather than on people or events. She can be pessimistic about her abilities and may be unaware of her potential in life to the extent of feeling inferior in comparison to others. She tends to be a perfectionist – setting impossibly high standards for herself (the fuel of greatness in any area she chooses) but becomes depressed when she fails to reach her own lofty expectations. A Melancholy is quite hard on herself, which tends to be a root cause of the negative self-perception that is perpetuated, simply, by her own thoughts.

Perception by Others. Although a Melancholy is adept at hiding her insecurities and projects an image of competence and confidence, she fears criticism and making mistakes. She can be friendly and outgoing with people who have earned her trust. Although she is compassionate and sensitive to other people's needs, her logical outlook may give the impression that she is cold or indifferent. As a result, she may be perceived as unfriendly or a "loner." A Melancholy is careful and precise in her communications and has difficulty with small talk or casual conversations. You may notice reluctance to share her knowledge with others, especially in large groups.

Perception of Others. Because of her fear of rejection, a Melancholy may be suspicious of other people's motives and may tend to project her negative self-perception onto others. She usually evaluates other people's words and behavior to determine whether she is being rejected and becomes silent or withdraws if she thinks she is being seen in a negative way. A Melancholy can be easily hurt, even by the innocent comments or actions of others. She rarely shows her emotions as emotions aren't always logical, and she avoids interpersonal aggression; in fact, she may be non-assertive even when her opinion is correct. She often applies her high standards to others and can become critical of those who fail to measure up.

Intellectual Orientation. A Melancholy is a creative thinker. She may score in the genius range on intelligence tests and has unlimited capacity to acquire new knowledge and skills. She is logical and analytical in her approach to life, collecting data before making decisions, and frequently asking questions to get all the facts. Very observant of people and her environment, she is always thinking, evaluating, and wondering. She sees vivid, detailed pictures in her mind whether of memories or just imagination. If she learns to control her thoughts, she can be highly productive and maintain a positive attitude. If her ideas are uncontrolled, she may experience emotional mood swings and often revisit adverse events in her mind. She may even go so far as to plot revenge tactics in her mind, but very seldom acts on those thoughts.

Emotional Orientation. Although a Melancholy is compassionate and empathetic toward others, she may equate emotional expression with loss of control and remain emotionally guarded, reluctant to express emotions too frequently. A Melancholy is a professional at disguising her real feelings to the bulk of society. Anger, for example, may be felt quite often towards herself or others, but she internalizes rather than expresses it, allowing anger to build over a period, and then explode over a minor situation. She does tend to hold grudges. This internalizing makes her moody and pessimistic, battle depression, and prone to stress-related physical ailments. She can become anxious if she is required to socialize frequently or for long time periods or if she is deprived of daily time alone. She prefers to avoid situations that require emotional openness instead of intellectual analysis. She possesses a strong need to actively avoid making mistakes and may feel anxiety if criticized. It is a grave offense towards a Melancholy if you "reveal" anything about them in front of other people. If you are speaking about them, do so only with their permission. It is best not to speak freely about her and if you do, it will violate her need for privacy. This is a quick way to make a dependable and loyal person your enemy and may hold that grudge for extended periods of time.

Work Orientation. A Melancholy is task-oriented rather than people-oriented or achievement-oriented. Let's talk this one out. Work environments could be perceived as a place where there is interaction with people and it takes conscious effort for a Melancholy to interact with people, thus building a skill, elevating the position that you are people oriented. Now let's assume there is a task to be performed and that task requires people interaction. Which part of those two would you genuinely prefer – the task or the interaction? Furthermore, if we remove the task and you're expected to just socialize and hang out, would you prefer the people interaction over the work, or the work over the people interaction? It may interest you to know that you lean towards tasks because you are analytical and approach functions in a logical and organized manner. People, however, are not always logical or organized! Your work makes sense, that's not always true of people. A Melancholy works well in a structured, daily routine. She has great ability to visualize projects from start to finish and works tirelessly to meet deadlines. She is very self-disciplined, independently driven and resists authoritarian leadership. To avoid making mistakes, she gathers facts before making decisions and may appear indecisive at times, but this permits her more time to collect data or refine a deliverable. While she is a perfectionist and checks work down to the smallest detail to ensure that it is error-free, she is rarely satisfied with the results. Possessing excellent leadership abilities in standard areas of responsibility (See the Leadership Profile for a detailed description of Melancholy Leadership skills), a Melancholy needs to gather and evaluate data before moving into unknown areas or responsibilities. In other words, training is crucial to her success. But once she attains her desired level of competency, she will produce quality results.

For a Melancholy, the hardest part about work is the people.

Motivation. Independent and self-motivated, a Melancholy needs to perform well to meet her high standards. She is strong-willed and can be very resolute (stubborn). She is not usually motivated by the promise of reward or the threat of punishment but may have an intense, healthy fear of economic failure; this can be a primary self-motivator in the workplace. Financial security is of utmost importance to a Melancholy, and she works hard within her areas of responsibility to ensure her employment and economy is secure.

Rejection/Acceptance Profile. Because a Melancholy has a severe fear of rejection, she is defensive, avoiding people and situations that cause her to feel rejected. She is very concerned about appearing incompetent and being criticized for her mistakes.

The Leadership Profile – Melancholy

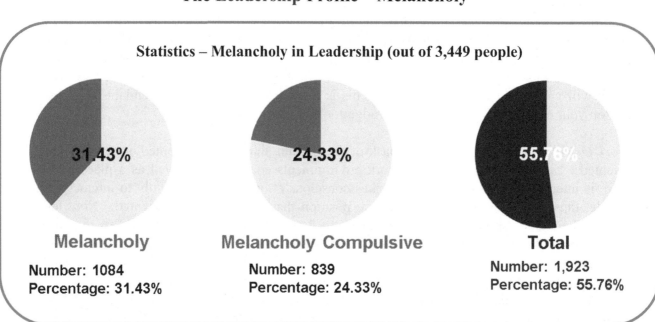

Statistics – Melancholy in Leadership (out of 3,449 people)

Melancholy	Melancholy Compulsive	Total
31.43%	24.33%	55.76%
Number: 1084	**Number: 839**	**Number: 1,923**
Percentage: 31.43%	**Percentage: 24.33%**	**Percentage: 55.76%**

A Note About the Leadership Profile

The Leadership Profile identifies the individual's ability to provide leadership, make decisions, and assume responsibilities. This Area outlines the individual's needs and desires for independence, achievement, and recognition. Because Leadership needs and desires are expressed through interacting with people, the Leadership Profile should not be evaluated alone. It should be interpreted with either the Social Profile or the Relationship Profile.

Evaluated together, the **Leadership Profile** and the **Social Profile** help determine the individual's career needs. By comparing the results with the individual's current employment situation, you can target conflict areas and help the individual maximize career skills.

Evaluated together, the **Leadership Profile** and the **Relationship Profile** help determine the individual's independence/dependence needs in close relationships. By comparing the results with the individual's current life situation, you can target conflict areas and help the individual enhance relationships.

Leadership Needs and Desires. A Melancholy is very independent, wanting minimal influence and control over people's lives and behavior while also resisting attempts by others to control her life. Because she has a high need to appear competent and avoid criticism, she prefers to avoid assuming responsibility and making decisions and may be strongly influenced by a fear of failure. While she has excellent leadership abilities and functions well in competent areas of responsibility, she avoids assuming new duties until she feels comfortable with them. Competency in her job skills alongside self-confidence is the winning combination for a Melancholy. Within the "sweet spot" of these two resources, there is relatively nothing she cannot accomplish, and she will shine as a leader within her areas of expertise.

Criteria for Relationships. Possessing a high need for privacy, a Melancholy rarely initiates friendships. Her fear of rejection prevents her from becoming involved with people. While she allows herself to become vulnerable only with carefully selected people, she is loyal and committed to the few people she chooses for friends. She tends to evaluate others intellectually rather than emotionally and values those who share her logical and rational approach to life. A Melancholy avoids aggressive or domineering leaders as well as conflict in interpersonal situations. Drawn to people with a similarly high need for independence, she is dependable, and values others who are committed to the same level of dependability (which she may refer to as "being responsible"). She is a hard worker and expects everyone on her team to be just as diligent. Be aware that if you do not measure up to the standards of a Melancholy leader, you will likely find yourself standing in the unemployment line.

Perception of Self. Although she is intellectually gifted and talented in many areas, a Melancholy is hindered by low self-esteem. Self-esteem is either nurtured or hindered within the environment that a Melancholy experienced, particularly her family of origin. If it was a healthy environment, she would be of good self-esteem and self-worth. If she was in an unhealthy environment, it impacted greatly the narrative of her thoughts, which she replays in her mind, yielding low self-esteem. She already tends to be introspective and self- critical, feeling inferior in comparison to others, and may endlessly analyze her behavior and perceived faults. Her perception of herself can defeat her due to her high need to be perfect in everything

121

she does. She could be out-producing and out-performing every other worker, but still perceive herself as a failure, feeling like she's not measuring up; all due to her low self-esteem. Her focus isn't on her output or the people around her, but rather on her thoughts. She lives in her mind so control of her thoughts is key, and while refocusing can be tricky, it is quite possible. Confident in common areas of responsibility, she may doubt her ability to excel in new areas of responsibility and avoids or resists the unknown to prevent making mistakes. As a result, it is important for a Melancholy to be permitted to assume new responsibilities at her own pace. Give her time to acclimate to the new tasks and responsibilities, providing proper guidance, resources, and training, and you will have a confident leader who produces.

Perception by Others. Fearful of criticism and making mistakes, a Melancholy projects an image of competence and confidence and is adept at hiding her insecurities. She can be friendly and outgoing with people who have earned her trust. A Melancholy's ideal leadership role is not in a team environment, but rather allowed to work independently within her area of expertise, supported by her superiors. However, if she is chosen to lead a team, it must be in a subject area in which she is competent. She will be respected by her team with her knowledge and qualifications. It is often easy to find a Melancholy in the workplace – look for the framed qualifications on her desk or wall for all to see. She is proud to display the competencies she worked hard to attain, proving she knows what she's talking about. You are always welcome to stop and admire these accolades.

Perception of Others. Because of her fear of rejection, a Melancholy may be suspicious of people's motives and project her negative self-perception onto others. She usually evaluates other people's words and behavior to determine whether she is being rejected and may become silent or withdraw if she perceives rejection. A Melancholy values people with good intellectual abilities, especially those who share her highly analytical approach to decision-making. She relates best to authority figures who are her intellectual equals or superiors. She is non-assertive even when her opinion is correct and avoids interpersonal conflict and aggression. She may apply her high standards to others and can become critical of those who fail to measure up.

Intellectual Orientation. A Melancholy is intellectually gifted, a creative thinker who may score in the genius range on intelligence tests. She possesses an unlimited capacity to acquire new knowledge and skills. In leadership positions, she prefers to research information to gain an edge and keep up-to-date with advances in her field. Logical and analytical in her approach to life, a Melancholy may view leadership as a series of tasks to be performed. She collects data before making decisions or beginning new jobs and is very observant of people and her environment. Always thinking, evaluating, and questioning, she sees vivid, detailed pictures in her mind and will be way ahead of others envisioning her approach and refining her skills. Importantly, if she controls her thoughts and doesn't get bogged down in negative thinking, she can be highly productive and maintain a positive attitude. If her feelings are uncontrolled, she may experience emotional mood swings and frustration causing her to want to isolate herself - stifling her abilities to shine as a kind and capable leader.

Emotional Orientation. Compassionate and empathetic toward others, a Melancholy can remain emotionally guarded, reluctant to share her emotions, often equating emotional expression with loss of control. As a leader, it wouldn't make sense to subject herself to the scrutiny of emotional expressions around her employees, certainly not around her peers. She may tend to be moody and pessimistic or struggle with depression unless she can train her mind to end her thinking process on a positive note of hope rather than the fear of the unknown. She often feels anger at herself or others but internalizes rather than expresses it. As a result, she may allow anger to build over a period then explode over a minor situation. A Melancholy can become anxious if required to interact with people frequently or for extended periods of time, or if deprived of daily quiet time alone. She has a strong need to avoid making mistakes and may become anxious if criticized. She also experiences stress if people pressure or attempt to control her.

A Note About Stinkin' Thinkin' For A Melancholy

It is essential here for a Melancholy to understand "stinkin' thinkin'" vs. healthy thinking. A Melancholy's mind is powerful. Because the mind is bent towards risk analysis for survival purposes and loves to bathe in familiar patterns of safe predictability, it is not always fighting on our side. Conscious awareness of the mind's natural "bodyguard" role is crucial to realizing it's always looking for a job. The mind wants to be keen to its surroundings and that will tend to pose itself as a skeptic, proposing the negative side of the ledger first in anything it approaches. Negative, skeptical thinking is not a bad thing; it's how a Melancholy uses a naturally skeptic thinking pattern that will decide whether it's helpful or harmful. (Listen to this) If I ask a Melancholy what she thinks of a new hire's resume, she will likely begin with a listed critique of the negative aspects. A Melancholy is looking for perfection. To end up with perfection one must first remove the negative aspects. Put simply, by eliminating imperfections one can find perfection! And that same subconscious, logical approach is applied to all aspects of life, which is why negative events are relived over and over in her mind. A gloomy disposition could be an easy symptom to recognize that too much time has been spent in negative mode. Bring back the positive! Find someone who can give a word of cheer or read affirmations, anything that trains your brain to helpfulness around your thought patterns. Your quality of life (and those around you) will improve dramatically in a short amount of time. It's worth consideration!

Work Orientation. Task-oriented rather than people-oriented, a Melancholy is highly analytical and approaches tasks in a logical, organized manner. She can visualize projects from start to finish and works tirelessly to lead her team to achieve goals and meet deadlines. She loves to mark progress by checking to-dos off her list. She is outstanding in maintaining quality control, viewing quality as more important than quantity. A perfectionist who checks work down to the smallest detail to ensure that it is error-free, she is rarely satisfied with the results. She works well independently and resists authoritarian leadership from her superiors. To avoid making mistakes, she will gather facts before making decisions. This may appear indecisive or that she is procrastinating at times, but that just means she needs to gather more information to be comfortable and sure her decision is accurate. She has excellent leadership abilities in her areas of expertise but needs to gather and evaluate data before moving into unknown areas of responsibility. She prefers not to take risks and will stall or rebel if pushed into unfamiliar areas before she has been trained. It is an insult to a Melancholy to demand performance without the opportunity to train – it sets her up for failure. Provide training and support and she will excel and produce beautifully. A Melancholy functions well in a structured daily routine and is highly organized. She knows where she is going and who and what she needs to get there.

Motivation. Independent and self-motivated as a leader, A Melancholy needs to lead and perform well to meet her high standards. She is strong-willed and can be stubborn and very tenacious. She is also dependable, a perfectionist, and competent in her areas of responsibility, which allows her to move confidently in her role and be quite satisfied at the end of the day with her performance. While she is usually not motivated by the promise of reward or the threat of punishment, she may have an intense fear of economic failure, which can be a primary self- motivator in the workplace. A Melancholy is one who greatly benefits from a bonus or raise for a job well done.

Rejection/Acceptance Profile. Because a Melancholy has a severe fear of rejection, she avoids people and situations that cause her to feel rejected. She can become defensive if criticized or corrected and is very concerned about appearing competent as a leader, drawing self-esteem from the accuracy and practical application of her leadership skills and performance results. She is pleased to work in areas where her team and her peers are dedicated to the same quality of output and support each other in doing so.

The Relationship Profile – Melancholy

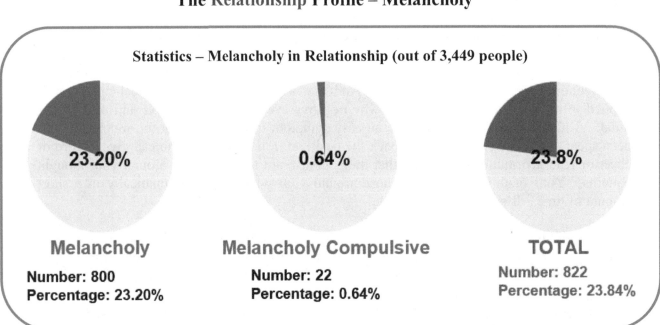

Statistics – Melancholy in Relationship (out of 3,449 people)

Melancholy	Melancholy Compulsive	TOTAL
23.20%	0.64%	23.8%
Number: 800	**Number: 22**	**Number: 822**
Percentage: 23.20%	**Percentage: 0.64%**	**Percentage: 23.84%**

A Note About the Relationship Profile

The Relationship Profile identifies your preferences for emotional involvement and shared affection on a one-to-one basis. This profile outlines your needs and desires for emotional sharing and relationships. For most people, the Relationship Profile is the dominant pattern that influences behavior in the Social and Leadership Areas.

By comparing the Relationship Profile with your current life situation, you can target conflict areas and meet essential emotional needs that are not being met.

Relationship Needs and Desires. A Melancholy is independent and has a high need for privacy. She expresses love and affection in minimal doses in close relationships, as love is more often shown through tasks or other non-expressive modes of connecting. She prefers minimal outward initiations from others in her close circle and may feel smothered if offered liberally. Although she may establish only a few close relationships in a lifetime, she is faithful and committed to those she loves, depending on them to meet all her needs for love. She needs acceptance and approval from others, but fear of rejection prevents her from becoming closely involved with most people. While she understands responsibility and dependability within close relationships, she may have difficulty understanding people. A Melancholy will "do things" for her significant others to show her love, devotion, and even affection. It's important to note that a Melancholy is independent and doesn't like to seem needy or demanding, so it's understandable that she does not want sole responsibility for another's happiness or well-being; a self-confident individual is far more appealing. Possessing a strong family orientation, she considers her home a sanctuary from the world and needs daily quiet time alone to counter the stress of being around people. Other Temperaments may allow a larger number of people to meet their inner needs, but a Melancholy looks to her family and maybe one or two close friends for her emotional fulfillment.

Criteria for Relationships. Because she has a strong need to develop trust in the other person before becoming emotionally involved, intimate relationships tend to grow slowly, and she allows herself to become vulnerable only with carefully selected people. At the same time, with the few people she chooses for friends, she is loyal, committed, and dependable, quick to make sacrifices for those she loves. She tends to evaluate people intellectually rather than emotionally and may have impossibly high expectations for herself and others. She avoids conflict in interpersonal relationships, valuing those who share her logical and rational approach to life; as a result, she will usually avoid aggressive or domineering people. It is not that a Melancholy doesn't become angry, it's that she doesn't want to "explode on you". If she does, she tends to get just as angry at herself for the explosion, as she will feel she has become the problem toward the person they blasted.

A Note About Parent-Child Relationships

Having talked about Criteria for Relationships, it's important we pause for a word about children. Not knowing a child's Temperament can cause far-reaching consequences between parent and child. Parents who are Melancholy and have extroverted children such as Sanguine, Phlegmatic and Choleric may have a difficult time raising children. Extroverted children cause emotional disturbances in Melancholy parents because extroverted children are so demanding socially, physically, and are very demonstrative, causing unrest for the introverted Melancholy parents that are emotionally reserved. These children want to be around people most of the time, if not always, and can emotionally drain a Melancholy parent very quickly from all the emotional activity. The older the children get, the more social they become and sooner or later will want people in their home as friends, guests, parties, etc. This is a major violation to the Melancholy parents' Temperament. These Temperament traits can be identified early in child-rearing. It is not rebellion on the part of the child it is a lack of Temperament understanding on the part of the parent. These issues are more likely to be a problem with a Melancholy parent than an extroverted parent because Melancholy children can escape to their rooms, and it is not evident to the parents that a problem exists. However, what becomes a problem is if the extroverted parents demand that the Melancholy child is socially active or force them to participate in activities where they interact with other kids regularly. This will cause them to be nervous, uptight, complainers and whiners. The children will not be able to identify that they don't want to go be with other kids but would rather be in the solace of their room doing their own thing, thinking, and pondering. The child will have very few friends and maybe only one or two close friends that they want to play with regularly.

I profiled a dear friend of mine and her 2 children, one of whom was 9 years old. He is Melancholy in the Social, Leadership, and Relationship Areas. Knowing how few close friends he desires in his inner circle, I decided to ask a trick question to check the accuracy of his profile. I asked, "So who is your best friend?" This would normally prompt an extroverted child into picking his favorite friend from the buffet of friends he has and label them as "best". Instead, he thought for a moment and answered, "I haven't found one yet." What an answer at 9 years old, and what a relief for a mother who can now understand who and what her son needs as a Melancholy at such a young age! (As a side note – she is quite extroverted and has very different needs, so this equipped her with the resources she would not have naturally known through good intentions, motherly love, or instinct.)

Perception of Self. Although she is intellectually gifted and talented in many areas, a Melancholy may feel inferior to others and hindered by low self-esteem and fear of rejection. She tends to be introspective and self-critical and may endlessly analyze her behavior and perceived faults. This perception stunts the development of her relationships. She often focuses inward on her thoughts rather than outward on people or events. Because she does not express feelings and emotions naturally, she doesn't receive emotional feedback from friends and close family members. She may be unaware of her potential in life and can be pessimistic about her abilities. The adolescent years for a Melancholy are lonely and very intimidating because she realizes she doesn't know that much and that makes her very uncomfortable; yes, competence matters even as a child. A perfectionist, a Melancholy may set impossible standards for herself and become depressed she failed to attain them within relationships. Without being educated about her own unique Temperament needs and those of other Temperaments, she will go through life feeling there is something drastically wrong with her. This is preventable with awareness, communication, and research – precisely why this very book was written. Temperament knowledge is the key.

Perception by Others. Projecting an image of competence and confidence, a Melancholy is adept at hiding her insecurities even though she fears criticism and making mistakes. She can be friendly and outgoing with people who have earned her trust, and although she is compassionate and sensitive to other people's needs, her logical outlook may give the impression that she is cold or indifferent. She communicates carefully and precisely, often having trouble with small talk or casual conversations. She often expresses love and care by "doing" rather than by outward expression. As a result, she is not inclined to be romantic and could be perceived as an unfriendly loner. A Melancholy may become defensive if criticized or demeaned by loved ones.

Perception of Others. Because of her fear of rejection, a Melancholy may be suspicious of other people's motives and project her negative self-perception onto others. She usually evaluates others' words and behavior to determine whether she is being rejected and may become silent or withdraw if she perceives rejection. She may fear rejection by those she loves, especially if she has suffered hurts in close relationships in the past. She can be easily hurt, even by the innocent comments or actions of others. As a result, she rarely shows her emotions. She is non-assertive even when her opinion is correct and avoids interpersonal aggression. A Melancholy may apply her high standards to others and can become critical of those who fail to measure up. The lack of outwardly expressive behavior toward others is a "catch-22" for a Melancholy. Others perceive her as not wanting to be approached, yet what a Melancholy perceives is that people do not engage with her because she is not approachable, likable, or loveable. Therefore, her understanding of others could be based on the mirrored reflection of what she projects onto them. Efforts to work on becoming emotionally expressive becomes a stressful, unnatural burden. It may feel that a Melancholy loses, either way.

Intellectual Orientation. Intellectually gifted, a Melancholy is a creative thinker and may score in the genius range on intelligence tests. She has an unlimited capacity to acquire new knowledge and skills, is logical and analytical in her approach to life, and frequently asks questions to get all the facts before making decisions. This systematic approach can be a "showstopper" in relationships because the intellectual orientation of the Melancholy can come across as being "better than you," or "smarter than you." A Melancholy is very observant of people and her environment and is continually thinking, evaluating, and questioning. She sees vivid, detailed pictures in her mind and can be very creative. If she learns to control her thoughts, she can be highly productive and maintain a positive attitude, sharing her gifts of ideas, dreams, and knowledge. If her thoughts (beliefs) are uncontrolled, she may experience emotional mood swings as she relives adverse events in her mind. This negative playback coupled with unexpected spiraling may make her far less tolerable, causing unwarranted damage to existing relationships. In general, a Melancholy is self-disciplined, task-oriented, and perfectionistic. Positive traits will surface largely within her few close relationships as her needs are acknowledged and met.

Emotional Orientation. Although compassionate and empathetic toward others, a Melancholy is reluctant to share her emotions, often equating emotional expression with loss of control. Her gift of high compassion is concealed by a high guard. She could sit in a movie theater and hold back tears during painful or moving moments, yet be defensive about expressing her feelings to others, even in close relationships. She may struggle with depression, often feeling anger at herself or others but internalizing rather than expressing it. She may allow anger to build over a period and then explode over a minor situation. A Melancholy will be stressed if she does not allow herself daily time alone. She may feel anxiety if criticized and has a strong need to avoid making mistakes. She prefers to avoid situations that require emotional openness instead of intellectual analysis. If a Melancholy loses a close connection for any reason, she may never wholly recover emotionally from the hurt. These seasons of grief and trying to heal can be a very lonely place for her because it's hard enough to express feelings within herself, much less to a friend or a counselor. Patience, zero judgement, and holding space for a Melancholy is always welcome for her heart and mind to find relief, even momentarily.

Motivation. Independent and self-motivated, a Melancholy needs to perform well in her close relationships to meet her high standards. She is strong-willed and can be stubborn. Usually, not motivated by the promise of reward or the threat of punishment. She resists controlling and being controlled in close relationships and may respond defensively if challenged or corrected.

Rejection/Acceptance Profile. A Melancholy has a severe fear of rejection and is fearful of appearing incompetent or being criticized for her mistakes, especially around those with whom she is close. As a result, she avoids people and situations that cause her to feel rejected and depends on her few close connections to meet all her acceptance needs.

A Note about Strengths & Weaknesses

The *Probable* Strengths & *Potential* Weaknesses section is located at the end of each of the 3 WIDP Profile Areas. An individual's Temperament may be different in one or all Areas, thus the Strengths & Weaknesses will coincide with their uniquely identified Temperament in that respective Area. It is important to interpret the labels *probable* and *potential* correctly. The difference of which characteristic is experienced or observed depends on several factors.

Any individual whose Temperament needs are actively getting met has the greatest chance of exuding their strengths. For instance, after we eat a meal, we are much happier, as our hunger need has been satisfied. The same is true with Temperament needs. Someone whose Temperament needs are getting met will tend to be a balanced and healthy individual, able to proactively participate within their strengths for a positive impact in their life.

However, if certain Temperament needs have been frustrated, the potential for negative performance could be experienced and observed, leading to unbalanced behavior and emotional instability.

> **Like a runny nose is a symptom,**
> **think of weaknesses as symptoms**
> **that indicate unmet Temperament needs.**
>
> ↓
>
> **Wiping our nose doesn't address the true problem.**
> **Instead, identify and treat the root cause:**
>
> **Meet Temperament Needs!**

Remember: No Temperament is automatically broken by design. Each Temperament is genetically wired with unique, specific needs that allow the individual to be mentally and emotionally healthy and functional within that context. Temperament makeup can be referred to as one's emotional biology.

Basic Strengths/Weaknesses of the Melancholy

Probable Strengths
- Intellectually gifted; possesses many creative abilities, can learn and specialize in anything of interest
- Analytical; is detail-oriented, methodical, and sequential
- Self-sacrificing; dependable to loved ones, goes above and beyond
- Diligent; works tirelessly to complete tasks and meet deadlines
- Faithful in relationships – committed and loyal
- Sensitive; has the deepest human compassion of all Temperaments, but express through tasks or service

Potential Weaknesses
- Moody; tends to be gloomy or depressed; focuses on negative
- Indecisive; fears making mistakes; is prone to procrastination causing indecisiveness, for fear of being wrong
- Critical; holds high expectations of people, impossible to please
- Sensitive to hurt and rejection; touchy and "thin-skinned", needs to be handled with care and expects to be appreciated
- Introverted; tends to be a loner; is usually unsociable and needs time to warm up to people, is suspicious of people

Become Aware of Your Natural Strengths and Learn to Use Them Wisely

Natural Strength	Strength Carried to Extreme	Avoidable Result
Programming	Cannot function without a scheduled plan	Obsessed with promptness
Physical conditioning	Overexertion, injury	Can become paranoid about physical appearance
Perfectionist	Unrealistic expectations of self and others	Critical, judgmental of self and others
Self-sufficient	Avoidance of socialization	Becomes narcissistic and egotistical

Decisions for a Melancholy

Decision-making for a Melancholy is a serious and deliberate process, as decisions must always be perfect. If a Melancholy lacks sufficient data to make a confident decision, she will procrastinate and go research/train/learn until she has accumulated enough data to make the most informed (right) choice. A Melancholy will put off decision-making over things in which she is not yet sufficiently knowledgeable.

Other Probable Strengths of the Melancholy

Analytical	Likes to examine the parts of their logical and proper relationships
Persistent	Sees one project through to its completion before starting another
Self-sacrificing	Gives willingly to help others meet their needs, doesn't have to know them personally to be willing to help
Considerate	Recognizes and regards the needs of others
Respectful	Treats others with defense, honor, and esteem
Sensitive	Intensely cares about others and what happens to them
Planner	Prefers to work out a detailed arrangement beforehand, and prefers involvement in the planning stages and finished product
Scheduled	Lives according to a thought-out plan, does not like for those intentions to be interrupted
Orderly	Has a methodical and systematic arrangement of things
Faithful	Consistently reliable, loyal, dependable, and steadfast, sometimes devoted beyond reason
Detailed	Does things in proper order with a clear memory of all the things that have happened
Cultured	One whose interests involve intellectual and artistic pursuits, possibly including symphony, ballet, theatre, and/or art itself
Idealistic	Visualizes things in their perfect form and seeks to measure up to that standard
Deep	Intense and often introspective with a distaste for surface-level conversations or pursuits
Musical	Participates in, or has sincere appreciation for, music; committed to music as an art form rather than the fun of performing
Thoughtful	Remembers special occasions and is quick to make a kind gesture
Loyal	Faithful to a person, ideal, or job, extending potentially beyond logic

Chart-maker	Organizes life, tasks, and problem-solving by making lists, forms, and graphs
Perfectionistic	Places high standards on self and others, desiring that everything be in proper order at all times
Behaved	Consistently conducts self within the realm of what is proper

Other Potential Weaknesses of the Melancholy

Bashful	Shrinks from drawing attention, derived from being self-conscious
Unforgiving	Difficulty releasing an injustice or forgetting a hurt done to them, apt to hold grudges
Resentful	Holds ill feelings from because of real or imagined offenses
Fussy	Insistent in calling significant attention to petty matters or details
Insecure	Apprehensive, lacks self-sustaining confidence
Unpopular	Intensity and demand for perfection tends to push people away
Hard To Please	Standards are set so high it is difficult to ever be satisfied
Pessimistic	Even in hoping for the best, sees the downside of a situation first
Alienated	Easily feels estranged from others due to insecurity; often feels that others do not enjoy their company
Negative Attitude	Feels that seeing the dark side or downside of a situation reveals a more grounded reality reflecting the inherent risk of all things, poses as sense of inner security but expressed in words or expression can lead to frustrated interactions
Withdrawn	Retreats to inner sanctuary, needs a great deal of isolation or alone time
Too Sensitive	Overly introspective and easily offended when misunderstood
Depressed	Feels down most of the time; downcast expressions reflecting inner thought patterns
Introvert	Thoughts and interests are directed inward, lives within self
Moody	Doesn't get much emotional altitude, quick to slip into valleys, often when feeling unappreciated
Skeptical	Disbelieving; questions the motive behind the words
Loner	Chooses to actively avoid crowds, interaction, and people in general

Suspicious

Distrusts others and/or their ideas

Vengeful

Knowingly holds a grudge and pursues payback toward the offender, even if just in the mind, even through subtle withholding of friendship, interaction, or affection

Critical

Constantly evaluating towards judgments, frequently thinking or expressing adverse reactions

Helpful Tips for the Melancholy

Things to Think About

As a Melancholy, you spend a reasonable amount of time alone - so, you have an excellent opportunity to study the following paragraphs to consider facts that will help you better understand yourself:

You are an introvert. Being an introvert, a loner, a recluse is okay. There is no reason for you to feel in the wrong about a lack of desire to meet and be around people; those are not the primary avenues to get your needs met. A Melancholy doesn't need to be with people for the sake of the company or conversation. You should not shut yourself off from people, but neither should you socialize like a Sanguine. Once you understand your Temperament, you can experience the liberation and freedom to be who you are without fear of disapproval from others, improving your quality of life dramatically. As a Melancholy, you require more detached time away from people to do what you do — think, dream, regenerate, analyze, and ponder issues of life, in general. The factory of your mind is working 24/7/365. And when you do go to sleep, there's a good chance you have a very active dream life.

There are times when you do need to put forth an effort to be with people; however, you also need to know that you do not need to socialize (assuming you are a Melancholy in the Social Area). Socializing is very low on your priority list because socializing is not a primary Melancholy Temperament need. To clarify, however, if you are "on a mission" you can socialize and do an outstanding job of it – recognizing you still are not socializing for the sake of socializing. To you, you are completing a task - you are working. It's good to remember that being with people can serve as a way of getting exposure if you have identified a particular person or persons with whom you want to interact. Just put your "task mask" on and take control. No one will ever know what you are doing because they cannot see behind your mask unless you allow it. Learning to harness this skill increases the social competence of a Melancholy without compromising the Temperament need of privacy, lending a balanced perspective and positive control of your mind in either circumstance. Doesn't that feel more realistic?

You are task oriented. You don't have to feel wrong about needing to keep busy doing tasks. If you stopped doing these responsibilities or jobs, you would feel little value and that you are wasting your time. When relationship-oriented people surround you, you may tend to feel that you are letting these people down if you do not stop "tasking " to socialize. But if you do stop tasking to socialize, your self-esteem starts feeling depressed as though you are not a responsible individual. Also, you will experience tremendous stress that builds moment by moment while socializing. The longer you are "non-productive" to the extent that you need to produce, the higher your stress will become. Conscious awareness of this can alter your perception of yourself in a more positive and intentional way. Work alongside a Certified WIDP Affiliate Manager to learn what to do when you feel conflicted (stressed/anxious).

You tend to live in your mind. Your mind is powerful. You are innovative and highly creative, even in your imagination. You hear narratives and can even "see" things that aren't there (like a skyscraper in an empty lot), all in your mind; it's part of being a Melancholy. This difficulty with your thoughts, if you look at the pattern, is that it tends to lean towards negative thinking. Because of this, you may push even your loved ones away from you. You can see very vivid pictures and scenes that are from your past or even create new ones as you think. You can re-examine past events over and over, revisiting the same experiences.

A common statement for a Melancholy is, "I can't turn my brain off." Obviously this is not true, but it feels that way because of the high activity. Constant thinking is normal for a Melancholy mind and is nothing to be alarmed over. The key is recognizing in that activity whether negative thinking has taken over without conscious action. The mask of negative thinking is trying to be "realistic" by removing imperfect obstacles so that you can become closer to being right and perfect. Relaxing your thinking or altering a downward spiral though process might be something as simple as studying something interesting, meditating, or listening to the wind or ocean waves. Watching clouds, birds, animals, insects, or exploring your surroundings can bring you peace. Reading a favorite book or just going for a car ride on the country roads can help "mellow you out." One helpful thing I have noticed is called "intentional thinking" where you simply focus on the task at hand and your intentionality behind it. Simple, but useful. Experiment with different ways to loosen up from thinking.

Most importantly to note when it comes to any thinking, positive and negative, thoughts about nothing or thoughts about serious matters, is that you control your thoughts, they do not control you. Being aware that you steer the ship is key. If you don't like the direction your thoughts are going, stop. Choose a different course. Set sail again. Negative thoughts do not belong to you until you take hold of the idea and start concentrating on it for extended periods of time. You need to learn to reject the negative thoughts and choose to consciously fill your mind with positive ones.

A Word About Financial Security

You have a fear of economic failure. Being careful with your money is okay. At the same time, you must learn to find and preserve a balance with your finances. Stockpiling cash when your husband, wife, or children need something is not maintaining a balance but instead, causes undue hardships on your family members, even with the best of intentions to provide security. If you do not maintain balance in the financial area, this fear can consume you to the point that others (including your family) will criticize you for being selfish and thinking only of your own immediate needs. Yet, your fear of economic failure is real and requires consideration by all concerned. In order for a Melancholy to really be in a mental state to enjoy and experience a quality life, economic security is critical. So, maintain a comfortable level of financial security while keeping balance with those under your charge, daily.

For you to have a tolerable level of financial security, you may need to do one or more of the following:

- Maintain a minimum balance in your checking or savings account.

- Keep several hundred dollars on your person or in your car.

- Refrain from charging or buying anything on credit as the thought of paying it back may cause anxiety. Even mortgages and car payments cause enormous stress for a Melancholy.

- Use credit cards as an asset, not a liability. Ensure whatever you spend can be paid off before the deadline of being charged interest. This builds proper credit and provides a safety net for unforeseen expenses.

- Wait until "specials" are running on things you want to buy.

- Sacrifice your wardrobe instead of spending more money on fashionable clothes.

- Buy a quality, reliable car a couple of years old, as a new car depreciates several thousand dollars when you leave the lot. Pay cash for the used car when possible.

- Live within a fixed budget that permits funding for all family members. Your monetary resources can work for you, but you must have discipline. So, make your plan and work the plan.

**You already budget for bills, food, and gas;
budgeting for entertainment is just another line item.**

**Your family will thank you for the fun!
(Even if they aren't thanking you for the electricity)**

How to Recognize Whether Your Child Is A Melancholy

Strengths	Weaknesses	Emotional Needs
Baby		
Likes routine, quiet, and somber	Cries easily, adheres to mother or father	Security, stability, and parental nurturing

Strengths	Weaknesses	Emotional Needs
Child		
Intellectual, intense, real friend	Belly-acher and irritable	Validation and support from parents

Strengths	Weaknesses	Emotional Needs
Teen		
Neat, creative, economically conscientious	Isolated, depressed, critical of others, bad attitude	Isolation from people, daily recharging/quiet time, stability

General Do's and Don'ts

DO'S

- Make quicker decisions (choose a stopping point to the research)
- Realize that your insecurities are due to your need to be perfect
- Relax your unrealistic standards for yourself and others
- Focus on the positive aspects of life and relationships
- Get the needed Time/Tools/Training before starting
- Be grateful you understand your Temperament
- Listen for evidence of "false humility"
- Realize no one likes "gloomy" people
- Learn from other Temperaments
- Realize you will never be perfect
- Respect other Temperaments
- Lighten up and enjoy life
- Look for the positive

DON'TS

- Procrastinate
- Look for trouble
- Become addicted
- Take life so fatally
- Forget to have fun
- Become a money tyrant
- Forget to set boundaries
- Look at life as a drudgery
- Justifiably criticize yourself
- Retreat from those who care
- Spend so much time planning
- Hide who you are behind a mask
- Put unrealistic demands on others
- Get caught up that one of these is out of order
- Just focus on tasks, people have talent, too
- Blame circumstances for negative thought patterns
- Focus on the negative aspects of life and relationships

Chapter 7: The Choleric

Steve is what you would call a "take-charge" kind of guy, a leader of leaders, ideas, and initiatives. Regardless of what needs to get done, he is ready to dive in. Although Steve prefers to be correct about everything, and may not admit when he's wrong about something, his primary motivation is to accomplish the goal. If he makes a decision and doesn't accomplish what he wants, he'll comfortably adjust by making another decision to fix the last decision and move on. For Steve, the end always justifies the means because he knows he can accomplish the vision he sees. The whole world could be against him thinking it can't be done, but that doesn't sway Steve; his resiliency is truly remarkable and a natural talent of mind.

Steve is a Choleric. He is a "mover and shaker" who tends to prefer the company of others who think as he does - on the grander scale of life rather than the mundane routine of the daily grind. He is anything but trivial as he thrives on big ideas, adventure, and exploration of concepts and potential while seeking to stand out and be the best. The world is truly his playground.

He is independent, a visionary, inspiring, productive, and strong-willed. Steve is great at making decisions quickly and is comfortable with the outcome, often defending his position even when it leads to failure. He exhibits strong leadership abilities and is an innovative problem solver. At work, Steve sets ambitious objectives for himself and his colleagues, blazing trails to meet objectives for his company, his team, and himself.

In his interactions and relationships, Steve enjoys the company of people he can lead, as this aids him to maintain control of his life and destiny. Steve can be fun and connects easily in crowds, lending to good communication and "people" skills. Yet, because of his achievement orientation, he has only a few true friends. He is quite open in his communications and others may feel he is a nice person, easy to make friends with. Some may even classify Steve as a friend, but that doesn't necessarily mean Steve sees them the same way.

Many people admire Steve, as he has a delightfully charming way about him, that is, when things are going his way. Yet, Steve also may show a different side when things aren't to his liking, to the point of becoming a bit of a bulldozer. When he is challenged or unsuccessful, Steve may use his anger as his primary motivation technique to "get people in line." While it alienates himself from others, Steve will act cold and indifferent about it, projecting an attitude of superiority and confidence. Steve thinks highly of his opinion and believes in what he's chasing after, even to the point that his opinion becomes the only one that matters to him. He may even challenge his supervisors when their agendas don't coincide with his.

Here's a true story of a powerful Choleric using less than healthy means of influence:

Frank works for a large computer company in the Northeast, with thousands of employees. He was one of the top six senior leaders in the organization. He had authority and power, and everyone knew it. The company had a facility in the South with over 600 employees. Frank and the Director of that facility were not in good standing with each other. In a meeting (with me), Frank mentioned he was traveling to the facility to correct a certain situation. "I'll show him who's boss," he commented. When I asked him the following week how the meeting down south went, he replied, "I closed his facility - told you I'd show him!" Frank had indeed closed the facility and put over 600 people in unemployment lines and was now bragging about it – just to get to one person.

This story reflects one Choleric who chose to cater to his weaknesses; other Choleric instances will be discussed later in this chapter.

> # When life seems like a puzzle,
> # use Temperament as the picture on the box
> # to guide each piece into its proper place.

Choleric — Demonstrated vs. Desired Behavior

A Choleric, by nature, is an active leader and not a follower. Look at the chart below. Notice that he demonstrates highly extroverted behavior but desires that people leave him alone. In other words, he is good at initiating expression but doesn't like expressions initiated toward him. This can be translated as expressive independence. What a powerful individual!

Their "Demonstrated Behavior" says

"I will be demonstrative toward you!"

Their "Desired Behavior" says

"I do not want you demonstrating toward me!"

Each Temperament Area explains the structure of the Temperament design (Demonstrate & Desire - this is discussed in detail in Chapter 8). For a Choleric, he is naturally expressive, but does not need others to be expressive towards him. In the Social Area, it means he can easily interact, but does not need to interact for the sake of interacting – there's always a reason he initiates conversation beyond simply social reasons.

The Social Profile – Choleric

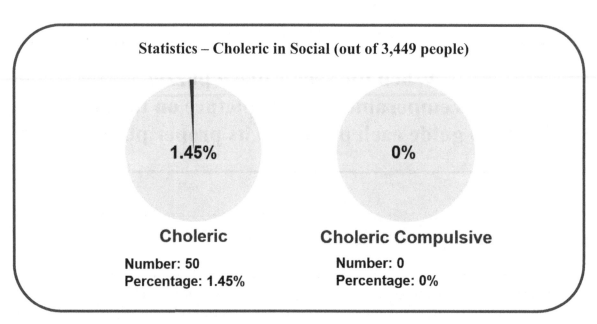

Statistics – Choleric in Social (out of 3,449 people)

1.45%

0%

Choleric

Number: 50
Percentage: 1.45%

Choleric Compulsive

Number: 0
Percentage: 0%

As you can see, a Choleric in the Social Area is quite rare. It may seem like a paradox that someone is wired with natural conversational skills and easily initiates with others yet has no need to converse. On the outside, such forward engagement could be interpreted as he is looking for relational interaction, connecting with others, possibly even that he is a people-pleaser at heart.

Yet, the true wiring of a Choleric in the Social Area points to a beautiful sufficiency in the world of social connection – you'll find he isn't desperate to fill silent air with words, even going all day without speaking to anyone, perfectly content. It's an attractive and intriguing quality that warrants a deeper look.

A Note About the Social Profile

The Social Profile outlines your needs and desires for light friendships, work/career associations, and other casual relationships. By comparing the Social Profile with your current life situation, you can understand conflict areas and achieve a comfortable level of interpersonal contact in your work and social environments.

Remember: The Social Profile should be applied only to your casual social/career contacts. To determine your needs and desires in close personal relationships, please consult the Relationship Profile.

Social Needs and Desires. Outgoing and personable in social settings, a Choleric appears to want a high degree of socialization with many people; in truth, he needs and wants only a few carefully selected friends but many casual acquaintances. He has a strong need for accomplishment and may choose activities and friendships that will assist him in attaining his goals, not for purely social reasons. He has a great need to be in control of his destiny. A Choleric in the Social Area will compete with another Choleric in a social setting, who will also likely compete whether he realizes it or not. These two can become mutual assets if they permit themselves not to be threatened by each other. The underlying need to achieve and conquer can also put on the mode of charm, calling attention to himself in social gatherings to build his social circle of connections. A Choleric who is aware of the needs of other Temperaments and is sensitive to those needs within social settings can learn how to enjoy other Temperaments and appropriately appreciate friendships and work relationships.

Criteria for Relationships. Achievement-oriented rather than people- or task-oriented, a Choleric depends on his knowledge and skills and has minimal need for close interpersonal relationships. He will be more energetic (fun) when an interaction is beneficial to him towards accomplishing his goals, which is always the primary motivator of interaction. A Choleric can talk about his pursuits at the drop of a hat – and he will drop the hat! If he determines you can be helpful to him in his idea or purpose, it will be a pleasant interaction. If you do not have the necessary skills, training, or knowledge he needs, you will find him disengaging rather quickly. Admittedly, this sounds quite selfish, but this focused drive is his wiring and the root of his need to accomplish what he's after. When he does develop relationships, he tends to seek out cooperative environments; those who can help accomplish his personal goals. He will be drawn to individuals who recognize and appreciate his accomplishments and may avoid close relationships with other strong-willed people. A Choleric can flip a mental switch that will take his approach from pleasant to indifferent, from engaging to apathetic. One must be careful when engaging with an unaware Choleric as he can treat you with great respect and in a moment seemingly become another person. He can "put on" whatever face he needs to accomplish his goal. However, a Choleric who is aware of his approach and mindset can provide thoughtful consideration for relating with other Temperaments, which takes a lot of conscious effort. Remember, a Choleric is designed to see potential and drive toward those goals.

Perception of Self. A Choleric projects optimism and confidence, can be centered on self, and seldom admits making a mistake. He is rooted in his ability to achieve whatever he desires. His high need for control of his environment and life path may lend little tolerance for emotions. To him, emotions are an inconvenience as he seeks the right path of success. Denial may be a tool of choice for a Choleric to buy time to find a solution or to push away criticism. He would rather put on mental and emotional armor as this is a more natural position of taking on the day or situation. A Choleric willfully represses facial indicators if he makes a mistake and quickly adjusts toward a workable solution. He possesses a resolute demeanor and is quite resilient no matter what the opposition. Energy and movement help him thrive as he sets high personal goals to help him, and his accomplishments, stand out from the rest. He maintains an attitude of competence and usually has an answer or solution to problems. He can adapt his behavior to circumstances and fill any role he feels necessary to achieve his goals. He can step into just about any vocational arena. Unlike a Melancholy, he does not, at first, require skill or education in the vocation as he will learn as he goes and will not look back on bad decisions or mistakes; he adjusts focus until he becomes competent in that area. Active and involved, he rarely spends time in self-introspection but tends to view himself only from a positive perspective.

Perception by Others. Possessing natural leadership abilities (willingness to accept responsibilities that other Temperaments would decline), a Choleric maintains resolute confidence. He has excellent social skills and can be outgoing and charismatic as well as physically affectionate. He often gives the impression that he desires close relationships with many people but is very selective in choosing his friends and may have little understanding of people's needs and emotions. He is usually the dominant figure in groups, often intimidating less confident people by his high energy and decisive manner. He may directly confront those who disagree with him and can be critical and argumentative. He may appear to be a braggart or as one who sees himself in a higher light than others do, perhaps being perceived as a "know it all". Yet in many areas he will be successful, competent, aggressive, and possesses a compelling desire to fulfill his vision.

Perception of Others. A Choleric is individualistic and does not need to please people, meet their expectations, or even seek their opinions. He distrusts people's abilities and is reluctant to delegate responsibility, often feeling the path of least resistance is to just do it himself (which he often can). He maintains high expectations of coworkers and friends, expects perfection from himself and others, and is intolerant of incompetence and weak-willed individuals. He values other independent individuals. His priorities usually involve goals, not people, resulting in a disregard of the rights and feelings of others while on his crusade for success. He likely will not remember names, referring to individuals as "the guy with the red car" or "the tall guy with glasses" or "the one that sat at the left of you". However, if he feels a person is important to him, he likely will remember that name, as he may need to call upon them later. He tends to motivate people through directing rather than guiding and rarely uses diplomatic reasoning. Social life for a Choleric will not be for social reasons, but rather to connect and network. He tends to like professional cordiality yet will yearn to get back to his work.

Intellectual Orientation. Highly intelligent and possessing excellent problem-solving abilities and communication skills, a Choleric is always envisioning new goals and challenges. He has an ambitious agenda, battling severe obstacles in his mind 24/7. He has an innate ability to develop and implement innovative techniques and makes quick, intuitive decisions. He is strong-willed and rarely changes his mind – even when he is proven wrong. He can have several projects going on in his mind (and in his life) at any given moment. He is diligent in searching out data that will provide him with an intellectual edge toward his cause. A Choleric who reads will primarily prefer self-development resources and seek new and better data to position himself more effectively towards victory.

Emotional Orientation. Showing few deep emotions and fearing loss of control over people and his environment, a Choleric can be repelled by emotional displays from others. Verbalizing loving emotions may take a lot of conscious effort and feel extremely awkward for him. His most prominent expressed emotion may be anger, which he tends to use to achieve and maintain control. He can be quick-tempered and may carry grudges and seek revenge for wrongs done to him. He may react with anger or hostility when his independence threatened or if people disagree with or criticize him. In fact, a Choleric has potential for exhibiting abusive outrage toward others. Becoming aware of this default mode of anger and expressive rage is very important for him in interactions and relationships, as it can occur suddenly even in what seem to be delightful interactions. Under pressure, he may tend to isolate himself from other people. While he feels emotions, you may rarely, if ever, see him cry.

Work Orientation. A highly productive, independent worker, a Choleric possesses excellent leadership abilities and problem-solving skills. He can assume and complete an impressive amount of responsibility and maintains a practical approach to tasks, overcoming obstacles that would discourage other people. He is the kind of person that will gain energy as he nears achievements and improves in competencies. You might even call him a "risk taker"; rather than go for the low hanging fruit, he prefers the top, where the best and brightest gather. A disciplined, well-organized perfectionist, a Choleric is easily bored with routine activities and needs constant challenges, as he finds them entertaining and worthy of his thinking and efforts. He works at a fast, efficient pace and is reluctant to delegate to others, leading to fatigue or burnout, a potential pitfall of every Choleric. He may equate criticism of his work with loss of approval. He resists authoritarian managers and is most productive when permitted to work independently, remaining in control of his schedule and activities. The quickest way to cause him great frustration and agony is to micro-manage him, ultimately resulting in seeking another employer where he has flexibility, freedom, and is not micro-managed. Ensure a Choleric is clear about where a company is headed and how to succeed within the department – his performance and productivity will improve exponentially when he has clarity of desired outcomes and end goals.

Motivation. Self-motivated by needs for accomplishment and recognition, a Choleric may direct many of his behaviors toward maintaining control of his life. He may be capable of changing his expression intensity or adopting bad behavior to maintain control and attain his goals. If threatened with punishment or loss of power, he may respond in anger but will not usually change. A Choleric is motivated toward the goals he deems worthy, ones that challenge and provide opportunities he aspires toward – the key is he must see the goal as worthy for himself, or it simply is not. Sometimes a goal's worthiness is determined by how reachable it is, along with how much recognition is involved. Uniqueness of accomplishment is a strong motivator. The greatest, however, is "vision". A Choleric is a great visionary, as he can see into the future and around corners where some of the other Temperaments only see what is in front of them. A Choleric may instantly spot an opportunity or goal that could take weeks, months, years, or even decades to accomplish. When he knows where he is going, he needs you to help him get there. If you want to motivate him, give him the "green light" on his vision and he is instantly motivated by your support. At that point, all he needs are the resources that will enable him to pursue his idea.

Rejection/Acceptance Profile. A Choleric is self-confident and does not fear personal rejection by others, nor need their acceptance. He does depend on people for support, then praise and recognition of his accomplishments. He can reject people who oppose his plans and may be unaware that people seek his approval. As a result, he may not easily compliment others or recognize their work. He can improve his relationship dynamics with his colleagues/team by giving them due recognition for their contribution to the project, as this is sound leadership in a team environment. Recognizing redundant tasks, administrative support, resource suppliers, subject matter experts in their field, and more, are just a few elements of a successful team that can be lauded regularly. Because a Choleric is self-reliant and self-sufficient, rejection by others positions him to act within his "island unto himself" mentality. This will debilitate efforts. Harnessing a team's ability to produce begins with the leader/manager and support at all levels to maximize performance for every Temperament and this will keep a Choleric properly engaged and productive.

A Note About Burn-out for a Choleric

Before continuing with the traits of a Choleric within the different Temperament Areas, it's important for any Choleric reading this chapter (or loved one of a Choleric) to understand the constant potential for burn-out in such a high-powered Temperament. This is a guaranteed risk, as it seems to blind-side he and his family time and again. With awareness, all can find and sustain balance.

Do you happen to know a person that accepts an assignment of high difficulty that others would not touch? The world calls on a Choleric because he has a reputation for being able to "always come through" and, of course, he wants to continue to look good in the eyes of those observing him. So, he takes assignments and finds himself working 80 hours per week with no private life. His family neglected and his mind in overload, he collapses from exhaustion. Why? Because he is driven internally with the mantra "I can do this"; yet even for a worthy goal, the strain will take its toll.

A Choleric is easy to recognize, as he has multiple "irons in the fire" or "spinning plates", even to the point of owning and operating multiple businesses (Wow!). Let's break down how the noble goal of changing the world with innovation and pure hard work can cause his world to come to a screeching halt:

Physically. A Choleric is expressive and highly energetic, active, and always on assignment. Therefore, he tends to overextend himself physically on a regular basis, which he justifies as necessary for accomplishing the goal. He expends an impressive amount of energy because he naturally possesses more energy than other Temperaments, pushing himself to the point of jeopardizing his health and in some cases his wellbeing and safety. The desire and drive to excel in whatever he does leads him onward. He can even motivate himself through competition – with himself! Awareness of physical limitations and listening to his body along the path of success is a great first step.

Emotionally. A Choleric could be considered the most emotionally challenging Temperament to understand. Consider the story of General George S. Patton when he visited a field hospital tent and reprimanded a soldier who was there because he was "afraid" of combat. General Patton slapped him with his gloves several times and yelled to get him out of his sight. This is one way a Choleric may handle expressing emotions, through anger; a familiar emotion that is subconsciously preferable to more conscious, vulnerable expressions. A Choleric is often repelled by open emotional displays and can cast disapproval on those who are emotionally expressive, as it portrays weakness to him. When a Choleric is focused on the goal and overextending himself to the point of emotional exhaustion, he'll feel defeated, downcast, beat up. Yet, a Choleric is not wired to sit in sorrow or self-pity, he is wired to think about how great it will be that he can rise above and resurrect himself in even greater achievement despite opposition. He will ignore internal indicators of depletion, loneliness, and feelings of hunger. Even within his closest relationships he may be quite hard and insensitive. Remember, it is not that a Choleric does not feel emotions or can't express compassion, empathy, etc. It is that his needs are not met through feelings because his needs are not relationally based.

Spiritually. A Choleric uses competent education & experiences combined with intuitive senses and "big picture" foresight to make quick decisions. It is possible he will not emphasize spirituality in his life due to the potential philosophical implications of being robbed of control of life and destiny, a root internal need. Living and "doing" in the shadow of chance or predestination is very demotivating to a Choleric. However, if he is rooted and grounded in spiritual awareness, he can contribute individually toward noble social and family purposes. By understanding how each Temperament fits within the larger context of creation and higher intention, he can thrive with glorious purpose. Sometimes, he learns tough lessons because of self-centeredness. It is the natural design of a Choleric to follow his internal set of rules as he understands them to be, so it cannot be automatically deemed narcissistic or ill-intended. He almost always will find a way out of his bad decisions, but even when proper behavioral corrections are made, the path can still hurt others. A Choleric typically leaves a large footprint of influence meaning he also has a wide blast radius when the plan doesn't go as intended. If he is functioning within true spiritual health, he will choose to be consciously aware of his impact and internal temperature - minimizing negative effects and increasing positive behavior and achievements worthy of a powerful, yet humble reputation.

Remember: Temperament is rooted in identifying what a person intrinsically needs, which motivates certain behaviors. When needs are being met, that Temperament will tend to operate within probable strengths. When needs are not being met, potential weaknesses likely will be observed. As you read about a Choleric in Leadership, seek to understand what it is he truly needs. Just like each of the other Temperaments, these needs are valid and necessary for this person to sustain proper health as well as mental & emotional functionality.

The Leadership Profile – Choleric

Statistics – Choleric in Leadership (out of 3,449 people)

12.03%

Choleric

Number: 415
Percentage: 12.03%

5.07%

Choleric Compulsive

Number: 175
Percentage: 5.07%

A Note About the Leadership Profile

The Adult Leadership Profile identifies your ability to provide leadership, make decisions, and assume responsibilities. This profile outlines your needs and desires for independence, achievement, and recognition. Because Leadership needs and desires are expressed through socializing with people, the Leadership Profile should not be evaluated alone but interpreted with either the Social Profile or the Relationship Profile.

– Evaluated together, the Leadership Profile and the Social Profile help determine your career needs. By comparing the results with your current employment situation, you can target conflict areas and maximize career skills.

– Evaluated together, the Leadership Profile and the Relationship Profile help determine your independence/dependence needs in close relationships. By comparing the results with your current life situation, you can target conflict areas and enhance relationships.

In a leadership capacity, a Choleric is good at giving orders, but not good at receiving them. However, the exception to this rule is that he can choose to submit to another authority for a certain length of time. A Choleric must either be in a role of leading (being responsible for) something that achieves reward or be in a position where he can work his way up the chain until he is in a place of leadership. Yes, of course, any woman who is a Choleric in the Leadership Area also has this need and drive.

Leadership has nothing to do with gender, but has everything to do with Temperament.

Leadership Needs and Desires. Independent, self-reliant, self-sufficient, and self-governing, a Choleric accepts little or no control from others but needs positive control over people and events in his life. The freedom to be himself (as a Choleric operating in leadership capacities), is essential for his mental and emotional health and success. He makes intuitive decisions, is discerning, spontaneous, and assumes (and completes) many responsibilities. He needs to promote his goals and visions and has a high need for success and recognition for his accomplishments. Just give him a set of endorsed guidelines and he will produce above and beyond your expectations.

Keep in mind, the Leadership Profile is always interpreted alongside either the Social Profile or the Relationship Profile, so be sure and look at true relational needs in conjunction with the Leadership Profile (contact a WIDP Affiliate Manager if you need a trained eye).

Criteria for Relationships. Achievement-oriented rather than task- or people-oriented, a Choleric depends on his knowledge and skills and has minimal need for close relationships beyond business-related interactions. Instead, he tends to develop relationships to help accomplish personal goals and seeks out people who can be influenced by him, especially those who can assist him. He's drawn to people who recognize and appreciate his accomplishments and may actively avoid interactions with other strong-willed people. If you put two Cholerics on the same project, there will be conflict as they both have an innate need to lead and be in control. However, with the WIDP Profile, you can eliminate problems before they start with well-defined roles and responsibilities. Ensure those definitions give clear distinction of responsibilities so that they do not bleed over into the other's area of responsibility. Just to note, while mutual agreement can be made and collaboration can be achieved, they will not become best friends because each need independence and will have this inner feeling the other Choleric is trying to invade their responsibilities and take over their area. Continue to nurture their relationship with recognition of their separate responsibility items and ensure they are equipped with what they need to succeed when you are a higher deciding authority (supervisor/manager).

Perception of Self. Projecting optimism and self-confidence, a Choleric can be egotistical and seldom admits making a mistake. He is confident of his ability to achieve whatever he desires even though his high need for control may mask inner fears. Thriving on challenges and setting high personal goals, he maintains an attitude of competence and usually has an answer or solution to problems. Sometimes his vision includes a timetable so far out that most people will not be able to see it. However, he can see it and that is all that matters to him. He can adapt his behavior to circumstances and fill any role he feels necessary to achieve his goals. Active and involved, he rarely spends time in self-introspection and may view himself only from a positive perspective. Most importantly, he sees himself as a high achiever and that gives him great satisfaction in his inner world. His daydreams (and night dreams) may include acts of heroism, nobility, and other symbolically high-achieving thoughts and themes. Encourage these, as inspiration is a powerful motivator for him and can reignite a dwindling flame in an instant.

Perception by Others. Possessing natural leadership abilities, a Choleric maintains an image of superiority and confidence. While he has excellent social skills and can be outgoing, charismatic, and physically affectionate, he may have little understanding of people's needs and emotions. His focus is completely on the target of accomplishing his vision, which may neglect the rights and feelings of others, no matter how close they are to him. Therefore, he could be perceived as being manipulative or coercive. He is usually the dominant figure in groups and may try to get as many listening ears as possible to tune into his vision. Less confident people can be intimidated by his high energy and decisive manner. He can be offensive to an Introverted Sanguine, Sanguine, and Phlegmatic. He may directly confront those who disagree with him and can be critical or argumentative, as being direct is his preferred method of addressing problematic situations; he will only choose diplomatic approaches if he is very aware of his Temperament characteristics and default modes.

Perception of Others. Extremely individualistic, a Choleric does not need to please people or meet their expectations. He is reluctant to delegate responsibility, seldom seeks the opinions of others, and distrusts people's motives and abilities. He maintains high expectations of coworkers and friends and is intolerant of incompetence, expecting perfection from himself and others. His priorities usually involve goals, not people; as a result, he may disregard the rights and feelings of others in his quest for success. He tends to motivate people through directing them and rarely uses calm persuasion or reasoning. While he values other independent individualists, he actively resists any control by others and tends to lose respect for weaker-willed people, even if he utilizes their assistance to contribute to his vision.

Intellectual Orientation. Possessing high mental abilities, a Choleric is always envisioning new goals and challenges. He has excellent problem-solving skills, is a good communicator, makes quick, intuitive decisions, and can develop and implement innovative and efficient techniques. Since he is so perceptive and operates without the mental interference of people-pleasing, he can see the potential of projects all the way to the end goal. Therefore, he is going to implement strategies that most other Temperaments (aside from a Phlegmatic) may not yet understand, which could be a frequently encountered resistance to his plans. Turn an ear and open mind to his recommendations and choose confidence and trust in his vision. Generally, he will have left a path of successes behind him, and you can conclude from those accomplishments that he is a dedicated visionary who can bring to pass what he sets out to accomplish. He is powerful and productive, strong-willed, resilient to setbacks and barriers, and will plow toward the goal long after others have stopped to take a breather.

Emotional Orientation. Showing few deep emotions and rarely verbalizing any deep or loving feelings, a Choleric can be repelled by emotional displays from others. His determination to move forward is for the objective, whatever it may be. He operates from a base of "achievement orientation" which translates into tasks, such that he will not be in a mindset that considers the emotions of those around him. A Choleric does fear loss of positive control regarding the influence of people and the influence of his environment. He is quick-tempered and the sentiment he expresses most often may be anger, which he may use to achieve or maintain power. When he is making great progress or accomplishes a small victory along the way, he will be in a great mood, feeding from the energy of progress. But, if you hear of someone leading with force, it will be a burnt-out Choleric (or at the edge) that has resolved to use his position of authority to control people around him (this could also be subconscious when a Choleric is tired or hungry). However, if he is leading from a healthy standpoint, it can take the form of "conviction" allowing him to consider and relate in a more positive way. If others criticize or disagree with him, he will feel opposed personally and react with hostility, especially if independence is threatened. He needs to be nourished by those in leadership over him without them displaying any control maneuvers or domination over him (certainly no micromanaging) as he will take that as a threat and become very hard-headed and stubborn.

Work Orientation. Achievement-oriented which translates to efficient tasking, a Choleric is a highly productive, independent worker. Give him a job to do with the people and financial resources to do it and then step back and watch him go. He has excellent leadership abilities and problem-solving skills and can assume and complete amounts of responsibility that will stagger the mind. His practical approach to tasks enables him to overcome obstacles that would discourage other Temperaments. He is not a quitter and will perform unimaginable feats with his natural mental & emotional talent. A perfectionist, he is disciplined and well-organized. Able to work at a fast, efficient pace, he needs constant challenges and is quickly bored with routine activities. He may equate criticism of his work with loss of approval and resists authoritarian managers, becoming very stubborn. He is most productive when permitted to work independently and remain in control of his schedule and activities. At the same time, his reluctance to delegate to others may lead to fatigue or burnout. There is just something about him that causes him to accept more responsibilities than any one person can handle. Delegation must become a learned skill for him to relinquish any authority. Once a Choleric realizes he can delegate authority, it excites him and empowers more vision and more responsibility. Everyone becomes a winner, as new projects and more jobs are created, just from his inspiration.

Motivation. Self-motivated by his needs for accomplishment and recognition, many Choleric behaviors revolve around maintaining control of his life. A significant motivating factor for a Choleric is being given more Leadership responsibility. Opportunity, challenge, and inspiration drive him. Yet the single greatest motivator (because of his mental ownership of it) is vision. A Choleric can see into the future and around corners where other Temperaments only see what is in front of them. He can see weeks, month, years, or even decades away. He knows where he is going, and he needs you to help him get there. Give him the green light on his vision and he is instantly motivated. He may be capable of changing his behavior or adopting negative behaviors to maintain control and attain his goals. If threatened with punishment or loss of control, he may respond in anger but will not usually change.

Rejection/Acceptance Profile. Self-confident, a Choleric does not fear personal rejection by others or need their approval. He depends on people for praise and recognition of his accomplishments. Unaware that people seek his support, he may not easily compliment others or recognize their work and can reject those who oppose his plans. For him, Leadership is his life, affecting every decision and interaction. If he is not able to lead or if you attack his administration, he will dismiss you and your attacks will roll off him like water off a duck's back. Challenge his Leadership and you are challenging the whole person to the core of his existence. Remember, the single-greatest way for a Choleric to be mentally and emotionally deflated is for responsibilities to be taken from him without his permission – it is like oxygen removed from his lungs.

The DeWalt Challenge
For
Joe the Choleric

Even though it was barely 20 degrees in mid-January in Massachusetts, the sweat was pouring off me. I was focused on one single task: to be the next "King of the Drill" for the DeWalt Million Dollar Challenge. I had been using DeWalt tools since I bought my first 9v cordless drill in 1994, continuing through 20 years of construction.

The challenge was to be the fastest to drive five 1 5/8" screws into a pine board with a 14.4v DeWalt cordless drill. To start the challenge, you hit the timer and, with the same hand, pick up the drill and get to work. When you finish, you hit that same timer with the bottom of your drill. The first phase of the challenge was a local preliminary qualifier held at home improvement centers around town, each event allowing one try-out per game. The contestant with the best time in each game would quality for the next match at the regional level.

It was 12:30 AM. I had been practicing for 4 hours to hit an originally set goal of 6 seconds or less, ten times. I knew every movement had to be calculated, every step seamlessly executed, every mental distraction thrown out – and if all these parts were not in place, it would result in 8 seconds or worse. With pun intended, I consider myself "driven" to perfection.

Looking back on the day of the competition, I was so nervous. My hands were cold, my insides knotted in anticipation. Everything in me was afraid of failing, even to the point of telling me to forget about it and go home, but obviously that wasn't enough to sway my drive to try. Finally, it was my turn.

I stepped up to the platform and a shiver went through me. I rubbed my hands to keep them from trembling and assumed the ready position as I had practiced countless times; my left hand hovering over the screws, my right hand over the timer...and with a deep breath, I slammed it down. The challenge had begun.

I grabbed a handful of screws, dropping most of them and working with the two that remained. The first screw bent over as I drove it, so I abandoned that one and drove the other successfully. I went back to the tray for more screws, juggled a few between my fingers, dropping 2 or 3 more. I had quick movements, but my execution was terrible. I drove another all the way in, then another, then another. Finally, with the last one sunk I hit the timer with the bottom of the gun. I looked up at the time: 15 seconds. My time was recorded, and the challenge representative said he would contact me if it held up.

I spent the rest of that day agonizing over my performance. But, to my amazement, that evening I opened an e-mail stating I had won and qualified for the regional competition!

At that point, my desire to be the best hit overdrive.

I decided to begin going to other local events and inconspicuously started taking notes: dimensions of the kiosk, timer size, type of drywall screws, and other details. I watched others fumble as I had, observed potential form improvements, even recognized critical success factors like ways to pick up screws. I decided to survey the screw tray before I started the timer to pinpoint which screws I would pick up first. I learned picking up two or three screws pointing in the same direction would dramatically improve my time.

Over the next month of observation and practice, I was in the 8-10 second range, though still aiming for 6 seconds or better. I built a practice kiosk with a diamond-plated lining, to the exact challenge dimensions. I even bought the same timer button, motivated to be the fastest drill in the country. It's interesting that I rarely ever thought of the prizes, which were substantial. The regional winner would get a 2003 Chevy Express van filled with DeWalt tools and a round trip to Phoenix, Arizona for the final competition; a $40,000 package. The "King of the Drill" grand prize winner would walk away with a fresh one million dollars. It's no surprise that more than 140,000 people entered the competition nationwide.

My practice regimen consisted of doing 20 – 25 runs per set, tracking my times in a notebook. By the end of the day, I had 150-200 runs logged and that's just the ones I wrote down - there were many more that were never logged, where I practiced technique instead of speed. Just before the regional event, 3 eight-hour days were spent fine-tuning every aspect of my performance. I had gotten my time into the low 7's, just shy of my goal, leaving me feeling a bit under-prepared the day I traveled to New Jersey to meet the other 32 contestants in the New England regional event. I took with me a mini version of the kiosk so I could practice right up to the last moment.

The next morning, I got up early to eat a good breakfast but thoughts on my performance outweighed my hunger. The event was held at a sponsoring Chevrolet dealership, and I was the first contestant to arrive, about 3 hours early, allowing me time to get loose and survey my surroundings.

I was surprisingly relaxed up until they called us all into a conference room and randomly summoned the first contestant. He set the pace, finishing at 12 seconds. Two contestants later shaved it to 11.26 seconds.

As the 10th competitor, I was escorted to the edge of the platform. I tested the drill, took a deep breath to calm my nerves and, remembering my strategy, I surveyed the screw tray for my initial grab. With another breath my right hand acted more by instinct, and I pressed the timer. I quickly grabbed three screws perfectly and drove them faster than I ever have. I reached back for two more screws, dropping one, so I drove the one that remained. I snatched the last screw and hit the timer. The crowd began cheering before I could even see my time. 10.23 seconds. I had stolen the lead.

Two hours and twenty-two contestants later, I was declared the New England regional winner! I won the van and the load of DeWalt tools; the thrill was unlike any other. I was moved by the cheering and the sportsmanship of the other contestants lining up to shake my hand. I was headed to the finals.

The months that followed were eventful as I prepared. I stepped up my practice times and enlisted the help of my wife and father-in-law who quickly became a valuable resource for my improvement. Within weeks we worked together, and my time fell below 7 seconds. Not long after I met my goal of 6 seconds, followed by my fastest time ever: 5.29 seconds. Having finally broken the ice, I regularly hit sub-6's.

At the finals in Phoenix, my wife and I had an excellent time, compliments of DeWalt. I placed third fastest time in Phoenix, falling just shy of the million dollars. While my motivation to succeed is unique, there were two in the nation that shared my unyielding determination. The winner truly deserved the title.

Later, I realized I had used over 200,000 screws in practice. Each one of those screws built confidence in me to accomplish anything I set my mind to achieve. Even though I lost the final event, I had conquered fear, nervousness, doubt, and so many other personal barriers, accomplishing more than enough to hold my head high.

Joseph Fodera
January 26, 2005

As we mentioned earlier in the chapter, it is unwise to view a Choleric in a negative light simply because of misunderstood needs of control and influence within his environment. That desire and drive is the same that reaches levels of success like in the story above. This is an example of a Choleric with a goal, believing he can achieve seemingly impossible things and learning the value and reward that process can bring. As a fun note, this is a true story, and the man in the story is my son-in-law, Joseph!

The Relationship Profile – Choleric

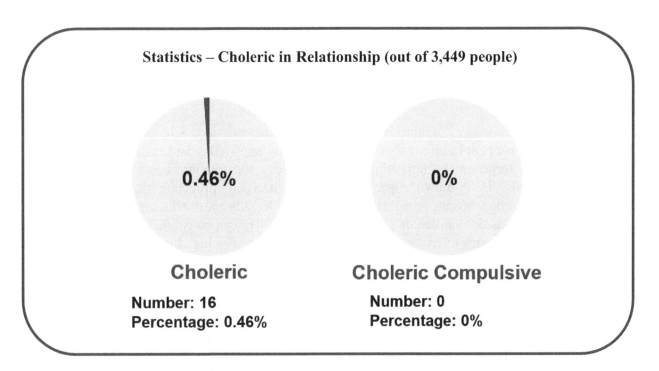

Statistics – Choleric in Relationship (out of 3,449 people)

0.46%   **0%**

Choleric   **Choleric Compulsive**

Number: 16   Number: 0
Percentage: 0.46%   Percentage: 0%

A Note About the Relationship Profile

The Adult Relationship Profile identifies your preferences for emotional involvement and shared affection on a one-to-one basis. This profile outlines your needs and desires for emotional sharing and relationships. For most people, the Relationship Profile is the dominant pattern that influences behavior in the Social and Leadership Areas.

By comparing the Relationship Profile with your current life situation, you can target conflict areas and meet personal needs that are not fulfilled.

Relationship Needs and Desires. A Choleric in Relationship is a rare person and may be confusing to many. Outgoing and personable, a Choleric appears to want a high degree of interaction people. However, he needs and wants close relationships with very few people. You don't find too many individuals that are this Temperament in this Area. Out of a database of 3,449 profiles, only sixteen (16) people were Choleric in Relationship. There were zero (0) Choleric Compulsives out of the same database. A Choleric Demonstrates high expression (6-7-8-9) but Desires low initiation from others (0-1-2-3) in the context of close intimate relationships. A person that Demonstrates high and at the same time Desires low doesn't make sense; he freely expresses love and affection but needs minimal open emotional expressions in return. He may define love as people's willingness to perform tasks for him and desires expressions of love on these terms, not solely with physical or emotional manifestations. To be in his inner circle (trust) means something very specific, just as it is for each Temperament. Since a Choleric has a high need for accomplishment and he may choose activities and friendships that

will assist him in attaining his goals rather than for purely relational reasons, the one who will attract his eye will be someone supportive of his needs and goals. Remember, still characteristic of a Choleric is the high need to be in control of his destiny, in close relationships. Ask him his intentions for his life and family and what his leadership in those environments will look like – he'll tell you! This will give you a good sense of the destiny he envisions and aims to achieve.

Criteria for Relationships. Highly productive and independent, a Choleric is achievement-oriented rather than people-oriented. He depends on his knowledge and skills and has minimal need for close interpersonal relationships, tending to develop relationships to help accomplish his personal goals. He is drawn to people who recognize and appreciate his accomplishments and seeks out people who can be influenced by him, especially those who are content to let him lead and make decisions on behalf of the relationship. He can cause difficult problems if he isn't aware of his modes of leading or of his deep needs within his closest relationships. It is possible a Choleric in Relationship has many unsuccessful attempts to relate intimately, simply due to behavior and frustrations rooted in unmet needs. This is where WIDP provides liberating insight. Increasing awareness will show him that he should avoid initiating or investing in close relationships with others that push their own agenda and, instead, seek a balanced and independent supporter of his goals and intentions (his leadership within that relationship).

Perception of Self. While a Choleric projects optimism and self-confidence, he can be egotistical and seldom admits making a mistake. Obviously this can be problematic for others but may not be for him. Confidence can come across as arrogance or pride, of which he may be unaware, because resolute confidence comes from knowing he can achieve anything he desires. His high need for control may mask inner fears of inferiority. He thrives on challenges and sets high personal goals. A Choleric maintains an attitude of competence and usually has an answer or solution to problems for all close relationship issues. These attributes do not make him right, but he certainly will believe he is. He can adapt his behavior to circumstances and fill any role he feels necessary to achieve his goals. His self-perception may be perceived as manipulation, but it is simply a Choleric being the self-motivated and confident driver that he is. Active and involved, he rarely spends time in self-introspection and may view himself only from a positive perspective.

Perception by Others. Possessing natural leadership abilities, a Choleric maintains an image of superiority and confidence. He has excellent social skills and can be outgoing, charismatic, and physically affectionate. While he often gives the impression that he desires close relationships with many people, he is very selective in choosing intimate friends. He is usually the dominant figure in groups; he can intimidate less confident people with his high energy and decisive manner. He may have little understanding of people's needs and emotions and often directly confronts those who disagree with him. He can be critical or argumentative and can be a perfectionist and demanding in close relationships. This may cause others to fear his anger and criticism or to become discouraged at their inability to please him and rightly so. He may appear to desire more close relationships than he wants based on his response to others but be aware that he does not let many people in his private world.

Perception of Others. A Choleric is individualistic and does not need to please people or meet their expectations. Of course, anyone in a close relationship wants a fulfilled and happy home (that's a goal, too, after all). While he values other independent individualists, his natural state is distrusting of people's abilities beyond his own, so he leads the decision-making and seldom seeks the opinions of others, remaining reluctant to delegate any responsibility within the relationship. Quickly bored with routine or mundane activities, a Choleric needs constant challenges. Intolerant of incompetence, he expects perfection from himself and others and maintains high expectations of close friends and family. Remember, "close" means within his inner circle, as distinct from casual acquaintances or people he has decided are of no value to him. His priorities usually include goals, not people, and he may disregard the rights and feelings of others in his quest for success. So, he will need to be quite educated on how other people perceive him; this may come with resistance until he accepts ownership of his design and his positive and negative natural tendencies. This awareness can be a noble goal and respectable project for him to digest. He will rarely use persuasion or reasoning and tends to motivate people by dominating/influencing them. Dominance, of course, will not work in close relationships, and he may suffer from many broken relationships due to this approach and this track-record won't be favorable to many. Begin awareness today and steer the ship in a positive direction for close relationships to thrive. A trained WIDP Affiliate Manager can guide a Choleric through correct insights and action steps based on his goals and dreams for his life in a significantly less amount of time than it would be for a Choleric to decipher on his own; all he must do is *choose* to submit to his design and to trust the trainer.

Intellectual Orientation. Possessing high mental abilities, a Choleric continually envisions new goals, perhaps even for his close relationships. He has excellent problem-solving skills and often develops and implements innovative techniques, but applying such techniques within close relationships may not always be welcome. Honest awareness of Temperaments with two-way conversation is the antidote. An excellent communicator, he makes quick, intuitive decisions. Having to learn to stop and get feedback from those he is involved with may need to be quite conscious and could cause him some anxiety. He adopts a practical approach to tasks and can assume and complete an impressive amount of responsibility. A Choleric is strong-willed and rarely changes his mind, even when proven wrong. This can be an obvious frustration within close relationships and hinder true intimacy. Awareness is the key.

Emotional orientation. A Choleric shows few deep emotions, if any, and can be repelled by emotional displays from others. Rarely verbalizing any deep or loving feelings, his most prominent expressed emotion may be anger alongside desires to move toward his goals. Because he tends to fear the loss of control of the people and situations within his environment, he may use anger to motivate within close relationships; this approach will not work long-term. He can be quick-tempered, even carrying a grudge or seeking revenge for wrongs done to him. He may react with anger or hostility if his independence is threatened or if those he is closest to disagree with or criticize him. You will quickly recognize that, when under pressure, he may isolate himself and disengage because he cannot withstand the emotional stress it puts on his close relationships. This will help silence undesired initiations for him to gather himself. Reflection on his tone, approach, and choices is time well spent. If harnessed, it can lead to choosing to revisit relational problems and conversations with a unified demeanor. One hint for a Choleric is to remind himself that his closest people are not against him personally, but are seeking what's best for the health of the relationship, not challenging whether he is fit to lead. Any leader is wise to consider his own needs as well as those whom he leads. Anything that is emotionally confusing (for a Choleric, that could be many things) can be discussed with a trained WIDP representative. Don't worry – they will know how hard it is for you to even ask for help, but the help to the relationship is worth it, and you will be the hero for seeking the best solutions possible.

Motivation. Self-motivated by needs for accomplishment and recognition, a Choleric has a high need to be approved and admired by those close to him. Many of his behaviors will be toward maintaining control of his life and the influence of his closest relationships. He may be capable of changing his tone or adopting new habits to control and attain his goals. Any close relationship will require much internal motivation, considering he feels most natural as a "one-man show". Yet, for the sake of his chosen few, he can choose to make some behavior modifications once he owns that it is a better goal for those relationships to be successful. If others choose to threaten punishment or loss of control, he may respond in anger but will not usually change. Threats often backfire in cold resilience. Importantly, anger will feel like a motivating, useful tactic, but he should be aware of how anger may work short-term but does not produce the long-term results he desires. The best way to motivate him is to spell out the desired result to achieve for the relationship and let him work through (take mental ownership of) how important emotional needs and different individual designs are within relating in a healthy, functional way. His desire for accomplishment and recognition alongside a picture of success will allow him to see that the goal is attainable and worthy of his time and conscious action.

Rejection/Acceptance Profile. Extremely self-confident, a Choleric does not fear personal rejection, even by those closest to him, nor does he need their approval. What he does depend on is praise and recognition of his accomplishments. Time spent telling a Choleric what he is doing well is magnificent for relational intimacy. Unaware that people seek his approval, a Choleric can be rejecting of people who oppose his plans and may not be the one to compliment or attentively recognize the extent of relational participation by those closest to him. He is also usually unaware that some of his independent behaviors could lead to relational difficulties. These, of course, can be adjusted with awareness of the needs of others and consideration that their needs are just as valid and important as his, and that the other Temperaments do need positive involvement in uniquely different, unfamiliar ways to him.

A Note about Strengths & Weaknesses

The *Probable* Strengths & *Potential* Weaknesses section is located at the end of each of the 3 WIDP Profile Areas. An individual's Temperament may be different in one or all Areas, thus the Strengths & Weaknesses will coincide with their uniquely identified Temperament in that respective Area. It is important to interpret the labels *probable* and *potential* correctly. The difference of which characteristic is experienced or observed depends on several factors.

Any individual whose Temperament needs are actively getting met has the greatest chance of exuding their strengths. For instance, after we eat a meal, we are much happier, as our hunger need has been satisfied. The same is true with Temperament needs. Someone whose Temperament needs are getting met will tend to be a balanced and healthy individual, able to proactively participate within their strengths for a positive impact in their life.

However, if certain Temperament needs have been frustrated, the potential for negative performance could be experienced and observed, leading to unbalanced behavior and emotional instability.

**Like a runny nose is a symptom,
think of weaknesses as symptoms
that indicate unmet Temperament needs.**

↓

**Wiping our nose doesn't address the true problem.
Instead, identify and treat the root cause:**

Meet Temperament Needs!

Remember: No Temperament is automatically broken by design. Each Temperament is genetically wired with unique, specific needs that allow the individual to be mentally and emotionally healthy and functional within that context. Temperament makeup can be referred to as one's emotional biology.

Basic Strengths/Weaknesses of the Choleric

Probable Strengths
- Independent; possesses strong leadership abilities
- Strong-willed; is determined; does not vacillate under pressure
- Visionary; challenged by the unknown; goal- or achievement-oriented
- Practical; is highly organized
- Decisive; judges people and situations intuitively
- Disciplined; highly productive, thrives on activity

Potential Weaknesses
- Unemotional; insensitivity to people's feelings
- Self-sufficient; difficulty delegating to others
- Impetuous; may assume more responsibilities than he can handle
- Domineering; can be manipulative
- Angry; hostile; sarcastic; inability to forgive
- Workaholic tendencies; susceptible to burnout

Become Aware of Your Natural Strengths and Learn to Use Them Wisely

Natural Strength	Strength Carried to Extreme	Avoidable Result
Visionary	Angry if people challenge his vision or leadership	Dictatorial and obsessive
Decisive	Makes decisions for everyone	Becomes manipulative to get his/her way
Independent	Reckless	Demotivating friends, colleagues, work efforts, and reputation
Productive	Works beyond the standard	Workaholic, neglecting all relationships

Decisions for a Melancholy

A Choleric is swift to decide on any problem, barrier, or situation. If a Choleric makes a wrong decision, he will "course-correct" by making another decision to correct the prior decision and move on. This makes for an influential individual; being adaptable to change is a much-needed talent in work and general life circumstances.

Other Probable Strengths of the Choleric

Adventurous	One who will take on new and daring enterprises with a determination to master them
Persuasive	Convinces others through logic and fact
Strong-willed	One who is determined to have his way
Competitive	Driven to be unique, to stand out and be the best or have the best resources
Resourceful	Able to act quickly and efficiently
Self-Reliant	An independent person who can entirely rely on his capabilities, judgment, and resources
Positive	Knows it will turn out right and keeps motivation high towards a worthy goal, unshaken by obstacles
Sure	Rarely hesitates or wavers
Outspoken	Speaks frankly and without reserve, direct with communication during conflicts
Forceful	A commanding demeanor where others may not persist if in the same situation
Daring	Willing to take risks, fearless, bold
Confident	Self-assured in their abilities
Independent	Self-sufficient, self-supporting, self-confident, and seems to have little need for help
Decisive	Quick, conclusive judgments once he has a good grasp of the "big picture"
Mover	Driven by a need to be productive, is a leader whom others follow, finds it difficult to sit still, gets anxious when stagnant
Tenacious	Holds firmly, stubbornly, and won't let go until the goal is accomplished

Leader	Natural-born director, driven to be in charge and finds it difficult to believe anyone else can do the job as well as he
Chief	Commands leadership and expects others to follow
Productive	Must continuously be working or achieving
Bold	Fearless, daring, forward, and unafraid of risk

Other Potential Weaknesses of the Choleric

Bossy	Can be domineering and overbearing in relationships
Unsympathetic	Finds it difficult to relate to the problems or hurts of others
Resistant	Hesitates to accept any other way but his own
Frank	Straight-forward, outspoken, and doesn't mind telling you exactly what he thinks
Exasperating	Finds it challenging to ensure irritation or to wait for others
Unaffectionate	Finds it difficult to verbally or physically demonstrate expressions of tenderness
Headstrong	Insists on having his way, believes in his vision and methods
Proud	One with high self-esteem who sees himself as always right and the best person for the job
Argumentative	Incites arguments generally because he is confident, right no matter what the situation may be
Nervy	Full of confidence, courage, and sheer guts, often in a negative sense
Workaholic	An aggressive goal-setter who must be continuously productive and feels very guilty when resting; is not driven by the task completion itself, but by the accomplishment and reward of the goal/vision
Tactless	Sometimes expressing himself in an offensive and inconsiderate way
Domineering	Compulsively takes control of situations and people, usually telling others what to do
Intolerant	Appears unable to withstand or accept another's attitudes, perspective, or way of doing things
Manipulative	Influences or manages shrewdly or deviously to his advantage, will get his way somehow

Stubborn	Determined to exert his own will, not easily persuaded, obstinate
Short-Tempered	Impatience-based anger and short-fused, especially when tired; anger expressed when others are not moving fast enough or have not completed what they have been directed to do
Rash	May act hastily, without thinking things through, generally because of impatience
Crafty	Shrewd, one who can always find a way to get to the desired end

Helpful Tips for the Choleric

You feel that you must be in control. While you can recognize a desire to be in control, acting as if you require to be in control can alienate you from acquaintances, business colleagues, friends, and those closest to you. Here are a few things you can do to exercise more conscious collaboration at work and at home:

1. *Respond to other leadership.* While it may be difficult for you to understand, you are not the only one who aspires to (and can) lead, especially considering another Choleric. When a Choleric bumps into another Choleric, whether in a social or work setting, they are immediately drawn in mutual respect and energy toward one another. When this happens, there is significant chemistry that takes place as they do understand each other's driven nature and can talk along the same lines, thereby reinforcing, invigorating, and energizing each other. Collaboration draws leaders closer together because now they have someone with whom they can identify. If you can get comfortable with another Choleric and not be intimated by them, you can learn a lot from them, and the relationship can be very beneficial to both parties.

2. *Don't look down on "the dummies."* Not everyone can be as quick on their feet as you are with decisions and solutions, but that doesn't mean other people don't have good ideas. A weakness a Choleric has is not respecting "weaker" Temperaments (as a Choleric would see it) and will openly criticize with no regard to feelings, especially in the absence of Temperament knowledge. However, if a Choleric will learn to delegate more responsibility, and in some cases invest time in training and teaching other Temperaments through example or walking them through their thoughts, productivity will increase, and productivity is always pleasing to a Choleric.

3. *Appreciate other Temperament types.* Those individuals not as fortunate as you in their Temperament makeup as leaders have different strengths than you as well. For example, the seemingly mundane issues that a Choleric has no tolerance to deal with can willingly be handled by other Temperaments who are capable and efficient. A Choleric needs the varying strengths of other Temperaments to support him and undergird his vision and goals, closing the gaps where he is otherwise unable.

4. *Stop manipulating other people.* You may think you're fooling people when you get them to do things they don't want to do; most people know when they're in a controlled situation – and they resent it. It is much more efficient to ask people to do things and then provide practical, constructive criticism of those results for a better overall outcome. A Choleric, through positive reinforcement, proper acknowledgment, and recognition of the efforts of those he is leading, will reap far more beneficial results of performance, morale, and willingness to continue.

You don't know how to handle people. Because you are driven to get things done, you have a strong tendency to use other people as means to an end rather than as valuable individuals who have their own intrinsic needs and desires. While it is challenging to make yourself more compassionate, you can apply a few simple principles and get along much better with others:

1. *Keep advice until asked.* I was once told, "I don't need a preacher, I need a friend." You are very prone to make quick decisions on your own without listening to other's input. You may have to bite your tongue, but listening to other ideas can provide crucial insight and direction that you otherwise would not have thought of alone. You will offer information into a situation whether asked or not and this can very often get you into complicated cases when the receiver didn't ask for advice. While it feels like you have the correct answer to every situation, it is very difficult to attend to another's best interests when you haven't taken the time to learn their true needs. Also, being able to learn on the fly doesn't mean a little education can solve every problem.

2. *Tone down your approach.* Chill out! Consciously control your words and expressions with intentional pauses and slower speaking. It is possible to be passionate about what you believe in and convey a sense of excitement without bulldozing the listener. Being a dynamic leader and misunderstanding the emotions and feeling of others is a significant deterrent to quality results. Dictatorial, hard-nosed, loud, angry approaches to a team or group is not received well. Recognize that you could seem like a bully through your approach. No one enjoys being treated as subservient.

3. *Stop arguing and causing trouble.* Argumentative, overbearing dictators aren't willingly followed. It is likely a Choleric will be in a leadership position anyway, and if not now then soon; the critical, judgmental behavior isn't necessary nor positively influential. It is advantageous and good leadership practice to develop a softer way of accomplishing the same goal but without the tension and disruption. Constant negativity or conflict is never an enjoyable work (or home) environment.

You are usually right, but you also may be unpopular. You may need to learn to be more humble in your approach. Everyone likes an ordinary, relatable colleague. As a natural leader or one in control, you don't have to be intimidated by anything! Surely you do not want to be unpopular, and it is easier to go forward when you have the endorsement from those that have the skills to take you to the finish line. With that in mind, here are a few things to consider:

1. *Let someone else be right.* Try sharing the glory for a change. You don't always have to be on center stage and get all the applause. Everyone enjoys a pat on the back occasionally. This small, genuine gesture will gain you tremendous leverage of goodwill for future projects. Alienating your employees to help you hoard credit is unwise leadership. Everyone is valuable to the team and needs to feel that their contributions are valuable and necessary. How about "Employee Suggestion Boxes"? This is free consulting from inside the circle of those that know what

needs to be improved within the organization. Practice listening to your co-workers.

2. *Learn to apologize.* Remember the slogan from the film, *Love Story*: "Love never has to say you're sorry"? Wrong in every way. If you do care about someone, and even if you don't, apologizing when you are wrong will do wonders for helping you build or repair damaged relationships. "Please forgive me, I am sorry." Although this is a hard phrase for a Choleric, it is beneficial and gains respect. Apologizing to someone shows humility, and situations could warrant a humble individual. Choose to be one.

3. *Admit you have some faults.* You may think you are perfect, but no one else does; we all have flaws. However, a Choleric rarely admits he has anything wrong with him. Truth is, he has an uncanny way of covering up errors or making it look like someone or something else is to blame. A Choleric is a quick thinker, the fastest of any Temperament. However, he may move so fast that actions get ahead of his thoughts. He may make decisions before thinks the issue all the way through. It happens along the task-filled journey to come upon a gross error. He realizes the error and must reroute his course of action. He knows he overlooked something or made a mistake, but instead of owning it, he makes an on-the-spot decision to adjust course and correct the deficiency and move forward. Most of the time no one will know it even happened and the project moves forward but could leave a scar somewhere in the fabric of the project. A Choleric should learn to slow down and take time to filter out all the pros and cons.

A Note About Workaholic Tendencies

It's okay for you to work hard, that's one of your most valuable strengths. However, learn to intentionally relax, take real time off, and recognize the feeling of needing to be in the driver's seat. Rest will relieve your pressure and those of your team. You work circles around the other Temperaments. Accomplishment is a good thing and that is why most Cholerics end up in leadership positions. But remember that a Choleric will always move up the ladder of success unless something is thrown out of balance within his life or within himself. You must learn to control the high energy drive of your Temperament. Realize when your Temperament is controlling your mood, tiredness, your failures, or even sensing a lack of progress. If harnessed and nurtured correctly, a Choleric can put his mind toward his goal and accomplish it with a healthy work-life balance.

How to Recognize Whether Your Child Is A Choleric

Strengths	Weaknesses	Emotional Needs
Baby		
Adventurous, gregarious, full of life, intelligent	Noisy, loud, strong-willed, challenging, dangerous	Needs validation for achievements, desires a pet, desires own space

Strengths	Weaknesses	Emotional Needs
Child		
Industrious, gung-ho, self-confident, responsible, dynamic	Controlling, unrelenting, taxing, inflexible, adamant, severe, harsh	Opportunity to express themselves and to be heard

Strengths	Weaknesses	Emotional Needs
Teen		
Dependable, in control, forceful, well organized, problem solver, an exhorter of others	Critical, rude and offensive, domineering, disliked, know-it-all, unremorseful, recluse	Acknowledgement of their strengths, feelings of being in control of their destiny

Do's and Don'ts for the Choleric

DO'S

- Let people offer opinions without cutting them off or putting them down
- Understand that others may have information you do not have
- Listen to what people are saying and allow your heart to open
- Learn to put others first and realize they have needs, too
- Allow others to be who they are and respect them for it
- Learn to receive friendliness and warmth from others
- Stay out of issues that are not your responsibility
- Learn to compromise and cooperate with others
- Schedule time off for relaxation and enjoyment
- Show the way without driving others like cattle
- Wait until advice is requested before sharing
- Admit the reality that you could be wrong
- Reflect on your approach before speaking
- Develop a plan for acknowledging others
- Be first to say thank you and I'm sorry
- Look for ways to encourage others
- Slow down so you don't burn out
- Greet people with a warm smile
- Plan fun things with your family
- Practice becoming less rigid
- Ask instead of command

DON'TS

- Neglect family time
- Speak before you think
- Think you know everything
- Bully everyone like a Drill Sergeant
- Forget to encourage and uplift others
- Believe an 80-hour work week is healthy
- Expect everyone to want to do it your way
- Think everyone wants to hear your opinion
- Believe your problems are bigger than others'
- Pressure yourself to accomplish more and more
- Take on more work than you have the time to deliver
- Expect the performance of others to be equal to yours
- Be so insensitive that you neglect the feelings of others
- Entangle yourself into responsibilities you can not handle
- Be so focused on the future that you miss out on the present
- Isolate yourself during difficult situations and lose connections
- Burn bridges by discarding people after they have assisted you
- Take advantage of those less skilled or knowledgeable than you
- Disregard the value of friendships and those who choose to be around you
- Pass opportunities to greet others with warmth and care for their lives, too

Chapter 8: The Three Areas of Temperament

Before we dive into the 3 Temperament Areas, let's seek to remove a potential barrier and discuss "labeling" individuals. Most people do not like labels and are offended by them, feeling as though they are being put in a box. As human beings, we have many complex areas of our inner being. These invisible, but very real, attributes are revealed within the context of Temperament and WIDP to provide insight into answering "why we do what we do". The possible Temperament combinations across mankind are vast, lending to very diverse individual characteristics and relational dynamics. Capturing and communicating Temperament information in a digestible way is difficult. Dr. Worley recognized logical groupings tied to the same core needs as he worked with individuals in a clinical setting. Those patterns and similarities are not just an infinite abyss of possibilities, those logically tied themes of needs are what WIDP explains as the 5 Temperaments.

So, when you think about your Temperament(s) or that of others, remember that they are logically grouped needs outlined within 3 Temperament Areas:

The Social Area

The Leadership Area

The Relationship Area

Some people happen to have the same Temperament in all 3 Areas, in which case their core needs are the same across each Area, and their preferences and behavior will reflect this. People with the same Temperament in all 3 Areas are typically referred to as "pure" types. Of course, this is not in contrast to "damaged" or any other negative connotation. It simply means they are the same Temperament in every Area. For example, to refer to one as a "Pure Melancholy" would mean they are Melancholy in the Social Area, Melancholy in the Leadership Area, and Melancholy in the Relationship Area. A person, then, with different Temperaments can be considered as having a multi-dimensional Temperament makeup; for example, a Choleric in the Social Area, a Phlegmatic in the Leadership Area, and Introverted Sanguine in the Relationship Area.

There are many possible combinations of Temperament across the 3 Areas. WIDP magnifies the characteristics of each Temperament breaking the 3 Areas down further into Regions in order to show the differences of demonstration (to others) and desire (from others) wired within each Temperament. We'll discuss Regions in more detail in the next chapter.

3 DIFFERENT AREAS OF ONES TEMPERAMENT

SOCIAL	LEADERSHIP	RELATIONSHIP
Surface-level relationships / society	Power and control / responsibility	Openness for close, intimate relationships

The information within WIDP enables an individual, family, team, clinician, or an employer to assess an individual's natural makeup quickly. From that insight you can target potential conflicts and develop sound strategies for future change to enhance self-understanding, family development, educational instruction, leadership development, hiring selections, employee progression, team development, marketing, sales development, or executive and staff coaching.

As any individual's understanding of needs is grasped, they will significantly increase their potential for a fulfilled and balanced life, with greater successes in all interpersonal relationships.

As a corporate application, the multifaceted use of WIDP will become an instrument of immense value to the overall operation of the diversity of groups mentioned above from many aspects. Its applications are cross-industrial and cross-culture because it is rooted in biological humankind, regardless of race, gender, or nationality.

What is the Social **Profile,**
the Leadership Profile,
and the Relationship Profile?

I. Social/Vocational Profile

The Social/Vocational Profile is the read-out describing the details within the Social Area. The Social Profile identifies the individual's Temperament needs and desires for socialization, work/school associations, and other superficial relationships. It explains whether an individual seeks to have *many* or *few* relationships socially and vocationally. The Social Profile helps answer the question,

"Who is in or out of a relationship with this individual?"

The Social Profile results should be applied to the individual's social and career contact level of acquaintances only and not to family, close friends, or intimate relationships.

The Social Profile describes needs and desires in surface-level interactions, as well as needs for acceptance and approval. Examples of this would be interacting with people in a work environment, at a grocery store, at the gas station, in the mall, at a trade show, conference, or just meeting or being around people in various places. It is society-at- large as you move through your daily activities.

An important note here, individuals in your work environment should not be automatically considered as close relationships, even if you know them well. However, some people can and do develop close relationships with their co-workers. At that point, the connection is no longer in the Social/Vocational arena, it has moved into the Relationship side. Interestingly, this link could now cause problems between them in the work environment in their dealings with each other, because of the specific needs in their Relationship Area as compared to the needs in their Social Area.

II. Leadership Profile

The Leadership Profile identifies the individual's Temperament needs and desires for influencing others, making decisions, and assuming responsibilities. Requirements in this Area may range from level of independence to level of dependence. The Leadership Profile helps assess and answer the question:

"Who maintains the power and makes decisions in a relationship with this individual?"

The Leadership Profile identifies leadership quite specifically. Leadership according to Temperament is the level of responsibility a person is naturally wired to handle. It also indicates how comfortable they are making independent decisions or depend on others in their decision-making process.

Let's look at 3 example individuals that will help explain how this works practically:

Jane - Social/Vocational Profile only
Mike - Leadership Profile only
Susan - Relationship Profile only

So, picture these 3 different people, all with their WIDP Profiles, and we are going to focus on only one Area with each individual. Since we are currently talking about Leadership, we will remove Jane & Susan from the room and solely focus on Mike, who is representing the Leadership Profile.

Jane - Social/Vocational Profile only
Mike - Leadership Profile only
Susan - Relationship Profile only

Now we say to him, "Mike, since you are a leader, I would like for you, right now, to lead."

Who is Mike leading? No one - and this illustrates how the Leadership Area works.

Jane (Social/Vocational) and Susan (Relationship) are not present, thus Mike has no one to lead, since Leadership plays out in either the Social or Relationship interactions. So, let's help Mike lead by bringing Jane (Social) back into the room. Jane is a co-worker with Mike.

Jane - Social/Vocational Profile only
Mike - Leadership Profile only
Susan - Relationship Profile only

Can Mike lead Jane? Of course, he now has someone to lead. Mike leads Jane in a Social or Vocational setting, as this Area speaks to the context of surface-level relationships, which is the case with Jane.

When you evaluate
the Leadership Profile and the Social/Vocational Profile together,
it helps to determine the individual's social or employment situation.

For Mike, his Leadership can now play out by leading Jane in the Social/Vocational arena..

Let's say that Mike is the Division Manager of a corporation and must meet with his Division team members. Jane (Social/Vocational) is in his department, and Mike is looking to implement new project goals. So, Mike is leading in the context of the Social/Vocational Area only.

Now let's remove Jane and bring Susan back into the room.

Jane - Social/Vocational Profile only
Mike - Leadership Profile only
Susan - Relationship Profile only

Based on what we've learned, describe the interaction of Mike (Leadership) and Susan (Relationship). Can Mike lead Susan? Yes! But the context of whom Mike is leading has changed.

Susan isn't Mike's co-worker, let's say she is Mike's wife. We have stepped outside of the Social/Vocational context of Mike's leadership interaction and moved him into leading within a close Relationship. Mike has the same Leadership needs and desires he had before, but do you think he will lead differently with his wife, Susan, than he did with Jane? We sure hope so!

Individuals in close relationships have quite a different relational dynamic than those in casual or work environments. While Mike's Leadership Profile will explain how he is naturally wired to handle responsibilities and make decisions, the *context* of leadership matters. You lead differently in the Social/Vocational arena than you lead in Relationships because of the different ways these two Areas are influenced when you interact. The impact of knowing how we lead with casual social acquaintances and how we lead with our close relationships is crucial to recognize and understand.

As you interact in the context of Leadership, you should always be aware that leading in your Social/Vocational arena can and should be different than how you lead in your Relationship arena, and we will discuss some critical issues of the Leadership Area & Relationship Area interactions next.

III. Relationship Profile

The Relationship Profile identifies an individual's Temperament needs and desires in the context of his closest relationships with family and friends; those he/she has chosen for his/her inner circle. Requirements in this Area may range from open emotional expressions and desire to connect with many people to minimal emotional expressions and very few deep connections desired to put within their closest circle. The Relationship Profile helps answer the question,

"How emotionally open or closed to deep relationships is this individual?"

WIDP defines these varying needs and desires not as "right" or "wrong," but as individual differences and preferences. If a person's life situation differs radically from their needs and desires in the Relationship Area (or any Temperament Area), they will be experiencing stress, conflict, and anxiety in their relationships. By teaching the individual about their unique needs, you can use WIDP to help bring balance and peace, restoring positive quality of life to all relational interactions, especially those closest to them.

For most people, the Relationship Profile is the dominant pattern that influences Temperament in the Social/Vocational and the Leadership Areas.

The power of the Relationship Temperament is a BIG issue that plagues corporations of all sizes from the "mom & pop" operations to the international corporations with thousands of employees scattered all over the world. Relationship Temperament dominance has crippled success and progress since the beginning of time. You may recognize it as the "Good Ole' Boy" system.

Scenario # 1

Most people will identify the Leadership Profile as the strongest of the three Temperament Areas, as it revolves around power and control as well as initiative. Watch what happens to the Leadership Profile as we move forward with this illustration.

Arthur and Rebecca meet at a social gathering after attending the annual town parade. After the ceremony, the community would gather at the town square filled with many nostalgic traditions and activities going on like ringing the courthouse bell, the prestigious Basketball Challenge, the slap-stick fun of knocking a clown off his seat, dart throwing contest, and many other competitive and fun events. Arthur and Rebecca get the same top score in the dart throwing competition and prepare for a tie breaker. They banter back and forth as they practice for the deciding round, one-upping the other with playful jabs to try and throw the other off focus. In the end, Rebecca wins first prize. Sorry, Art!

So, let's break down this coincidental meeting to illustrate Relationship Dominance. Notice we begin the meeting in the Social arena.

Phase 1   Art and Rebecca meet at a social gathering

Well, Arthur liked what he saw in Rebecca, and there seemed to be chemistry between them as they playfully teased each other. Rebecca tells Arthur the least she could do is buy him a cup of coffee to celebrate her victory and his defeat. Arthur accepts the invitation.

Phase 2   They have coffee together

The **Leadership** Area becomes an issue here because most people like to be in control of their destiny and determine how much power they will give to someone else when it comes to their life decisions, especially their personal time and energy. For Arthur and Rebecca to agree to coffee together means there is some level of attraction between them. Otherwise, the invitation would not have been offered or the request would have been declined. Therefore, both Arthur and Rebecca gave up some of their Leadership to mutually, but individually, allow for coffee to happen.

So, what is happening is both are also allowing the **Relationship** side of their Temperament to move in, gradually replacing the Social/Vocational side. There are feelings and heart emotions beginning to get involved, as they both see something in the other person that attracts them.

Obviously the cup of coffee is not the objective, the aim is to get to know each other a little better. Sure enough, during their outing Arthur becomes even more interested in Rebecca, and decides to ask her out to dinner. They are now even further away from the Social/Vocational Temperament Area and moving deeper into the **Relationship** Area.

Phase 3   *They have dinner a few times*

So, what has happened to the relationship at this point? Remember, they both are releasing a certain amount of Leadership so they can have dinner and be together more frequently in an interest of developing their Relationship.

The Relationship Temperament Area is the realm of your heart needs.

After they have had dinner a few times together, they come out of the restaurant holding hands, hugging each other, very much closer emotionally, moving into Phase 4:

Phase 1   *Couple meets at a social gathering*
Phase 2   *Couple has coffee together*
Phase 3   *Couple has dinner a few times*
Phase 4   ***Couple holds hands, hugs, and kisses***

Then they escalate their Relationship further:

Phase 1   *Couple meets at a social gathering*
Phase 2   *Couple has coffee together*
Phase 3   *Couple has dinner a few times*
Phase 4   *Couple holds hands, hugs, and kisses*
Phase 5   ***Couple gets married***

The value of understanding what is happening inside each person is yet another value of understanding Temperament. It does happen that people stay married for 10-20-30-40-50 or more years, but the opposite also happens. Awareness of Temperament affords couples the possibility of saving themselves from much pain and increases chances for success because they know how things work and what is important to each person no matter the phase of the process.

Reviewing these five phases, notice each person began independently in control of their life not knowing each other and ended up at the marriage altar relinquishing that powerful independence for the sake of unification of their lives. Do you see the power of the Relationship Temperament Area? When it comes to matters of the heart, in any environment, the Relationship Temperament will dominate.

Let's look at another set of five phases of Relationship Dominance and see what happens when Leadership enters back into that same Relationship.

Scenario #2

Phase 1   *Couple argues*

Arthur and Rebecca are having a discussion over the bills, and the conversation becomes heated, resulting in an argument. What is the very next thing that happens?

Phase 2   *Couple takes back control*

They each begin to take back their independent Leadership (power). Arthur slams down his fist on the table and says he is not going to pay the bills the way Rebecca wants him to, and Rebecca stands up and insists that he is not going to speak to her with an angry, demeaning tone. She walks off bitter, and he goes in the opposite direction just as upset. Now, we have a broken Relationship while Leadership is given precedence and they issue the non-speaking mode of asserting themselves.

Next comes the making up, because neither of them wants to remain heartless, of course:

Phase 3   *Couple reunites*

Arthur apologizes to Rebecca for his loss of control, and she accepts his apology. They compromise on the issue of paying the bills and they move back into Relationship. Recognize the Leadership and how, for the sake of Relationship, they both choose to relinquish individual control. And so with things calming down and balancing, they move forward in their marriage.

Then one day Rebecca comes home from shopping with the kids and is so excited to share her purchases with Arthur. She's been having to handle four children all day but is so proud that she made some accomplishments and is gleaming with excitement.

Before she can utter a word and without even looking up, Arthur asks, "So how much money did you spend?"

Phase 1   *Couple argues*
Phase 2   *Couple takes back control*
Phase 3   *Couple reunites*
Phase 4   **Couple argues with no reconciliation**

Rebecca begins explaining that she tried to get the best deals with clearance items and end of season leftovers, finding every item at a 75% discount. Arthur repeats his question, "How much money did you spend?" She tells him "$147." He immediately launches into a tirade about how she must take the clothes back, how the money was rent money. All four of the children are screaming because mommy and daddy are fighting, and are scared, hungry and tired. Threatening divorce and making very hurtful remarks to each other, Rebecca decides to load the kids and head to her parents' house for the night.

So, what just happened? Once again, they chose to take back their Leadership and moved entirely out of Relationship focus with each other. Now emotions are suppressed or absent entirely, and they feel miserable and no motivation to continue in Relationship.

They separate, and regress to the point of the final phase of this scenario:

Phase 1	*Couple argues*
Phase 2	*Couple takes back control*
Phase 3	*Couple reconciles*
Phase 4	*Couple argues with no reconciliation*
Phase 5	**Divorce**

The complete opposite progression of Arthur and Rebecca's development into Relationship is being experienced. But, why? The **Relationship** Profile is the dominant pattern that determines where connections end up. If the person chooses to push the other person away from their heart to their outer circle, they will have a different influence and mode of interaction, especially if that person is a different Temperament in that Area. Although most people consider **Leadership** to be the strongest (most powerful, most controlling, most influential) amongst the 3 Areas, it is the **Relationship** Profile that is the Dominant pattern. Where the heart decides to go, the rest will follow. What insight!

Scenario #3

Considering that the Relationship Temperament can dominate at any time, what does that look like in a corporate setting? Again using a five-phase structure, we'll illustrate the progression of Leadership undermined by the more internally influential Relationship Area.

Phase 1   You are the Division Manager

Let's say that you are the Division Manager within a large corporation. You have been there for ten years and have established yourself as a successful manager. Your work situation is excellent, and you are very comfortable and secure in your position.

Phase 2   Work with a close friend

Philip came into the company two years ago, and you developed a bond of friendship with him. You and Philip have a lot in common and spend free time together for some golf or rock climbing in the surrounding areas on the weekends. You become best friends.

Phase 3   Given authority to promote two people within your Division

Philip comes to you and mentions, "Hey, I heard a certain position just opened! I've been telling you for months if that spot ever opened, up I'd be perfect for it." You feel a tug of obligation, but in a good way, to offer Philip the promotion because, after all, he is your best friend, and you don't want to offend him and the good times you could have. You both would get to be in leadership positions, and don't want to sacrifice this wonderful friendship.

Phase 4   You promote your best friend under the "Good Ole Boy" system

So, Philip is promoted to the new position because of his Relationship with you. He is happy, and you are perceived as a fantastic friend for supporting (Leadership) him.

Phase 5   Your best friend is incompetent

Philip does not have the necessary experience or skills to handle the responsibility of the new position. As a result, the Division suffers and loses valuable production while only gaining frustrated employees due to Philip's inadequacies. Now you, as his superior, are forced into a significant decision. What are you going to do with Philip? Demote him - fire him - give him another position somewhere in the company - or just let the company losses keep piling up (giving you a bad name) crippling the organization further. This is tough - he is your best friend, after all.

You can see the negative impact that the **Relationship** Area can have at the organizational level with no awareness of what's taking place internally. Unfortunately, this happens all the time at every level of management. Relationship dominates, and the organization suffers the loss. It can be prevented as easily as it can be predicted.

WIDP and Temperament knowledge are vital resources to position people confidently and reliably in places of responsibly. Remember that you cannot assign, promote, hire, or employ solely for **Relationship** reasons. The proper selections need to be analyzed considering an individual's Social/Vocational Profile and their **Leadership** Profile. A great fit for the role can be found for all the right reasons with the right insight. The right insight ignored or used in the wrong context will cost, substantially.

Likewise, building any successful interpersonal relationship involves moving through the three Areas of Social, **Leadership**, and then **Relationship**; quite a logical sequence of progression. People typically begin relationships by discussing Social issues to determine if the connection is safe and potentially compatible. Then they progress to **Leadership** issues, identifying a mutually comfortable way to handle power and control between them. If the first two Areas resolve satisfactorily and run efficiently, people could "graduate" another person into the heart side of **Relationship** for deeper emotional closeness with each other. This is how trust is truly built.

Now that we have a better understanding of how the Areas operate and are used, let's move to a more granular level of each of the Areas, which are the Demonstrated & Desired Regions, in the next chapter.

Chapter 9: The Two Regions: Demonstrated and Desired

SCORING

The WIDP report further breaks down each of the three Areas of Social/Vocational, Leadership, and Relationship into two Region Scores: The Demonstrated Score and the Desired Score. Each may rate anywhere from zero (0) to nine (9) scale, as seen below.

0-1-2-3 4-5 6-7-8-9

The individual's scores can be found next to their name at the top of the WIDP Report. There are 6 total numbers that represent each Region.

Let's recall the Chess analogy from Chapter 2, where we explained that looking at Temperament is like looking at six separate chessmen, which make up the components of Temperament in each Area (the numbers used within the charts are just for example purposes):

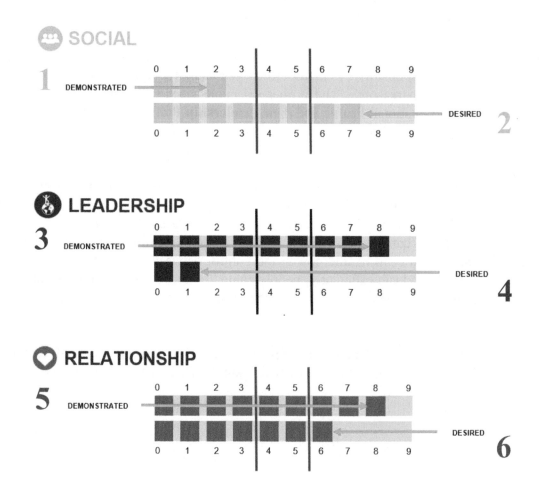

Demonstrated Score

The Demonstrated Score within each Area indicates:

How the individual prefers to act toward other people

This behavior <u>can be observed</u> and is the representation that a person presents to others. The Demonstrated Score in each Area is the most natural way a person feels comfortable to:

😀 **Get Together With Others**
            DEMONSTRATED Socializing

🕺 **Have Their Way With Others**
            DEMONSTRATED Leadership

♡ **Be Close to Others**
            DEMONSTRATED Relationship

Because WIDP uses numbers to represent Temperament, it's important to interpret these numbers properly – they are neither positive nor negative:

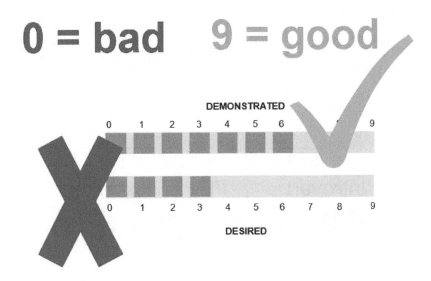

Rather, Numbers used in WIDP indicate an individual's Temperament level:

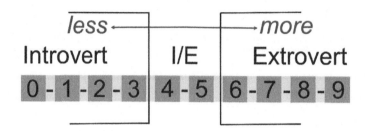

There is no such thing as "good/high" or "low/bad" Numbers or Temperament. These numbers simply are a numerical representation to help understanding the dynamic of your individual Temperament as we Demonstrate toward others and Desire from others.

Remember: Temperament is your intrinsic wiring – you were born this way, coded genetically, and Temperament does not change throughout your lifetime. are as you were coded genetically in your mother's womb at conception.

Yes, your environment and your culture can influence your personality and character, but your Temperament does not change throughout your lifetime. Recall the differences of personality, character, and Temperament in Chapter 1 and feel free to revisit it as often as needed to thoroughly grasp the structure of your emotional biology. Life circumstances can change dramatically over time. You can adopt new values, new beliefs, even new ethics from your experiences. But what a relief it is to know what can change about you and within you, and what cannot. This gives you the freedom to move through life and experience those changes while never losing the sure footing of who you truly are.

Introvert | Introvert/Extrovert | Extrovert

An **Introvert** number of 0-1-2-3 refers to individuals that fall within this range of numbers in one or more of their Temperament Regions (6 total possibilities of having an Introvert number in that Region).

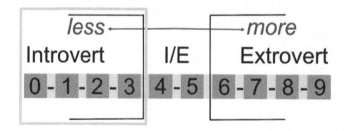

These are very rational people who need very little people interaction, preferring to spend most of their time thinking things through.

An **Introverted/Extrovert** number of 4 or 5 refers to individuals that have this range of numbers in one or more of their Temperament Regions. They can function well in either environment as an Introvert or Extrovert, comfortable with both situations.

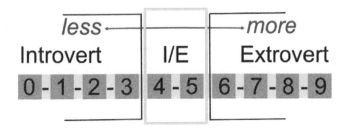

An **Extrovert** number of 6-7-8-9 refers to individuals that have this range of numbers in one or more of their Temperament Regions. They are very outgoing who have a need and desire to be with people frequently if not always.

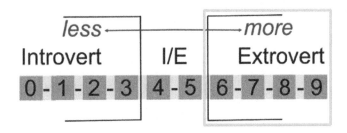

Let's look at the ranges of Demonstrated numbers in closer detail.

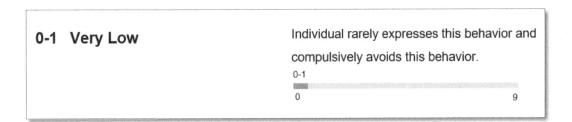

Consider someone who scores a "0" in the Demonstrated Region of their Social Area. What does this mean? It means that they will not initiate toward you. It also means they do not want you inviting them to social events of any kind. They will find it difficult to be the one starting conversations or even sharing thoughts and ideas. You may find them to be extremely private individuals or at least they will look like they are.

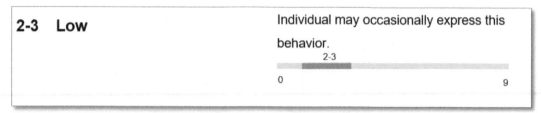

Individuals that score either a two (2) or three (3) in any of the three Areas will accept a little interaction with others, but still demonstrate introverted characteristics most of the time (in the context of that Temperament Area).

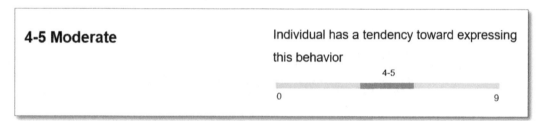

Those who score either a four (4) or five (5) in any of the three Areas can interact and initiate comfortably as an Introvert and as an Extrovert. However, they will bounce back and forth from wanting time with people to wanting time alone. Too much of either will create stress for them, so they must balance themselves with moderate amounts of both.

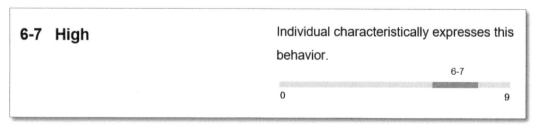

A high number of 6 or 7 indicates an individual that will most often actively initiate interaction in the context of that Area.

8-9	Very High	Individual **compulsively** expresses this behavior.

An individual with "Very High" numbers of 8-9 will always be looking for people and places to interact. They likely draw energy from interaction and are quite expressive with their thoughts and feelings in the context of that Area.

Desired Score

The Desired Score indicates:

How the individual prefers others to behave towards them

The Desired Score is <u>not possible to determine through observation alone</u>. This can only be determined through a WIDP assessment.

The Desired score in each Area is the level of behavior the individual prefers others to use in their approach toward them to:

😊 Get Together With Him/Her
DESIRED Socializing

🏃 **Have Their Way With Him/Her**
DESIRED Leadership

♡ **Be Close to Him/Her**
DESIRED Relationship

We just examined the Demonstrated Regions of each Temperament Area and what that Demonstration looks like depending on where an individual scores, which determines the level of expression and initiation toward other people.

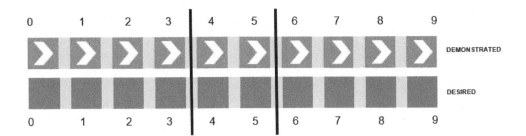

The Desired Regions of each Temperament Area, which can only be assessed, means that a person may or may not differ (even significantly) from their public displayed image. The Desired Score is the action from others this person most prefers.

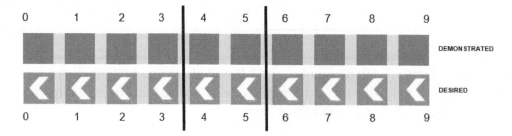

Let's look at the ranges of Desired numbers in closer detail.

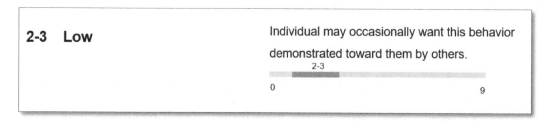

An individual that scores either a zero (0) or one (1) in any of the three Areas of will compulsively avoid possibilities of demonstrations by others. Let's say someone scores a "0" in the Desired Region of their Social Area. What does this mean?

It means that they do not desire for you to initiate towards them. An Introvert does not want you to drop by to visit at work or home without an invitation. They will do everything to send you messages telling you that they don't want to. To put it bluntly, they aren't saying "Don't approach me", more accurately they are saying "Don't even THINK about approaching me".

Individuals that score either a two (2) or three (3) in any of the three Areas may want this behavior every so often by other people, but it's still a rare thing.

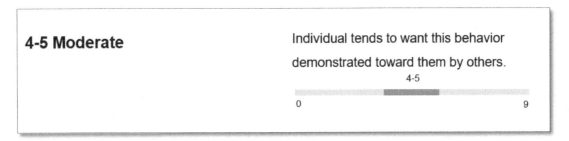

Those who score either a four (4) or five (5) in any of the three Areas can function well settings with people or without people. However, they will need a moderate amount of both in proper balance to maintain proper functional health. The key word here is "moderation".

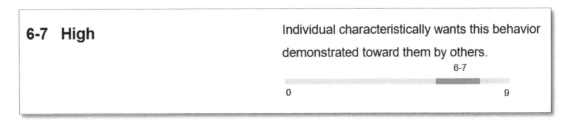

A high number of 6 or 7 indicates an individual that characteristically wants this behavior expressed towards them – they Desire that others are willing to initiate, interact, and demonstrate toward them a lot.

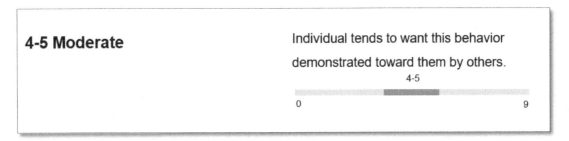

An individual with "Very High" numbers of 8-9 likely has their shoes by the door, compulsively needing to be in environments and create situations where others can interact with them. This person does not ever get tired of you Demonstrating toward them, seeming as though they can never get enough.

Introvert | Introvert/Extrovert | Extrovert

We have used the term "compulsive" in discussing the low and high end of the number scale; 0- 1 and 8 – 9.   Let's clarify exactly what the term "compulsive" means. To do so, we will identify the "compulsive" numbers for each Temperament.

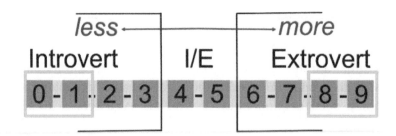

A Temperament with a compulsive set of numbers, it is indicated by a small "c":

ISc	Introverted Sanguine Compulsive	the compulsive numbers are 08, 09, 19
Sc	Sanguine Compulsive	the compulsive numbers are 89, 99, 98
P	*Phlegmatic*	*HAS NO COMPULSIVE NUMBERS*
Mc	Melancholy Compulsive	the compulsive numbers are 00, 01, 10
Cc	Choleric Compulsive	the compulsive numbers are 80, 90 91

Looking at the WIDP Scoring Chart below you will see there are dark colors in the four corners This is where the compulsive numbers are, at the extreme corners farthest from the middle of the chart as possible.

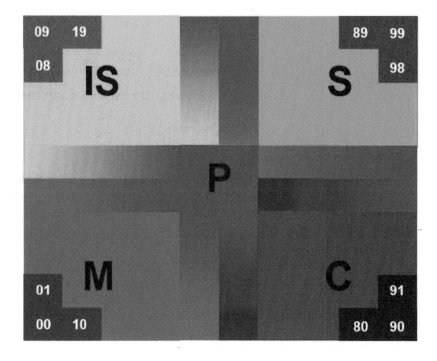

It is important to notice that the P = Phlegmatic HAS NO COMPULSIVE NUMBERS. Although they do not have compulsive numbers, it's said that they are "compulsive" about not being compulsive. A Phlegmatic sees to it that they are not excessive in any direction due to having to protect their limited energy. "Moderation" is their motto, balance is everything.

Compulsive in this context is not used in a negative sense like militant, neurotic, out of control, or hopeless. "Compulsive," as employed in WIDP, indicates that the person's living patterns are, first and foremost, focused on the various characteristics of that Temperament need, whatever Temperament they may be compulsive in. Yes, it is possible to have a compulsive Temperament in each of the three Areas.

Individuals who are Melancholy compulsive (Mc) in their Social Profile are incredibly introverted. They have an overriding need to maintain their privacy away from other people. Melancholy compulsive people are also reclusive. Likewise, Choleric compulsive individuals in Leadership, focus on keeping being command of themselves, their surroundings, and people within their surrounding at all times.

This compulsiveness does not insinuate terrible conduct. However, individuals who are compulsive in one or more Areas of their Temperament makeup can be very complicated people in any arena due to their innate focus on these needs, whether they be a staff member, colleague, adolescent, boss, leader, spouse, client, manager, etc. There is no limit to where you might find a compulsive Temperament.

WIDP is a groundbreaking Temperament resource to thoroughly understand the dynamics within the context of the three Areas of Social/Vocational, **Leadership**, and **Relationship**. WIDP identifies each's unique needs, desires, and likely behavioral responses. The compulsiveness is just another factor to consider in the overall understanding of people and Temperament. It is not right or wrong. Individuals with compulsive Temperaments can, and most generally do, become an asset when positioned in the right role, at work and at home.

In general, the greater the differentiation between the Demonstrated Score and the Desired Score, the higher the chance that the individual is experiencing conflict in this Area. Since WIDP provides a broad interpretation of these scores in the different profiles, representation of these invisible tendencies using numerical data assisted in clearer understanding.

An individual can read their profile and glean a tremendous amount of new knowledge about who they are. However, with a good debriefing from a Certified WIDP member, there is so much more clarity by understanding the impact that the three profile Areas have on each other.

Because of variations within scoring ranges, a few details of WIDP may not apply precisely to the individual (a sentence or statement here or there). However, the overall high reliability of WIDP is unparalleled in the field of assessment instruments. With a proper debriefing, the WIDP Profile data is extremely reliable for the rest of your life. Most generally, patterns will be around 96 – 98% stable and in some cases, there have been reports that WIDP is 100% safe and reliable.

Chapter 10: WIDP Graphically Represented

Throughout this chapter, we'll be using a graphic representation chart of what WIDP Profile Results look like for individuals. WIDP Numbers can be written or displayed in the following ways:

As an Example: **Meet Johnny**

SOCIAL = 2/7 (27)

LEADERSHIP = 1/2 (12)

RELATIONSHIP = 8/6 (86)

Alternatively, it can also look like this:

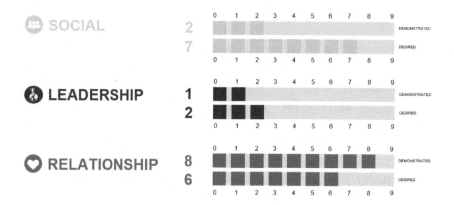

The Demonstrated Score is **always** the first number within each of the 3 sets of numbers.

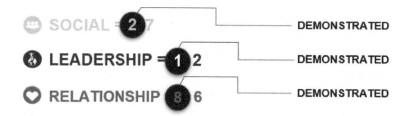

The Desired Score is **always** the second number within each of the three sets of numbers.

SOCIAL = 2 **7** ——————— DESIRED

🏃 LEADERSHIP = 1 **2** ——————— DESIRED

♡ RELATIONSHIP = 8 **6** ——————— DESIRED

When together, it reads: **27 12 86**. This indicates a person's unique Temperament in all 3 Temperament Areas profiled by WIDP. With these 6 numbers, we have our chessmen.

Are you curious about YOUR Temperament? Send an e-mail to info@widp.org or visit www.widp.org. After completing the WIDP Questionnaire online, you can get your results immediately, log in anytime you want to re-read it and study it (your WIDP Profile is good for life), and even print it out or share it. It's all there as soon as you are ready to gain Inside Insight about your unique design.

The WIDP Questionnaire can be taken in three languages: English, Spanish, or Portuguese. If you are an Adult or Youth (ages 6 – 16), you can take WIDP and discover your Temperament Numbers.

As you study your numbers, it's fascinating to read about yourself. It is also helpful to have a perspective of where your numbers are in relation to other people. They may be designed similarly where you will have much in common, or very differently where communication or relating to that person may have a different dynamic.

To show the relationship between WIDP Numbers, we use a wonderful tool – The WIDP Scoring Chart.

Plotting Your WIDP Results

So, how do we use this chart? It can seem overwhelming at first but will make sense pretty quickly. We're going to walk through an activity of plotting your WIDP Numbers. To do so takes two things:

- ✓ Your WIDP Profile Results
- ✓ The WIDP Scoring Chart (below)

At the top of your WIDP Results will read something like this:

Profile for Johnny Example – 271286

Write the results of your WIDP Profile here:

Social	Leadership	Relationship

Johnny Example's first two numbers are 27. Find your first set of numbers "??" and locate those on the WIDP Scoring Chart and circle them. Put an "S" beside it indicating that this is your Social Temperament Numbers. Johnny's Social Score of "27" falls into the section known as the Introverted Sanguine. Where do your numbers fall?

The second set of numbers for Johnny Example is "12". Find your second set of numbers "??" and locate those on the WIDP Scoring Chart, circle them, and put an "L" beside it indicating that this is your **Leadership** Temperament Numbers. Johnny's Leadership Score of "12" is in the Melancholy section. Where are your Leadership Numbers?

The third and final set of numbers for Johnny Example is "86". Find your third set of "??" on the WIDP Scoring Chart, circle them, and put an "R" beside it indicating that this is your **Relationship** Temperament Numbers. "86" for Johnny falls into the Sanguine section. What about yours?

Now you have your WIDP Profile results plotted on your WIDP Scoring Chart. This shows your Temperament in each of the 3 Temperament Areas. It also shows the possibility of the numbers of others, giving us a broad perspective of just how diverse an individual can be.

How do you accurately verbalize your WIDP Scores to another person, alongside the Temperament for each one? Johnny would say: "My WIDP results are: 27-Introverted Sanguine, 12-Melancholy, 86-Sanguine. As you and those around you begin speaking Temperament terminology more and more, it is easy to ask someone for their numbers and they simply respond, "27, 12, 86." And you will both know what that means.

Good job!

Chapter 11: Temperament Blends

While plotting your numbers in the previous chapter, you may have recognized some Temperament sections on the chart have a forward slash (/) and are located in between the Temperaments. These numbers belong to a Temperament makeup called a "Blend". What is a "Blend"?

Here's a list of some of the characteristics of a Blend:

- o The first thing to remember is that the Phlegmatic Temperament is the only Temperament that Blends with the other four Temperaments. Look again at the chart below and notice the different possible combinations. The Phlegmatic quadrant falls precisely in the center of the WIDP Scoring Chart and is composed of the numbers 44, 45, 54, and 55. The other four Temperaments surround the Phlegmatic quadrant.

o If you look closely at the WIDP Scoring Chart, you will find that there are two rows of shaded areas that run from top to bottom and from side to side. These sections directly in the middle of the chart are where the Blends exist. The Phlegmatic Temperament blends with any of the other four Temperaments to make unique Demonstrate & Desire dynamics, possible in any Temperament Area.

o Whenever you see a blend, think "BALANCE".

o An individual could be a Blend in any of the 3 Temperament Areas of Social, Leadership, or Relationship.

o Yes, it is possible to have a "Blend" in two or all three of the Temperament Areas.

o Blends give the person a "softer" presentation of the Temperament Area with which they have blended.

o There are eight possible blend combinations. Remember, the Phlegmatic is the only Temperament that blends with the others.

The "Blends" are listed in their long and short forms below. Find each one on the chart to familiarize yourself with where they are and how each Temperament blends with the Phlegmatic:

- Introverted Sanguine / **Phlegmatic**   IS/P   0-1-2-3 / **5**

- **Phlegmatic** / Introverted Sanguine   P/IS   **4** / 6-7-8-9

- Sanguine / **Phlegmatic**   S/P   6-7-8-9 / **5**

- **Phlegmatic** / Sanguine   P/S   **5** / 6-7-8-9

- Melancholy / **Phlegmatic**   M/P   0-1-2-3 / **4**

- **Phlegmatic** / Melancholy   P/M   **4** / 0-1-2-3

- Choleric / **Phlegmatic**   C/P   6-7-8-9 / **4**

- **Phlegmatic** / Choleric   P/C   **5** / 0-1-2-3

The blends are quite simple to understand. Let's study these one at a time.

Introverted Sanguine (0-1-2-3) / **Phlegmatic (5)**

09	19	29	39	49	59	69	79	89	99
08	18	28	38	48	58	68	78	88	98
07	17	27	37	47	57	67	77	87	97
06	16	26	36	46	56	66	76	86	96
05	15	25	35	45	55	65	75	85	95
04	14	24	34	44	54	64	74	84	94
03	13	23	33	43	53	63	73	83	93
02	12	22	32	42	52	62	72	82	92
01	11	21	31	41	51	61	71	81	91
00	10	20	30	40	50	60	70	80	90

You read the blends by the first number, the Demonstrated Score, which is the Introverted Sanguine 0-1-2-3, which means they will not be Demonstrating toward you and if they do, it will be just a little. Assume this person was IS/P in Social. This person would be uncomfortable to actively initiate towards others but would prefer a moderate amount of initiation from others. The Desired number is 5 indicating Phlegmatic, and they will vacillate being an introvert and then swing to be an extrovert. This maintains proper balance. Remember, a Phlegmatic is moderate in everything and, in this case, Desires in moderation.

IS

Demonstrated
INTROVERTED SANGUINE
People-oriented
Gentle
Diligent
Loving
Compassionate
Supportive
Loyal

P

Desired
PHLEGMATIC
Calm
Friendly
Objective
Diplomatic
Practical
Humorous
Dependable

Phlegmatic (4) / Introverted Sanguine (6-7-8-9)

09	19	29	39	49	59	69	79	89	99
08	18	28	38	48	58	68	78	88	98
07	17	27	37	47	57	67	77	87	97
06	16	26	36	46	56	66	76	86	96
05	15	25	35	45	55	65	75	85	95
04	14	24	34	44	54	64	74	84	94
03	13	23	33	43	53	63	73	83	93
02	12	22	32	42	52	62	72	82	92
01	11	21	31	41	51	61	71	81	91
00	10	20	30	40	50	60	70	80	90

The Demonstrated number is 4, which will vacillate back and forth between Demonstrating as an introvert and then swing to Demonstrating as an extrovert. They are comfortable functioning either way for a limited period, as the Phlegmatic is moderate in everything. The Desired numbers are 6, 7, 8, or 9 indicating a high or very high need for you to Demonstrate toward them. The P/IS blend is a very outgoing individual if they feel safe in the interaction/relationship.

P — Demonstrated

IS — Desired

PHLEGMATIC	INTROVERTED SANGUINE
Calm	People-oriented
Friendly	Gentle
Objective	Diligent
Diplomatic	Loving
Practical	Compassionate
Humorous	Supportive
Dependable	Loyal

Sanguine (6-7-8-9) / **Phlegmatic (5)**

09	19	29	39	49	59	69	79	89	99
08	18	28	38	48	58	68	78	88	98
07	17	27	37	47	57	67	77	87	97
06	16	26	36	46	56	66	76	86	96
05	15	25	35	45	55	65	75	85	95
04	14	24	34	44	54	64	74	84	94
03	13	23	33	43	53	63	73	83	93
02	12	22	32	42	52	62	72	82	92
01	11	21	31	41	51	61	71	81	91
00	10	20	30	40	50	60	70	80	90

The Demonstrated numbers are 6-7-8-9, which are all extroverted. They will have high or very high Demonstration. They will initiate interaction easily and genuinely like people. The Desired number is 5 indicating they will vacillate between being an introvert and then to being an extrovert. This maintains proper balance. Remember, a Phlegmatic is moderate in everything and, in this case, Desires in moderation.

S	P
Demonstrated	**Desired**
SANGUINE	**PHLEGMATIC**
Outgoing	Calm
People-oriented	Friendly
Engthusiastic	Objective
Responsive	Diplomatic
Talkative	Practical
Loving	Humorous
Compassionate	Dependable

Phlegmatic (5) / Sanguine (6-7-8-9)

09	19	29	39	49	59	69	79	89	99
08	18	28	38	48	58	68	78	88	98
07	17	27	37	47	57	67	77	87	97
06	16	26	36	46	56	66	76	86	96
05	15	25	35	45	55	65	75	85	95
04	14	24	34	44	54	64	74	84	94
03	13	23	33	43	53	63	73	83	93
02	12	22	32	42	52	62	72	82	92
01	11	21	31	41	51	61	71	81	91
00	10	20	30	40	50	60	70	80	90

The Demonstrated number is 5, which will vacillate back and forth between Demonstrating as an introvert and then swing to Demonstrating as an extrovert. They exhibit a balanced expression and pleasant demeanor, and they genuinely like people. They will limit their exposure due to a need for moderation. The Desired numbers are 6, 7, 8, or 9 indicating a high or very high need for Demonstration from others. The P/S blend is a very outgoing individual and wants people-oriented activities but will eventually grow tired and need to recharge.

P — Demonstrated

S — Desired

PHLEGMATIC	SANGUINE
Calm	Outgoing
Friendly	People-oriented
Objective	Engthusiastic
Diplomatic	Responsive
Practical	Talkative
Humorous	Loving
Dependable	Compassionate

Melancholy (0-1-2-3) / Phlegmatic (4)

09	19	29	39	49	59	69	79	89	99
08	18	28	38	48	58	68	78	88	98
07	17	27	37	47	57	67	77	87	97
06	16	26	36	46	56	66	76	86	96
05	15	25	35	45	55	65	75	85	95
04	14	24		44	54	64	74	84	94
03	13	23	33	43	53	63	73	83	93
02	12	22	32	42	52	62	72	82	92
01	11	21	31	41	51	61	71	81	91
00	10	20	30	40	50	60	70	80	90

The Demonstrated numbers are 0-1-2-3, which are all introverted. That means they will not be Demonstrating toward you or, if they do, it will be just a little. The Desired number is 4 indicating introvert/extrovert, and they will vacillate being an introvert and then swing to being an extrovert. This maintains proper balance. Remember, a Phlegmatic is moderate in everything and, in this case, Desires in moderation.

M

Demonstrated
MELANCHOLY
Creative
Analytical
Gifted
Self-sacrificing
Compassionate
Perfectionist
Disciplined

P

Desired
PHLEGMATIC
Calm
Friendly
Objective
Diplomatic
Practical
Humorous
Dependable

Phlegmatic (4) / Melancholy (0-1-2-3)

09	19	29	39	49	59	69	79	89	99
08	18	28	38	48	58	68	78	88	98
07	17	27	37	47	57	67	77	87	97
06	16	26	36	46	56	66	76	86	96
05	15	25	35	45	55	65	75	85	95
04	14	24	34	44	54	64	74	84	94
03	13	23	33	43	53	63	73	83	93
02	12	22	32	42	52	62	72	82	92
01	11	21	31	41	51	61	71	81	91
00	10	20	30	40	50	60	70	80	90

The Demonstrated number is 4, which will vacillate back and forth between Demonstrating as an introvert and then swing to being an extrovert. They are comfortable functioning as either an introvert or an extrovert. Remember, a Phlegmatic is moderate in everything. The Desired numbers are 0-1-2-3 indicating introversion; they do not Desire for others to be Demonstrative toward them.

.

P	M
Demonstrated	**Desired**

PHLEGMATIC	MELANCHOLY
Calm	Creative
Friendly	Analytical
Objective	Gifted
Diplomatic	Self-sacrificing
Practical	Compassionate
Humorous	Perfectionist
Dependable	Disciplined

Choleric (6-7-8-9) / Phlegmatic (4)

09	19	29	39	49	59	69	79	89	99
08	18	28	38	48	58	68	78	88	98
07	17	27	37	47	57	67	77	87	97
06	16	26	36	46	56	66	76	86	96
05	15	25	35	45	55	65	75	85	95
04	14	24	34	44	54	64	74	84	94
03	13	23	33	43	53	63	73	83	93
02	12	22	32	42	52	62	72	82	92
01	11	21	31	41	51	61	71	81	91
00	10	20	30	40	50	60	70	80	90

The Demonstrated numbers are 6-7-8-9, which are all extroverted. They will have high or very high Demonstration. They express and initiate freely. The Desired number is 4 indicating introvert/extrovert, meaning they can accept you Demonstrating toward them in moderation. They are comfortable functioning as either an introvert or an extrovert. Remember a Phlegmatic is moderate in everything and, in this case, Desires in moderation.

C	P
Demonstrated	**Desired**
CHOLERIC	**PHLEGMATIC**
Independent	Calm
Visionary	Friendly
Productive	Objective
Decisive	Diplomatic
Inspiring	Practical
Determined	Humorous
Strong-willed	Dependable

Phlegmatic (5) / Choleric (0-1-2-3)

09	19	29	39	49	59	69	79	89	99
08	18	28	38	48	58	68	78	88	98
07	17	27	37	47	57	67	77	87	97
06	16	26	36	46	56	66	76	86	96
05	15	25	35	45	55	65	75	85	95
04	14	24	34	44	54	64	74	84	94
03	13	23	33	43	53	63	73	83	93
02	12	22	32	42	52	62	72	82	92
01	11	21	31	41	51	61	71	81	91
00	10	20	30	40		60	70	80	90

The Demonstrated number is 5, which is introvert/extrovert. They will sway back and forth between being and introvert and being an extrovert. They are very comfortable with functioning either way. Remember, a Phlegmatic is moderate in everything. The Desired numbers are 0-1-2-3 with are all introverted. That means they no not Desire that you be Demonstrative toward them and, if you do, that it be slight.

P	C
Demonstrated	**Desired**

PHLEGMATIC	CHOLERIC
Calm	Independent
Friendly	Visionary
Objective	Productive
Diplomatic	Decisive
Practical	Inspiring
Humorous	Determined
Dependable	Strong-willed

Chapter 12: The GAP Theory

G = Great
A = Anxiety
P = Present

We're deepening our knowledge further now with more insight into how Temperaments interact with each other. Sometimes a potential conflict between the Demonstrated and Desired Regions can occur within an individual's Temperament. This is called The **GAP** Theory (**G**reat **A**nxiety **P**resent). This knowledge will not only help you understand yourself better, but certainly strengthen your situational awareness with others regarding all interactions.

When looking at WIDP Profile results, be aware of a profile "G-A-P"; a four (4) or more point spread between the Demonstrated Score and the Desired Score. This could be within any of the three Temperament Areas.

In the GAP Chart below, you can see WIDP Temperament Numbers within their regular colors do not have a GAP of four (4) or more. However, all numbers in the brown colored part of the graph experience a GAP of four (4) or more within their Temperament makeup. They have a GAP!

Most of the GAP numbers are either in the Introverted Sanguine quadrant or the Choleric quadrant, with the exception of a few Blends.

We now have a keen awareness of understanding that the Introverted Sanguine and the Choleric have a pre-disposition to experience conflict with many of their relationships simply due to their Temperament makeup. Even blended Temperaments with a GAP can feel this internal conflict.

The wider the GAP, the more anxious, intolerant, insensitive, sensitive, stressful, blunt, stubborn, indifferent, cold, and driven the person will be.

The widest GAPs found in the WIDP Scoring Chart are 90, the Choleric Compulsive in the bottom right-hand corner, and 09, the Introverted Sanguine Compulsive in the top left-hand corner.

Not only is this to be understood in your internal context, but you must also consider that others you associate with might have a GAP of their own with which you will have to compete.

Using the Choleric Compulsive, as an illustration; Let's say that you, a 90 Cc (Choleric Compulsive) in Leadership, have been promoted to a position where you must work with another 90 Cc in Leadership who has equal authority. Both Cholerics want to run the show and be in charge. Do you think there will be a conflict between them? Of course, that conflict will occur quite regularly. Why? Because both are very high in Leadership, and both want to lead the way you see fit. To put it into a picture, the two of them will be "jockeying" for first place all the time.

Does this mean that they cannot work together? No. What it does mean is that the Supervisor over these two individuals needs to be aware of each Temperament to have a positive impact on them both.

It is very common to have more than one Choleric that is in the same department and both wanting to run the operation. However, if you know Temperament information, you can assign each of them a territory of responsibility and give them free reign to run that section without interference from any other Choleric, coworker, peer, and in some cases, upper management.

To put some images to this concept, let's look at the following regarding the GAP Theory.
- The Horizontal GAP within your Temperament and another person
- The Vertical GAP within your Temperament and another person
- The Cross-Section GAP between your Demonstrated to their Desired and from their Demonstrated to your Desired.

1. Consider the Horizontal View of your Social Profile with another person.

For this exercise I will be using the following Temperament sets of numbers: Your Social Profile is 90 and the Social Profile for the Other Person is 21.

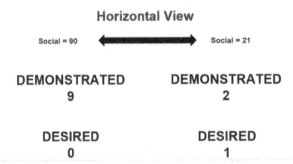

As you look at the graph, notice the blank lines between the arrows and consider the following:

- Do you see a GAP of four (4) or more between your Demonstrated number (9) and their Demonstrated number (2)? Yes, we have a GAP here of seven, and that is a severe GAP. Will there be a conflict between them? GAP - Yes, there will be conflict.
- Do you see a GAP of four (4) or more between your Desired number (0) and their Desired number (1)? No, there is no GAP there, so these two individuals are OK in their Social Desired numbers. No GAP - No Conflicts.

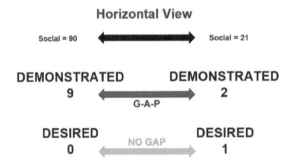

Now let's put your Demonstrated and Desired numbers in the blanks, and see if there's a GAP:

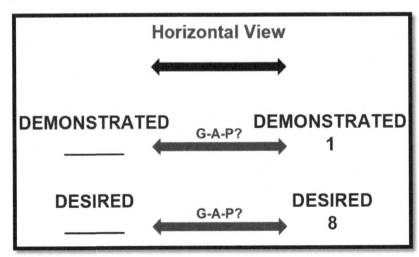

2. **Consider the Vertical View of your Social Profile and another person's profile.**

Using the same set of numbers, yours 90 and theirs 21, we will set it up the same way and observe from the Vertical View.

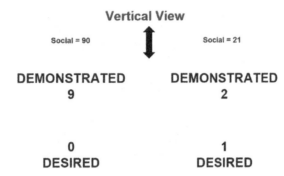

- Do you see a GAP of four (4) or more between your Demonstrated number (9) and your Desired number (0)? Yes, there is a GAP of nine, so this indicates that you have a severe internal struggle as well as you are experiencing stress and anxiety with other individuals. GAP - Yes, there are internal and external Conflicts.
- Do you see a GAP of four (4) or more between their Demonstrated number (2) and their Desired number (1)? No, they only have a GAP here of one, and that is not a problem for that person. No GAP – No Conflicts internally.

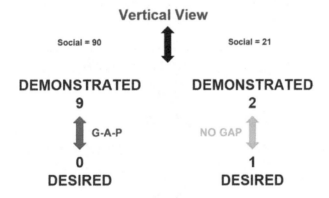

Now let's put your Demonstrated and Desired numbers in the blanks, and see if there's a GAP:

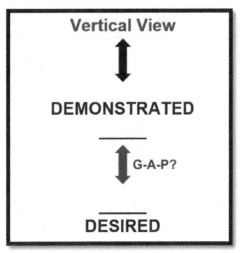

3.   Consider the Vertical View of your Social Profile and another person's profile.

Once more let's use the same set of numbers, yours 90 and theirs 21, we will set it up the same way and observe the Cross-Section GAPs.   The Cross-Section GAPs look at your Demonstrated (9) to their Desired (1) and their Demonstrated (2) to your Desired (0).

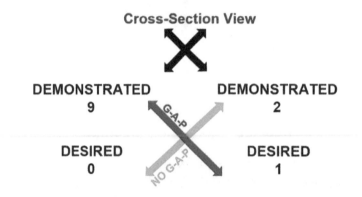

- Do you see a GAP of four (4) or more between your Demonstrated number (9) and their Desired number of (1)?   Yes, there is a GAP of eight (8) so this indicates incompatibility and, thus, stress and anxiety as you Demonstrate with this person. GAP – Yes, there will be Conflict.
- Do you see a GAP of four (4) or more between their Demonstrated number (2) and your Desired number (0)?   What you are Demonstrating and what they Desire is compatible.   No GAP – No Conflict.

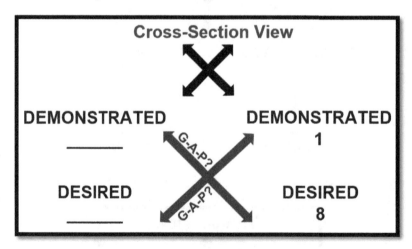

At this point, you can complete the same exercise above and apply it to the Leadership and Relationship Areas.   Use a red marker for the GAP's and a green marker for the ones without a GAP. Seeing you and another person side-by-side from a Temperament perspective can immediately identify potential problem areas.

You can also do this for several individuals at one time. It is beneficial for team development, determining what person to use on marketing or sales assignment, even new hire screening. This also functions as a conflict resolution tool as you can see clearly where the conflicts are and begin to form solutions with this awareness.

Activity #1 – Identify the Team Leader

Identify the Team Leader

Jim	2 0	**9 2**	**6 6**
Brenda	3 0	**3 1**	**2 4**
Dennis	1 0	**0 1**	**2 3**

Because it is in a Leadership capacity, we want to first determine who can lead and who can not. With this group, we see that they are all capable of Leadership.

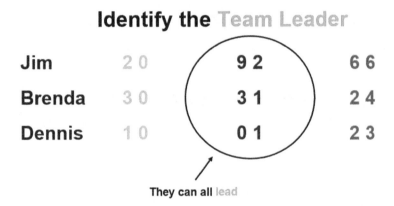

Identify the Team Leader

Jim	2 0	9 2	6 6
Brenda	3 0	3 1	2 4
Dennis	1 0	0 1	2 3

They can all lead

Remember in a work setting to be careful not to try and select based on the Leadership & Relationship – this will cause trouble!

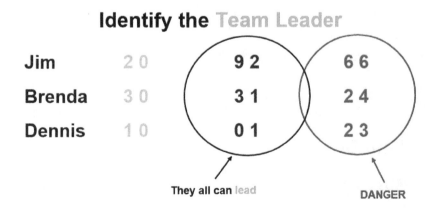

Identify the Team Leader

Jim	2 0	9 2	6 6
Brenda	3 0	3 1	2 4
Dennis	1 0	0 1	2 3

They all can lead   DANGER

So, who is the best Team Leader & Why? In this case – **Jim** is the best choice. All 3 can lead and all 3 are Melancholy in their Social Area. Since Jim has a better natural design for responsibilities that include other people; he would be the best choice to lead the team.

Activity #2 – Identify the Best Team Leader

Who would make the best
Team Leader **and why?**

Joe	2 1	**9 0**	**0 1**
Sue	0 2	**4 5**	**5 4**
Tom	6 7	**9 1**	**8 9**

Activity #3 – Identify the Best Team Leader

Who would make the best
Team Leader **and why?**

Kim	2 6	**3 4**	**0 2**
Barb	3 1	**2 0**	**1 2**
Jane	0 1	**1 2**	**0 5**

Activity #4 – Leader Profiles – Identify the Best Leader and Why:

Leader Profiles

John Doe	1 0	**5 0**	**2 5**
Mary Doe	1 0	**1 2**	**3 7**
Jim Doe	3 6	**7 0**	**4 6**
Don Doe	5 0	**8 0**	**5 5**

Chapter 13: Psychometrics of WIDP

Psychometric Evaluation Results
of
WORLEY'S ID PROFILE

This presentation of the psychometric properties of the WIDP Temperament Profile will begin with a discussion of the instrument and its structure, reliability, and validity, and conclude with a general summary of its utility based on findings.

The **Worley Identity Discovery Program (WIDP)** is a software system (now web-based) utilizing a sixty (60) item inventory questionnaire developed by me, John W. Worley, Ph.D. I intended to produce an instrument that would yield a quick but detailed summary of individual Temperament to aid in the facilitation of an individual's development and self-understanding.

The **WIDP** interprets reports based on sixty simple questions answered online or can be administered using a printed questionnaire and is manually entered into the system by a Certified WIDP Representative.

WIDP provides three detailed assessments that provide a comprehensive identification of needs, desires, and interpersonal behaviors in three crucial Areas of life (Social, Leadership, and Relationship) and those three Areas divided into two additional Regions each (Demonstrated and Desired):

Social Profile	**Demonstrated**
	Desired
Leadership Profile	**Demonstrated**
	Desired
Relationship Profile	**Demonstrated**
	Desired

This information enables the person to assess their individual's strengths quickly and weaknesses, target potential conflicts and develop sound beneficial strategies for future change. The person's understanding of self will be enhanced, increasing the possibility of a fulfilled and balanced life. With improved insight and self-awareness, they will enjoy greater success in interpersonal relationships.

I. Social Profile

The Social Profile identifies the individual's Temperament needs and desires for socialization, work/school associations, and other superficial relationships. Requirements in this Area may range from demonstrating and wanting minimal socialization, to showing and craving constant socialization. The Social Profile helps answer the question, **"Who is in or out of a relationship with this individual?"**

II. *Leadership Profile*

The Leadership Profile identifies the individual's Temperament needs and desires for influencing others, making decisions and assuming responsibilities. Requirements in this Area may range from independence to dependence. The Leadership Profile helps assess, **"Who maintains the power and makes judgments in a relationship with this individual?"**

III. *Relationship Profile*

The Relationship Profile identifies the individual's Temperament needs and desires in close relationships with family and friends. Requirements in this Area may range from emotional connections and expression of relationships with many people to isolation from relationships. The Relationship Profile identifies, **"How emotionally open or closed to relationships is this individual?"**

WIDP defines these varying needs and desires, not as **"right"** or **"wrong"**, but as individual differences and preferences. If the person's life situation differs radically from their needs and desires in one or more of the Areas, they are experiencing stress, conflict, and anxiety in relationships. By teaching the individual about their unique needs, they can use **WIDP** to help themselves restore balance and peace to their lives and relationships.

Building any successful interpersonal relationship involves moving through the three living Areas - Social, Leadership, and Relationship - in sequence. People typically begin relationships by setting social issues, to determine if the connection is safe. They then progress to leadership issues, establishing a mutually comfortable way to handle power and control. If the first two Areas resolve satisfactorily, people can move into a relationship, an area of emotional closeness with each other. Many interpersonal conflicts arise because Social and Leadership issues need to be fixed, yet people are attempting to function in an area of personal Relationship with each other.

Scoring

The report generated for each of the three Areas based on two scores: The Demonstrated Score and the Desired Score. Each rating may range from zero to nine. The individual's scores are recorded at the top of the **WIDP Report**.

The Demonstrated Score indicates how the individual prefers to act toward other people. This behavior can be observed; it is the image presented to others. The Demonstrated Score in each Area is the level of action the individual feels most comfortable in using to bring people together (Demonstrate Socially), to get his/her way (Demonstrate Leadership) and to be close to others (Demonstrate Relationship).

Scores are interpreted as follows:

Demonstrated Score

0 – 1	**Very Low**	**The individual rarely expresses this behavior and compulsively avoids this behavior**
2 – 3	**Low**	**The individual may occasionally express this behavior**
4 – 5	**Moderate**	**The individual tends toward expressing this behavior**
6 – 7	**High**	**The individual characteristically expresses this behavior**
8 – 9	**Very High**	**The individual compulsively expresses this behavior**

The Desired Score indicates the person's preferred behavior from others toward him/her. It is an indicator of the individual's inner needs and desires, which may differ significantly from their public image. The Desired Behavior in each Area is the action the person prefers others use in their approach to getting together with them, (Desired Social), to get their way (Desired Leadership) and to be close to them (Desired Relationship).

Desired Score

0 – 1	**Very Low**	**The individual rarely wants this behavior demonstrated toward him/her by others, and compulsively avoids situations where it may occur**
2 – 3	**Low**	**The individual may occasionally want this behavior demonstrated toward him/her by others**
4 – 5	**Moderate**	**The individual tends toward expressing this behavior**
6 – 7	**High**	**The individual characteristically wants this behavior demonstrated toward him/her by others**
8 – 9	**Very High**	**The individual will compulsively seek to have this behavior demonstrated toward him/her by others**

In general, the more significant the discrepancy between the Demonstrated Score and the Desired Score, the higher the probability that the individual is experiencing conflict in this Area. Since **WIDP** provides a comprehensive interpretation of these scores, numerical data is provided for your interest only.

WIDP describes Temperament characteristics found in individuals with specific rating patterns. Because of variations within scoring ranges, a few details of **WIDP** may not apply precisely to the individual. However, the overall high reliability of **WIDP** is unparalleled in the field of assessment instruments.

WIDP includes the individual's Temperament type or Temperament Blends, according to the theory first developed by Hippocrates and updated by contemporary professionals. These five basic types (Melancholy, Choleric, Sanguine, Introverted Sanguine and Phlegmatic) and various Blends (e.g., Melancholy-Phlegmatic, Phlegmatic-Choleric, Introverted Sanguine-Phlegmatic) can accurately describe the individual's inner needs and desires. Two of the types, the Melancholy and the Phlegmatic, express along the continuum of introverted behavior. The Choleric and the Sanguine both express as extroverts. The Introverted Sanguine demonstrates as a Melancholy (introvert) but desires as an extrovert. Listed below are the variations of the behaviors and the behavioral blends with their numerical values:

FIVE TEMPERAMENTS:

IS	Introverted Sanguine
S	Sanguine
P	Phlegmatic
M	Melancholy
C	Choleric

BLENDS:

P/IS	Phlegmatic/Introverted Sanguine
IS/P	Introverted Sanguine/Phlegmatic
P/S	Phlegmatic Sanguine
S/P	Sanguine Phlegmatic
M/P	Melancholy Phlegmatic
P/M	Phlegmatic Melancholy
C/P	Choleric Phlegmatic
P/C	Phlegmatic Choleric

COMPULSIVE*: (Small c = compulsive)

ISc	Introverted Sanguine Compulsive
Sc	Sanguine Compulsive
Mc	Melancholy Compulsive
Cc	Choleric Compulsive

*Compulsive** in this context is not used in a negative sense like fanatic, obsessive, uncontrollable, or incorrigible. Instead, it indicates that the person's living patterns will focus on the various characteristics of that Temperament need, whatever they may be, within either of the three Temperament Areas of Social/Vocational, Leadership, or Relationship.

For example, individuals who are Melancholy compulsive (very introverted) in the Social Area, have a paramount need to maintain their privacy, away from other people. Melancholy individuals are timid. Likewise, Choleric compulsive individuals, in the Leadership Area, focus on always maintaining influential control of their environment and of others in contact with them.

This compulsiveness does not insinuate lousy behavior. However, individuals who are Compulsive in one or more Areas of their Temperament makeup can be complicated people, especially as employers, leaders, managers, and within close relationships.

WIDP is an innovative Temperament resource that, combined with professional communication skills, identifies an individual's unique needs, desires, and behavioral responses. This information applies to humankind from a biological foundation.

To assess the psychometric properties of **WIDP Profile**, I collected a database of 585 administrations of the instrument. The database was evenly split between males and females (280 men and 305 women). The average age of the participants was 36 years (37.2 years men and 34.7 years female), with a mean education level of fourteen (14) years for both genders.

RELIABILITY

When defining the psychometric properties of an instrument, the term Reliability is used in some ways. The most common use being the consistency with which an apparatus measures over time or occasions. This form of reliability, referred to as *Coefficient of Stability or Test-Retest Reliability*, is assessed by calculating the relationship between two or more sets of scores produced by the same group of individuals across a time interval. To assess WIDP Test-Retest Reliability thirty-nine (39) people were given two administrations of the measure with a four (4) month interval between assessments. The average relationship between scores on the six scales of the WIDP across the two administrations was found to be r '.7 (Pearson Product Moment Correlation). The psychometric evaluation confirms that WIDP has excellent stability over time, and therefore will provide consistent results between administrations.

> **NOTE:** **The average Test-Retest Reliability of similar types of instruments over a one-month period is between .7 and .8. The WIDP's - r .7 over four months is outstanding.**

Another measure of reliability used in assessing instruments properties is the *Measure of Internal Consistency Reliability*. On the individual scale level (the WIDP has six) this is an indication of how well the items in a scale measure the same thing. Because the elements on the WIDP six levels scored dichotomously (an article gave a value of one [1] or zero [0] based on specific response possibilities), the ***Kuder-Richardson Formula 20 (KR-20)*** was used. The average internal consistency of the six scales was ***KR-20*** '.54. To put this result in perspective, consider that the average internal consistency of the 10 Minnesota Multiphasic Personality Inventory - 2 (the most widely used psychological measure today) Clinical scales and the three-validity scale is .52.

Conclusion: The WIDP is very sound on instrument reliability.

VALIDITY

How valid is the WIDP? We can think of validity to the extent to which a test measures the characteristics it is designed to measure. Establishing the validity of the WIDP was accomplished by two methods. The first of these methods (concurrent validity) was to compare the WIDP scores between individuals not currently in counseling with those who have been diagnosed with specific psychological problems by clinical psychologists. Diagnosable issues carry known behavior patterns that should be demonstrated by mean scale scores found on the WIDP. Descriptions of the results presented by diagnosis:

Major Depression:

Individuals with this diagnosis are typically withdrawn socially and lack the energy to pursue relationships actively. The WIDP Profiles for this diagnosis indicate that they seldom initiate interaction with others, and they rarely want others to socialize with them. The average Desired interaction score for this group is zero (0). Further, they report less than half of the willingness to make decisions or assume responsibility than that of non-diagnosed individuals (Desired and Demonstrated Leadership is Low).

Obsessive Compulsive Disorder:

Relationships for persons with this disorder are complicated. They typically lack intimacy in relationships and struggle in making decisions often to the point of wanting others to make decisions for them. WIDP Scores for this diagnosis indicate that their Desired Relationship (what they desire from others within close relationships) is much higher than that of the average person. Also, their Demonstrated Leadership scores show that they seldom want to make decisions and to take responsibility.

Marital Problems

While not considered an actual psychological disorder, marital problems are a diagnosed condition. Often the problem that couples face is of intimacy and control. Struggles over who makes decisions and who is responsible are everyday decisions. Blaming one another for what is missing in the marriage is the norm. The scores on the WIDP are consistent with these common issues. These individuals tend to Desire that their Relationship initiate Demonstrations towards them much more than does the average person. WIDP results with higher-than-average scores within Desired Leadership indicate that they would like their spouse to own more responsibilities than they themselves. Their Low scores within Demonstrated Social reflect the lack of desire to be socially involved and a tendency to be withdrawn.

Alcohol Dependence

Individuals who are alcohol dependent are often found to be lacking in their desire to be responsible and isolating from meaningful social situations. The WIDP Profiles of this diagnosis indicate that their Demonstrated Social Profile is less than half of the usual response style. They rarely express Desired needs for Socialization. Their Desired Leadership scores (near zero) indicate that they do not wish others to make decisions for them or attempt to influence them. Their Low Demonstrated Leadership score further means that they do not want to make decisions.

Note: Even though the WIDP Profile is an analytical tool, the results of the comparison of mean responses with known characteristics of the established diagnoses above indicate that the scales have concurrent validity. That is, they measure what they intend to measure.

The second method of establishing validity focuses on the position that the WIDP scales reveal different types of efficient functioning. If this were true, we would expect to find a broad range of response styles in the average population. During the sampling of individuals, I administered the Rosenberg Self-Esteem measure to eighty-two (82) of the participants. If the hypothesis is correct that healthy people can present many different scores on the six scales, then the scales will have little or no relationship with self-esteem. Results indicate that only Desired Leadership is related (marginally) with self-esteem. The other scales correlated zero (meaning no connection). Do not misinterpret this result to suggest that the WIDP is intended to present a complete profile that involves the interaction between the three domains of Social, Leadership, and Relationships; also, between the Demonstrated and Desired elements of each of the domains. The results do indicate that self-esteem is not related to any of the Temperaments found on any of the scales themselves, but as I have proposed, it is a product of the difference between scales.

Chapter 14: Case Studies Using WIDP Temperament Profile

Introverted Sanguine Compulsive in Leadership

The Unwanted Promotion

Michael was Assistant to the Director of Purchasing for a large university. The Purchasing Department was responsible for a $40,000,000 annual budget. Michael was very active and functioned quite well for fifteen years. In this role, he did what he was instructed to do by the Director, mainly administrative tasks. Since Michael's primary responsibilities did not require him to make a lot of crucial decisions or manage a lot of people, Michael found himself successful and comfortable with his job.

Everything was going great, then Michael's boss, the Director of Purchasing, got relocated. Michael was automatically promoted to fill the vacant position of Director of Purchasing! Seeming like the most logical move that was right for the university, it was very wrong for Michael. Immediate stress, anxiety, and frustration became visible in Michael's life with the unwanted promotion. Michael's life and world turned upside-down. Along with managing twenty-seven staff members also came the chief responsibility over the $40,000,000 budget. After two agonizing years as Director of Purchasing, Michael was exploring the possibilities of early retirement due to the enormous daily pressure.

After struggling with the situation, Michael sought assistance from a business consultant. They administered the WIDP Profile to Michael and the results revealed that Michael was an Introverted Sanguine in Leadership! This means that Michael functions best as a true second-in-command. Since one of the characteristics of an Introverted Sanguine is a desire to not handle decisions by himself, no wonder he was stressed out as the Director!

With the insight provided by the WIDP results, Michael realized his areas of weakness as well as his strengths and they developed a strategy for coping with decision making and managing the staff members. The group divided into thirteen teams with two members each. One member is the buyer and one is the seller. The two of them assist each other with decision-making issues. Each has their autonomous area of responsibility, thus eliminating the need for constant oversight. Only the decisions that they cannot make as a team are brought to Michael. The extra person, the twenty-seventh, is a floater and fills in where needed when someone goes on vacation or sick leave. The implementation of this model reduced the decisions Michael had to make by 85% and gained assistance from some of his key team members for the other 15%.

Michael's strategy worked for the next five years, and became eligible for retirement, but felt he'd like to stick around a few more years until his children graduated from college.

Success for Michael and WIDP!

Sanguine

Stereotyped Female Attorney

Robin was a female attorney from Connecticut who had been practicing law for several years as a court-appointed attorney for those who could not afford legal representation. She was very unhappy with her profession and with her lifestyle. Robin felt she just was not the attorney type and that the occupation was stifling her personal growth. She felt obligated to dress and act the part, which made her attire feel out of place and unacceptable in the industry in which Robin worked each day. She was depressed and very distraught with her life and vocation and did not know how to change the situation. In desperation, Robin sought assistance from the Human Resource Department in hopes that they might provide some insight.

On her first visit, Robin was given the WIDP Profile Questionnaire to complete; a standard procedure for everyone who seeks their assistance. Robin's Profile results revealed that she was Sanguine.

One of the greatest fears of a Sanguine is rejection by other people. Robin felt that she should model the appearance of the stereotyped attorney, and she had been dressing to accommodate that look. Robin was single, 5' 9", and wore her shoulder-length chocolate brown hair in a twisted bun on top of her head in a five-pronged pitchfork style hair clip. She wore heavy black-rimmed glasses with the beaded chain attached to the lenses for hanging around her neck when not needed for reading. She wore no makeup. She donned a plain black pleated button-up dress that extended all the way to the throat and finished the look with black platform shoes. Her well-worn black briefcase carried the battle scars of many years of service. While she could have posed as Mona Lisa's sister, Robin was perhaps a bit more inconspicuous in a dress.

After reviewing her WIDP Results, she was told: "Robin, why don't you let your hair down, get yourself some new high fashion glasses, buy yourself a bright flashy multicolored dress, maybe several, some pairs of high heeled shoes, and put on some makeup. Let's start wearing the friendly and outgoing woman that you are, for a change. Once you have those, go home and have a celebration by burning everything in your closet that isn't this woman.

Robin started crying. When she finally gained control of her emotions where she could speak, she asked, "So, I can dress like that?" Robin was a stifled Sanguine wanting acceptance as an attorney but hid her true self behind the expectations of the stereotype. A Sanguine is a very outgoing individual who brings excitement and fun to the world no matter where they are. A Sanguine makes life tolerable for the other Temperament types that are more serious and focused on accomplishing tasks. Robin's voluntary standards were unnecessary, unhealthy, and violated her true person because it forced her into being someone other than herself.

Guess what?   Robin only needed one session with the Human Resource Department to transform her life forever.   As it turned out, she did go home and have that celebration. Burning the clothes she was wearing that very day! The results of the WIDP set her free to be, on the outside, the Sanguine that she had always been inside.

Success!

Phlegmatic

Power vs. Status Quo

The Director of a non-profit organization needed assistance from a consulting firm to figure out a quick solution concerning a piece of property the group currently had under their control. The property had three buildings, was debt free, and valued at $500,000. Under the property agreement, the organization could keep the property so long as personnel occupied the premises. The personnel presently occupying the property were part of their group but had allied with another team that had visions of taking over the land and the buildings. So, the five-person Board had to decide, within three days, whether to hold this property in order to secure it legally.

The Director approached the consulting firm as an aggressive, focused, take charge person who was able to make quick, intuitive decisions and go forward. He did not waiver in conflict and was very direct and bold in his communications. However, the other four members of the leadership group were Phlegmatics. They were all very dependable, steady, task-oriented, and middle-of-the-road-type people. These members rarely make quick changes to anything and prefer changes to happen slowly, over an extended period, with everyone agreeing to the modification. The mindset is: "If it worked for this long, why change it now?" Without consensus on a solution, any issue could be postponed indefinitely.

The Director, having been alerted of the potential loss of the property to another organization via an anonymous phone call, organized a response plan consisting of arranging personnel from his organization to occupy the property and organizing a locksmith to put new locks on the buildings the following morning. With these response plans drafted, he only lacked approval from the other four members of the board. In an emergency meeting, all of the Phlegmatic members did not want to engage in conflict with or even question the integrity of the person who was currently occupying the property. They had difficulty believing the other organization would actively move to take the property and, so, the members chose not to permit the expense of changing locks on the buildings even as a safeguard. Remember, a Phlegmatic does not like to waste money and saw this as an unnecessary expense.

What happened? The other organization did take control, changed the locks, and walked off with $500,000 worth of property. Why?

There are essentially two rights that happened: The Phlegmatics were right in their stand against the Director who wanted to jump in, take over, and control the situation, which is why a board is in place; to help gain consensus on situations involving the organization. This board was an element of a more substantial parent organization, which also happened to be run by a Phlegmatic, and the pulse of the leadership was content to run as a status quo organization. The Director, who offered a reasonable aggressive response for an aggressive move by another organization, was simply out of place in a Phlegmatic-heavy board.

As a result, the Director chose to resign and, candidly, the Phlegmatics rejoiced.

Melancholy

A Manager of the Wrong Group

Lela was a middle Director of a more massive corporation on the East Coast. She had been in this assignment for five years and was experiencing extreme stress and depression, so she sought assistance from her Human Resource Department. Interestingly, Human Resources referred her to a psychiatrist – which was the same psychiatrist she had been in therapy with for twelve years. The past years of therapy had offered Lela little relief, so she pursued Worley's ID Program.

During her first visit, she completed the WIDP Profile Questionnaire, and her results revealed that she was a Melancholy Compulsive (on the MBTI she was an ISTJ) who was dealing with chronic depression and extreme anger. She had been on medication of Elavil 100 mg, Prozac, Zoloft 250 mg, and Wellbutrin 450 mg over the course of thirteen years. She was presently taking 150mg of Trazodone per day for mental distress. Her medication record began in 1981 and continued until the day she began WIDP. Her mental condition had been diagnosed as having suicidal tendencies. According to Lela, she only had two stable elements within her life: God and her husband.

After consulting with her psychiatrist, Dr. Worley recommended that all medication be eliminated and that her needs as a Melancholy Compulsive Temperament type be addressed instead. The psychiatrist agreed, and the process of decreasing medication began immediately.

Lela was unable to function at work, had a breakdown during a staff meeting, and broke out in a fit of rage. Immediately STD (Short Term Disability) was sought and granted. A treatment plan was implemented to reduce her medication to none as quickly as possible and to be seen three times a week.

For a clinical report, the following was established:

Essential features: Lela is experiencing a reactive depression of severe proportions. She displays consistently and notably a depressed mood, and she reports a loss of interest in all vocational and social activities including those that involve immediate family members. She is very sad, dissatisfied, angry, irritable, self-punishing, and very argumentative. Her emotional behavior is usually that of being in tears and a state of despair and hopelessness.

Associated features: Additional symptoms include sleep and appetite disturbance, loss of energy, difficulty in concentrating, slowed thinking, periodic loss of memory, and thoughts of suicide or death.

Social/vocational adjustment: Lela has withdrawn from friends and family members and prefers to avoid all interpersonal involvement whenever possible. Her situation is severe enough that she cannot function socially or vocationally.

Complications: The most severe difficulty of her depression is suicide ideation combined with her Melancholic Temperament and her co-dependency, which is cruel.

Treatment recommendations: Therapeutic intervention, graduated, of six to twelve weeks, will usually improve client's condition. Self-recognition, behavioral modification, stress reduction, and stress management therapy focusing on the results of the WIDP Profile.

It was uncovered during the treatment process that she needed to transfer out of her vocational position. Her management position required her to interface daily with multitudes of people dealing with various issues. She needed a job that was stable, steady, and routine, a place that did not require her to interface with people all day long. A lateral transfer within the company worked. Within ninety days, Barbara was back at work, entirely off medications, no longer angry, and quite happy in her new position. Therapy was no longer needed.

A huge success for Barbara, a Melancholy.

Choleric

A Leader Out of Leadership

Renee was a twenty-six-year-old scientific engineer in a fast-growing company. She had been there three years and felt like her true skills were not being exercised in the enterprise, and she was very frustrated. This was causing such extreme anxiety and severe drop in performance that her supervisor strongly recommended therapy. Renee did not know that she had natural leadership abilities based on her Temperament, only that she suffered with internal anxiety and frustration in her profession and was snowballing into her marriage.

She scheduled an appointment with WIDP, took the WIDP Profile, and it revealed that she was a Choleric in Leadership. A separate assessment also revealed that she was co-dependent. At the time of her first therapy session, her primary focus was on the issue of wanting to divorce her husband. They had been married for nine months and had a seven-month-old daughter.

She also had a deep longing to reconnect with her mother. Her mother had chosen to leave her and her father when she was fourteen. Since that time, her mother had lived with fourteen different people and was now living with the fifteenth.

Renee vulnerably expressed that she was also interested in another man within the company. She had shared lunch with him a few times, but they were not yet actively engaged in a romantic relationship. Both desired a more intimate relationship.

She was very emotional and crying during her first three therapy sessions, but the tears diminished with each new session. Confusion was present in her thinking, and she was unable to make decisions or come to any conclusions without assistance from someone. She had no close friends that she could communicate with, so she spent most of her time in isolation as a very anxious and frustrated woman longing for her mother and wanting out of her marriage.

In her marriage, she felt that her husband was not acknowledging her abilities to participate in any marital decisions and that he was intimidated by her success as a scientific engineer. She made more money than he did and had more education. So, he ruled the marriage by dominating her. These issues, along with an inability to realize her leadership potential in the corporate world, called for a total re-orientation of her life. The following approach was taken:

A. She was encouraged to begin exercising her abilities as a leader in the marriage and at work, giving Renee a sense of freedom that she had never experienced.

B. She was instructed to consider herself as an equal individual, with equal opportunities, regardless of her gender. For Renee, this was a new and unexplored concept for her work or home mentality.

C.   Regarding her marriage, it was recommended that she first come to a better understanding of herself based on her WIDP Profile, and then begin communicating this new understanding of herself to her husband. She was also encouraged to take a vacation together with her husband. The guidance for Renee reduced her anxiety and frustration level very quickly.

D.   Renee was advised to contact her mother by phone and then write to her a lengthy, detailed letter explaining how much she needed her mom in her life. She had never considered approaching her mother before.

As she implemented these changes, she immediately felt liberated as a leader in her marriage and vocation. She and her husband spent a week together in Maine. During that time, she decided she did not want a divorce. She wrote her mother a letter, feeling like a new person just being able to express the love and longing she had for her in her heart. She commented, "Even if she won't visit me or establish a relationship with me, I don't feel like I'm tormented over this issue anymore." She is considering the possibility of completing her Masters' degree in engineering and receives encouragement from both her husband and her supervisor.

All of this ended in seven sessions using the WIDP Profile. Success for the Choleric!

Public School Second Graders

Do Teachers and Students Always Connect?

An evaluation to determine the applicability and the effectiveness of WIDP was conducted in a public school on the east coast. Those participating in the evaluation were as follows:

Students:	Twenty-two students, 12 males and 10 females
Grade:	Second grade
Age:	Seven years old
Nationality:	Mixed
Teachers:	One female
Teacher Aides:	Two females
Special Education Teacher:	One female
Assistant Principals:	Two (One from another school)
Principals:	One female
School counselors:	Two females (One from another school)
Consultant:	One male

The contract completed in the following phases:

Initial Meeting:	3 hours Work with Principals designing approach.
Teacher Instructions:	4 hours Instruction outside of the classroom on the understanding of WIDP.
Profiles:	1 hour Twenty-two (22) Youth Profiles administered in the classroom.
Review Profiles:	2 hours This included (1) Consultant, (1) Principal, (2) Assistant Principals, (2) Counselors, (2) Teachers, (2) Aides.
Classroom Observation:	6 hours Two (3 hrs. each) classroom observations regarding interaction between teachers and students.
De-briefing:	2 hours All staff present.

Chapter 636 Information for this school district:

K-8 Students:

2000 - Special Education
3000 - Bilingual
4000 - Chapter 1 (Title One)
3000 - Mainstream

Requirements needed from the school before implementation of the project

1. Parental Release Form on each child.

   (Example)

   The children in Mrs. _____ & Mrs. _____ rooms will be working on a class project that will help children find helpful ways to solve problems and resolve conflicts. The teachers will be working with a Consultant, _____, to learn some new methods about conflict resolution. As part of the plan, each child will be given a questionnaire to see how they presently solve problems, assume leadership, and makes friends. The Consultant and Faculty will develop new methods for children and staff to work together with this information. Please sign the permission slip below and return it to the school as soon as possible. Thank you for your attention to this matter.

   PERMISSION SLIP

   I give my child, _____ permission to be included in this project.

   Parent Signature   Date

2. Classroom seating arrangement diagram with each student identified.
3. Diagnosis and prognosis, from the counselor, on each student that is presently seeing a Counselor.
4. Name of medication and dosage prescribed for each student.
5. Identify any student that may be or has been diagnosed with Attention Deficit Disorder (ADD) or Attention Deficit Hyperactivity Disorder (ADHD).
6. Any other pertinent information relative to unusual classroom behavior and/or known physical, mental, or sexual abuse.
7. Approved and signed a Contract with a purchase order number.

Findings During Testing

The teachers and aides were worried as to whether the children could understand and follow the questions on the questionnaire and provide proper responses from the six different response choices. The teachers developed three sets of picture cards and three response clocks as visual aids for the children to refer to when needed. The picture cards and clocks were placed strategically around the classroom.

The teachers also felt that it would be essential to allow the children more time to respond to the questions by providing breaks every ten questions. Time breaks would require an additional fifty minutes for testing as there are sixty questions on the questionnaire.

The teachers were amazed that the students did not refer to the picture cards or the response clocks. Neither did the children need breaks after every ten questions. They were provided one ten-minute break after completing half of the questions.

The children enjoyed the challenge of the project and participated without any complications. One of the male children became very anxious during the last fifteen minutes. This child had been diagnosed with Attention Deficit Hyper Disorder (ADHD).

During the debriefing session, the teachers and staff acknowledged that they were quite impressed with the reliability and predictability of the WIDP Results. They were immediately able to identify how the implementation could be advantageous in many different applications with the children and with other peers and school staff.

One teacher, when asked if she had trouble interacting with one particular child, revealed that she had a deep emotional dislike for this child. The WIDP Results identified this inner conflict between the teacher and this child. The teacher began crying and said she felt like a failure, as a teacher, because she did not like this child. The issues were corrected immediately by re-assigning the child to the other grade teacher who felt very comfortable with this child, and the problem was resolved.

The results also detected that some students were more compatible with other students and would become more academically productive simply by changing the seating assignments. With that change implemented, the classroom behavior calmed down immediately.

The most important revelation was that the core participants realized how much more efficient they could relate to the students. Having a new understanding of their needs and desires, based on their individuality, gave them a deeper insight into the value of WIDP. Teachers and staff also identified other high need applications of WIDP within academic institutions, such as:

1. Leadership training
2. Staff-to-staff relationships
3. Staff-teacher relationships
4. Teacher-to-teacher relationships
5. Staff and teachers relating to parents, grandparents, and stepparents.

6. Suggestions that all school counselors and educators receive training on the WIDP.
7. Staff and teacher selection process; make completing the WIDP a mandatory part of the interview and evaluation process.
8. All students tested upon entering the school system during their enrollment process; to be retested every two or three years.
9. WIDP Profile considered for all high school students.
10 A class in instructing students on the value and application of their WIDP Results.
11. Further applications of conflict resolution, team building, determining a leader(s), & project management.

The two public schools that participated in this project were very satisfied with the results. They began applying for educational grants for further developing other WIDP initiatives within their schools.

CHAPTER 15: WIDP vs. Taylor-Johnson Temperament Analysis

(WIDP vs. T-JTA)

T-JTA Data

The comparison of the WIDP to the T-JTA Regular Edition revealed a great simplicity to understand the differences. The T-JTA is a diagnostic, counseling, and research instrument. T-JTA is primarily a Marriage Counselor's tool used in identifying patterns of personality traits that represent the individual feelings and emotions at present time. The T-JTA evaluation, however useful at that moment, is very temporary and subject to change within days, hours, or even minutes.

It serves as a convenient method of measuring some essential personality traits which influence personal, interpersonal, scholastic, and vocational functioning and adjustment. It is especially appropriate for premarital, marital, and family counseling purposes. The questions are constructed in such a way that the test can be taken not only on yourself, but also by a comparison of one person and another using a T-JTA Criss-Cross fashion. The age range of T-JTA is 13-64, and there are 180 response items within the tool.

T-JTA Secondary Edition is a specialized tool used only for self-testing with junior and senior high school students or adults who have attained a minimum of a fifth grade reading level, but less than an eighth grade reading level. Special Adult Reading Deficiency Norms (ARD) has been developed for use with Secondary Edition, Form S Question Booklet, with an age range of 7-12, and 180 response items.

T-JTA, Regular Edition, focuses on the **feelings** of individuals. This emphasis, as stated in the T-JTA training materials, is:

> **"…designed primarily to provide an evaluation in a visual form showing a person's feeling about himself/herself _at the time when he/she answered the questions_."**

This focus immediately differentiates the T-JTA from WIDP. The WIDP and the T-JTA are so different in their application of behavioral and Temperament understanding that it is better described as "apples to oranges". Most notably, T-JTA is focused on temporal feelings of the moment while WIDP is based on one's core, permanent Temperament.

WIDP Data

WIDP measures and determines individual intrinsic needs and desires relative to his/her base Temperament and gives you a detailed summary of people Social, Leadership, and Relationship Areas.

I.	**SOCIAL PROFILE**	**General social/work orientation**
II.	**LEADERSHIP PROFILE**	**Independence/leadership needs**
III.	**RELATIONSHIP PROFILE**	**Emotional involvement in close relationships**

The report generated for each of the three Areas is further divided into two Regions; the Demonstrated Score and the Desired Score.

The Demonstrated Score indicates how the individual prefers to act toward other people. This behavior, the image presented to others, generally can be observed. The Demonstrated Score level is each Area of action the individual feels most comfortable in using to:

Get together with others	**Demonstrated Social**
Have their way with others	**Demonstrated Leadership**
Be close to others	**Demonstrated Relationship**

The Desired Score indicates the preferred behavior from others toward them. This indicator of the individual's inner needs and desires may differ significantly from their publicly presented image. The Desired Behavior in each Area is the action the person prefers others to use in their approach to:

Get together with him/her	**Desired Social**
Have their way with him/her	**Desired Leadership**
Be close to him/her	**Desired Relationship**

In general, the **greater the distance** between the individual's Demonstrated Score and Desired Score, the **higher the probability** that the person is experiencing conflict in the measured/examined Area.

Additional data on the T-JTA

The T-JTA **Criss-Cross** analyzes five profile categories and their relationships between two individuals. The five categories are:

1. **Husband**
2. **Wife**
3. **Couple**
4. **Husband by Wife**
5. **Wife by Husband**

The five profiles portray a complete T-JTA marital Criss-Cross testing. The two top profiles depict the **Husband** as he sees himself and the **Wife** as she sees herself. The center **Couple** profile combines the two self-tests to show the interrelationship between the two personalities. The two bottom profiles, **Husband by Wife** and **Wife by Husband,** again depict the two self-tests, but also portray the results of the tests that each spouse completed on the other.

This set of profiles provides the counselor with vital information as to how each person sees himself or herself as well as how each person perceives the other. Similarities, differences, or areas of misunderstanding become clear. The T-JTA can also be administered in Criss-Cross fashion between various family members.

The purpose of the T-JTA is intended to serve as a quick and convenient method of measuring some essential and comparatively independent personality variables or tendencies. The test is designed primarily to provide an evaluation in a visual form showing a person's feeling about himself/herself at the time when he/she answered the questions. The T-JTA also makes possible the early identification of emotionally troubled individuals.

While the test was not designed to measure severe abnormalities or disturbances, it does provide indications of extreme patterns which require immediate improvement. There are four shaded zones on the T-JTA and clinical value for each zone are: Excellent, Acceptable, Improvement Desirable, Improvement Needed. The profile is designed to indicate the standard range of individual differences and is in no way intended to be diagnostic in the case of psychotic states.

Overview of the T-JTA Temperament Analysis Traits

Using "traits" as the form of identification, the tool uses **traits** to indicate a constellation of behavioral patterns and tendencies sufficiently cohesive to be used and measured as a unit. There are nine sets of traits in the T-JTA as follows:

T-JTA TEMPERAMENT TYPE TRAITS

Trait	**A**	**Nervous vs. Composed**
Trait	**B**	**Depressive vs. Lighthearted**
Trait	**C**	**Active-Social vs. Quiet**
Trait	**D**	**Expressive-Responsive vs. Inhibited**
Trait	**E**	**Sympathetic vs. Indifferent**
Trait	**F**	**Subjective vs. Objective**
Trait	**G**	**Dominant vs. Submissive**
Trait	**H**	**Hostile vs. Tolerant**
Trait	**I**	**Self-Disciplined vs. Impulsive**

Trait A   Nervous vs. Composed

Nervous: A state or condition frequently characterized by a tense, high-strung, or apprehensive attitude.

Composed: Characterized by a calm, relaxed, and tranquil outlook on life.

Questions in this category are designed to measure nervousness, whether induced by internal or external stimuli, and whether it is experienced internally or manifested in external signs and symptoms. The items used include such indications of nervousness as the inability to concentrate, the presence of undue worry or anxiety, excessive concern about health or physical well-being.

Some of the more obvious external manifestations of nervous tension are excessive excitability, natural loss of composure, excessive smoking, eating, drinking, indigestion or loss of appetite, the regular use of relaxant medications, and such nervous mannerisms as nail-biting, foot tapping, and restlessness.

Composure is measured by a sense of calmness or serenity, freedom from excessive worry and anxiety.

Nervous appears to be more variable in its manifestation than most other traits. It is mostly a measure of anxiety, especially when combined with high scores in **Depressive**, **Subjective**, and **Hostile**, and a low score in **Self-Discipline**.

A high **Nervous** score may be temporary when it results from immediate, acute stress.

Trait B   **Depressive vs. Lighthearted**

Depressive: Pessimistic, discouraged, or dejected.

Lighthearted: A happy, cheerful, and optimistic attitude or disposition.

The items which directly measure depressive states or reactions include feelings of apathy, despair, disillusionment, or pessimism; depressive preoccupation with problems, or misfortunes; emotional exhaustion and the contemplation of suicide.

The items which provide indirect indications of depression include feelings of being unwanted, of not belonging, of fearfulness, of being unimportant or unappreciated,
as well as a tendency to be easily disheartened by criticisms and discouraged because of a lack of self-confidence or a sense of inferiority.

Lightheartedness is a sense of well-being and optimism.

Depressive is found to correlate positively with **Nervous**; improvement in either trait appears to improve the other.

High **Nervous** and high **Depressive** scores are usually evident in persons seeking psychological assistance. While the cause of this pattern is frequently found to be subjective in nature, medical examination and cooperation may be advisable.

When the **Depressive** score is extraordinarily high and **Self-Disciplined** low, caution is indicated.

Trait C   **Active-Social vs. Quiet**

    Active-Social: Energetic, enthusiastic, and socially involved.

    Quiet: Socially inactive, lethargic, and withdrawn attitudes.

Active-Social is a feeling of energy and vitality, the briskness of movement, keeping on the go, and being considered a go-getter, finding enjoyment in activity and excitement, being a tireless and industrious worker, enjoying a wide variety of activities and interests, and keeping in condition with regular exercise.

Quietness is a preference for a stable, restful, quiet life, for being alone rather than with people, and for little participation in social events or activities.

A high score in **Active-Social** usually indicates a liking for people and a need for companionship and group participation. High scores are considered admirable unless they are combined with a high **Hostile,** high **Nervous,** and a low **Self-Disciplined.**

A low **Quiet** score suggests a withdraw tendency.

Trait D   **Expressive-Responsive vs Inhibited**

    Expressive-Responsive: Spontaneous, affectionate, demonstrative.

    Inhibited: Portrayed by restrained, unresponsive, or repressed behavior.

Expressive-Responsive is the ability to be friendly and responsive in contact with people, to be talkative and to express oneself with animation, enthusiasm, and gestures, to have many friends, and to be thought of by others as being an expressively warm-hearted and outgoing person.

The items which measure the more personal forms of expressiveness include the ability to show affection without embarrassment, to be warmly demonstrative with members of one's family, to be able to express tenderness, sympathy, or pleasure, and to be willing to share one's joys or sorrow with another person.

Inhibited is the inability to express tender feelings, and by a tendency to be reserved, restrained, repressed, and self-conscious.

The trait **Expressive-Responsive** is a measure of freedom to express the natural sense of warmth and affection and to respond to such feelings in others. It involves the desire to be liked.

Trait   E   **Sympathetic vs. Indifferent**

Sympathetic: Empathetic, kind, compassionate, sensitive to the needs and feelings of others. Showing concern for the welfare of those who are less fortunate, aware of the another's need for encouragement, kindness, or understanding, and feared for children, animals, and the elderly.

Indifferent: Is a lack of sympathetic interest in other people, a tendency to be strict, thoughtlessly inconsiderate, and slow to recognize the needs of family and friends.

Since sympathy involves compassion and concern for others, it is especially influential in creating healthy courtship, marriage, and parental relationships.

Trait F   **Subjective vs. Objective**

Subjective: Emotional, illogical, self-absorbed.

Objective: Fair-minded, reasonable, and logical in attitude.

The items include those indications of conflict or emotionality which tend to interfere with the ability to think objectively and impartially. Specific topics include tendencies to be overly sensitive, introspective, jealous, suspicious, or self-conscious, as well as the tendency to daydream, hold grudges, be easily embarrassed, or to misinterpret the motives of others.

Subjectivity, when extremely high, may indicate severe emotional disturbance. It seems to suggest that inner feelings tend to create bias and a distortion of the ability to be logical in the appraisal of reality and life situations.

Objective is the capacity to be analytical, impartial, dispassionate, not preoccupied with introspection or plagued by internal doubts and fears.

Trait G   **Dominant vs. Submissive**

Dominant: Confident, assertive, and competitive. Indicated ego-strength, such as being influential with others or desiring to influence or change their thinking.

Submissive: The tendency to follow, to rely too much on people, to give way to their wishes, to avoid complaining, to seek peace at any cost, and to be easily persuaded or taken advantage of by other people.

When interpreting the profiles of a married couple, an analysis of the interrelationship between the self-evaluation scores in **Dominant** may be of more importance in counseling than the location of the ratings.

Trait H   **Hostile vs. Tolerant**

     Hostile: Critical, argumentative, and punitive.

     Tolerant: Accepting, patient, and humane in attitude.

The **Hostile** tendency is to be superior, overbearing, impatient, sarcastic, argumentative, and unreasonable, as well as being contemptuous of weakness in others, quick to show temper, to tell others off, and to evidence a hostile reaction to people in general.

Hostility, which is directed inward, against the self, is not exclusively measured by this one trait score but may be reflected in an inferior score in any one or more of the other categories.

Trait I   **Self-Disciplined vs. Impulsive**

     Self-disciplined: Controlled, methodical, persevering.

     Impulsive: Uncontrolled, disorganized, changeable.

Neatness, orderliness, and the ability to organize and plan; to have endurance and perseverance, the inclination to set goals, make plans well in advance, to be methodical and deliberate, to keep things in place, to budget, to think before acting, to avoid frequent shifts of interest and goals, and to have good self-control is **Self-disciplined**.

The **Impulsive** tendency is hastiness in making decisions, vacillation, reduced ability to plan, a trend towards taking chances and easily tempted, to get into trouble because of hasty acts, as well as the inability to break bad habits.

A low level of self-discipline, (**Impulsive**) indicates poor control and, in some cases, a tendency to act out. Such individuals tend to sway, seldom follow through on projects, even those of their choosing, and are prone to change jobs frequently.

Impulsive individuals find it difficult to persevere in counseling or therapy.

From the material presented it is evident to see that the T-JTA and WIDP cannot be respectably compared due to the base differences of what they each measure. However, it is clear that the more reliable and dependable of the two for measuring fundamental needs and desires that are foundational to the individual is WIDP.

CHAPTER 16: WIDP vs. Myers-Briggs Type Indicator

(WIDP vs. MBTI)

The personality system presented here is known formally as **"Jung's theory of personality type"** (hereafter referred to as **"personality type/types/typing"**), first developed by Carl Jung in the early 1920's and more recently resurrected and made into a useful instrument by Myers and Briggs. Sometimes, this system referred to as the **"Myers-Briggs Type Indicator"** (or **MBTI**), but in a rigorous sense, the MBTI is a test vehicle for personality typing.

Personality typing is not used nor studied much within the psychiatric, research/academic, or psychological communities because it is, first, rejected by some schools of thought on fundamental philosophical grounds (e.g., cognitive psychology). Also, many counseling psychologists do not find it useful for their purposes because it does not measure mental health. However, this does not mean that practicing doctors eschew personality typing. Many counselors do use this system for their patients/clients, particularly for helping people to **"find themselves"** and similar, non-mental health-related purposes.

Outside of the psychological community, however, personality typing (typified by the MBTI) is the most widely used model of human personality. It is used extensively in career counseling and development, business, and education. Its penetration into these areas stems partly from the fact that it does not touch upon the tricky aspect of mental health, which are dealt with by trained counseling psychologists and psychiatrists.

In a nutshell, personality typing mostly assumes that our whole nature can be divided into four independent areas or scales: Energizing, Attending, Deciding, and Living (defined in detail below). Within each scale, we prefer one of two opposites that determine the range (also described below). A total of 16 different combinations (2x2x2x2), each of which represents one particular and unique personality type.

This summary will cover the following subjects:

1. Description of the Four Scales
2. Preferred Vocabulary for Each of the Four Scales
3. A Short Summary of the Sixteen Personality Types
4. Correlation of Personality Typing to the Four Temperaments
   The **"Four Temperaments"** comprise very well-known and often used models that divide up human personality into four major groups or temperaments. Hippocrates developed the first system in ancient Greece (where the four temperaments are better known as the Four Senses of Humour). Recently, there have been more modern and refined **"Four Temperament"** models, such as Keirsey and Bates, who found that the sixteen personality types can be summarized into four temperaments which parallel (if only approximately) the four Hippocratic senses of humor of Sanguine, Melancholic, Choleric and Phlegmatic.)

DESCRIPTION OF THE FOUR SCALES

In each of the following four scales, every person usually prefers one of the two different choices (designated by a letter). This does not mean that they do one to the exclusion of the other, most people go both ways depending on the circumstances. However, most people usually do have an overall preference. Where a person does not perceive a clear and resounding choice, the letter 'X' is used to designate this **"I don't know"** condition.

Important Note: The following scale descriptions are simplifications (and perilously close to oversimplification) of quite complex, rigorous, deep, and hard to understand reports presented by Jung (see recommended literature section for references).

1.   ENERGIZING   **How a person is energized:**

Extroversion	**(E)**	Preference for drawing energy from the outside world of individuals, activities, or things.
Introversion	**(I)**	Preference for drawing energy from one's internal world of ideas, emotions, or impressions.

Note: In a deeper sense, Energizing is only one facet of this scale It is a measure of a person's whole orientation towards either the inner world (I) or the outer world (E).

2.   ATTENDING   **What a person pays attention to:**

Sensing	**(S)**	Preference for taking in information through the five senses and noticing what is actual.
Intuition	**(N)**	Preference for taking in information through a "sixth sense" and seeing what might be; Jung calls this "unconscious perceiving".

3.   DECIDING   **How a person decides:**

Thinking	**(T)**	Preference for organizing and structuring information to decide in a logical, objective way.
Feeling	**(F)**	Preference for organizing and structuring information to decide in a personal, value-oriented way.

4.   **LIVING**   **Lifestyle a person adopts:**

Judgment   **(J)**   Preference for living a planned and organized life.

Perception   **(P)**   Preference for living a natural and flexible life.

Note: An alternative definition of this scale is "Closure: whether or not a person likes an open-ended lifestyle".

PREFERRED VOCABULARY FOR EACH OF THE FOUR SCALES

There seems to be a specific vocabulary associated with each preference for the four scales. By reading the word list on the left and the right for each scale and determining which list you like the sounds and meanings of the phrase better, may indicate your preference for that scale. This vocabulary list will also help you to understand better what the four scales measure or denote.

Also included with each scale is the percentages of the total population (in Western culture) who hold that preference; studies have shown the four scales to be substantially independent of one another.

EXTROVERSION | INTROVERSION PREFERRED VOCABULARY

Extroversion (E) 75% of Population	**Introversion (I) 25% of Population**
sociability	territorial
breadth	depth
external	internal
extensive	intensive
interaction	concentration
expenditure of energy	conservation of energy
interest in external events	interest in internal reaction
multiplicity of relationships	limited relationships

SENSING | INTUITION PREFERRED VOCABULARY

Sensing (S) 75% of Population	**Intuition (N) 25% of Population**
experience	hunches
past	future
realistic	speculative
perspiration	inspiration
actual	possible

down to earth	head in clouds
utility	fantasy
fact	fiction
practicality	ingenuity
sensible	imaginative

THINKING | FEELING PREFERRED VOCABULARY

Thinking (T) 50% of Population	Feeling (F) 50% of Population
objective	subjective
principles	values
policy	social values
laws	extenuating circumstances
criterion	intimacy
firmness	persuasion
impersonal	personal
justice	humane
categories	harmony
standards	good or bad
critique	appreciates
analysis	sympathy
allocation	devotion

JUDGEMENT | PERCEPTION PREFERRED VOCABULARY

Judgement (J) 50% of Population	Perception (P) 50% of Population
settled	pending
decided	gather more data
fixed	flexible
plan	adapt as you go
run one's life	let life happen
closure	open options
decision making	treasure hunting
planned	open-ended
completed	emergent
decisive	tentative
wrap it up	something will turn up
urgency	there's plenty of time
deadline	what deadline?
get show on the road	let's wait and see

A SHORT SUMMARY OF THE SIXTEEN PERSONALITY TYPES

The two preferences for each of the four scales give 16 different combinations (2x2x2x2). If one includes the 'X' preference (which means either the person has no clear-cut choice, or that they do not know it yet), there can be as many as 81 different combinations. However, each 'X' choice is usually handled by blending and carefully studying the two associated preferences. The order of designating the letters is: Energizing, Attending, Deciding, and Living

Here's a summary of the overall personality for each of the 16 types as determined from various studies:

ENFJ: **"Pedagogue"**   Outstanding leader of groups. Can be aggressive at helping others to be the best that they can be. 5% of the total population.

INFJ: **"Author"**   Strong drive and enjoyment to help others. Complex personality. 1% of the total population.

ENFP: **"Journalist"**   Uncanny sense of the motivations of others. Life is an exciting drama. 5% of the total population.

INFP: **"Questor"**   High capacity for caring. Calm and pleasant face to the world. High sense of honor derived from internal values. 1% of the total population.

ENTJ: **"Field Marshall"**   The basic driving force and need is to lead. Tend to seek a position of responsibility and enjoys being an executive. 5% of the total population.

INTJ: **"Scientist"**   Most self-confident and pragmatic of all the types. Decisions come very easily. A builder of systems and the applier of theoretical models. 1% of the total population.

ENTP: **"Inventor"**   Enthusiastic interest in everything and always sensitive to possibilities. Nonconformist and innovative. 5% of the total population.

INTP: **"Architect"**   Greatest precision in thought and language. Can readily discern contradictions and inconsistencies. The world exists primarily to be understood. 1% of the total population.

ESTJ: **"Administrator"**   Much in touch with the external environment. Very responsible. Pillar of strength. 13% of the total population.

ISTJ: **"Trustee"**   Decisiveness in practical affairs. Guardian of time-honored institutions. Dependable. 6% of the total population.

ESFJ:	**"Seller"**	Most sociable of all types. Nurturer of harmony. Outstanding host or hostesses. 13% of the total population.

ESFJ: **"Seller"**   Most sociable of all types. Nurturer of harmony. Outstanding host or hostesses. 13% of the total population.

ISFJ: **"Conservator"**   Desires to be of service and to minister to individual needs and is very loyal. 6% of the total population.

ESTP: **"Promotor"**   Action! When present, things begin to happen. Fiercely competitive. Entrepreneur. Often uses shock effect to get attention. Negotiator par excellence. 13% of the total population.

ESFP: **"Entertainer"**   Radiates attractive warmth and optimism. Smooth, witty, charming, clever. Fun to be with. Very generous. 13% of the total population.

ISTP: **"Artisan"**   Impulsive action. Life should be of impulse rather than of purpose. The action is an end in itself. Fearless, craves excitement, master of tools. 5% of the total population.

ISFP: **"Artist"**   Interested in the fine arts. Expression primarily through action or art form. The senses are keener than in other types. 5% of the total population.

CORRELATION OF PERSONALITY TYPING TO THE FOUR TEMPERAMENTS

Other systems have been developed to model human personality. The most well-known and often used ones are those that divide human personality into four major groups, or temperaments. Hippocrates in ancient Greece described the first four temperament system, also known as the **"Four Humours"**: Sanguine, Melancholic, Choleric, and Phlegmatic. More recently, Keirsey and Bates took the sixteen personality types and categorized them into four recognizable temperaments based on certain combinations of three of the four scales: SJ, SP, NT, and NF. Also, they named each temperament after a Greek god from mythological legends who best symbolized the personality attributes of that temperament: Epimetheus (SJ: **"Hindsight"**), Dionysius (SP: **"Let's Drink Wine"**), Prometheus (NT: **"Foresight"**), and Apollo (NF: **"Reach for the Sky"**).

Additional Data on Kiersey-Bates' and the Hippocratic Humours

There are some correlations between the Hippocratic Humours and the Keirsey-Bates temperaments, but the fit is nowhere near perfect. To complicate matters, the understood definitions of the Hippocratic Humours have, themselves, changed over time; there is no generally agreed upon definition. Thus, here we will focus on the Keirsey-Bates system and seek to correlate it to a modern description of the four Hippocratic Humours (as defined in the book Personality Plus by Florence Littauer) for a more general sense of contextual comparison.

(**Important Note**: The lists of focus/needs/beliefs/behaviors for each temperament are an aggregate list; this means that any one person of that temperament will exhibit or have only some of these attributes. The other two scales play a role in this.)

The Keirsey-Bates system is summarized as follows:

SJ: DUTY/COMMERCE/ECONOMIC (Epimetheus)

Key Focus/Emotional Need: Responsibility, Tradition, and To Maintain Order

Beliefs/Behaviors

1.   Conserves heritage and tradition or establishes new ones.
2.   Can be very analytic (especially 'T' types).
3.   Belief in the hierarchy; subordination and superordination.
4.   Rules; compelled to be bound and obligated.
5.   My duty is to serve, give, care, save, share.
6.   "Shoulds" & "Oughts"; "be prepared".
7.   Fosters and creates social units: clubs, church groups.
8.   Management Style: Traditionalist, Stabilizer, Consolidator.
9.   Most likely Hippocratic Humour (modern usage): Melancholic.
10.   Spiritual Style: St. Ignatius.

SP: JOY/ARTISTRY/AESTHETIC (Dionysus)

Key Focus/Emotional Need: Freedom, Independence, Spontaneity, and To Have Fun

Beliefs/Behaviors

1.   Impulsive.
2.   Can be very expressive (esp. if an 'E').
3.   To do what I want, when I want.
4.   Action to fulfill my current needs, impulses, not an investment for long term need.
5.   Works dramatically and quickly in a crisis.
6.   Hungers for action without constraints.
7.   Tremendous stamina.
8.   Management Style: Troubleshooter, Negotiator, Fire Fighter.
9.   Most likely Hippocratic Humour (modern usage): Sanguine.
10.   Spiritual Style: St. Francis of Assisi.

NT: SCIENCE/THEORETICAL (Prometheus)

Key Focus/Emotional Need: Competence, Knowledge, and To Lead and Control

Beliefs/Behaviors

1. Tries to understand "whys" of the universe (especially if a 'P').
2. Very demanding of self and others.
3. Goal setter.
4. A driver (especially if a 'J').
5. "Should have known" and "Should have done better."
6. Coolly objective; straightforward and logical in dealing with others.
7. Reluctance to state obvious; little redundancy in communications.
8. Work is for improvement, perfection, and proof of skills.
9. Love of knowledge.
10. Management Style: Visionary, Architect of Systems, Builder.
11. Most likely Hippocratic Humour (modern usage): Choleric (esp. if a 'J').
12. Spiritual Style: St. Thomas Aquinas.

NF: SPIRIT/ETHICS (Apollo)

Key Focus/Emotional Need: Search for Self, and Peace and Harmony

Beliefs/Behaviors

1. "How do I become the person I am?"
2. Value relationships.
3. Harmony with others can be very amiable.
4. The desire to inspire and persuade.
5. Need to live a life of significance.
6. Search for unique identity.
7. Tend to focus on the good in others.
8. Especially abhors "evil," if it violates cherished values.
9. Management Style: Catalyst, Spokesperson, Energizer.
10. Most likely Hippocratic Humour (modern usage): Phlegmatic.
11. Spiritual Style: St. Augustine.

CHAPTER 17: Temperament vs. Personality

(WIDP vs. DiSC)

The development of a person's Temperament, character, and their personality based upon the following three steps:

Step One: Genetic **TEMPERAMENT** make up was determined while you are in your mother's womb, that is **inborn or genetic.**

Step Two: Then comes the formation of your **CHARACTER** which you shape and design, affected by your family of origin and the influences of people, learned behavior, and your environment.

Step Three: Finally comes the formation of your **PERSONALITY** which is self-selected; a mask. You only reveal what you prefer others to see, the standard presentation we each present to those around us.

The DiSC Profile focuses on (and measures) personality. The DiSC only reveals the outward (observable) side of the person's personality, which is not the real person. Personality is a chosen mask presented to you based on what the person wishes to reveal to you about them.

Temperament, the intrinsic (subjective) self is what WIDP focuses on (and measures). Temperament is not alterable or fluid like the personality.   A person's Temperament is static despite their environmental focus. Therefore, an individual who understands their Temperament can understand themselves and their specific needs as well as those of others. Each person is extraordinary based upon their genetic/inborn makeup. God uniquely designs people.

AN OVERVIEW OF PERSONALITY

The design of personality training is to identify individual styles of personality in a certain setting or environmental focus, implying that your personality **changes** depending upon your environment.

They developed the Personal Profile System (DiSC) to increase understanding, acceptance, and respect for individual differences in the work or social environment, which has expanded to even more specific environmental habitats like Sales, Management, or other general Leader environments. Their system is based on the DiSC model of behavior as developed in the 1920s by William Moulton Marston and John Geier. This model identifies four distinct types of personalities people use to meet their needs and desires, depending on their environment. All people could use all four of these tendencies. However, individuals use some behaviors more than others.

We briefly define the four behavioral tendencies as:

D   **DOMINANCE:** People with a high **"D"** behavioral tendency seek to meet their needs by controlling their environment through direct, forceful action, often overcoming opposition in hostile or antagonistic situations.

i   **INFLUENCING:** People with a high **"I"** behavioral tendency seek to meet their needs by persuading others to work with them to accomplish results. They function effectively in favorable, supportive environments.

S   **STEADINESS:** People with a high **"S"** behavioral tendency seek to meet their needs by cooperating with others to carry out their respective tasks. They function effectively in stable and consistent environments.

C   **CAUTIOUSNESS:** People with a high **"C"** behavioral tendency seek to meet their needs by working with existing circumstances to provide quality and accuracy. They strive to achieve their standards for results, even in unfavorable environments.

Personality training deals with a person based on an environmental focus during evaluation. Persons answering the behavioral profile will respond one way

- as an employee
- as a spouse
- at the family picnic
- in a conflict situation
- in an intimate relationship.

The DiSC assessment process will give you five different personality profiles for the same person. Nevertheless, each requires the individual to fill out another separate questionnaire to evaluate each of the varying environmental focuses. In the examples above, the individual may have different or even significantly different results, as personality changes at will. When using DiSC for solutions to environmental problems, remember, the solutions are only good for that environment; temporary, at best.

DiSC is the **masked** approach which always creates a situation where others only see what an individual wants them to see. DiSC measures the self-selected image, it does not measure the true person behind the mask.

Chapter 18: The Contrast Between WIDP
vs.
Tim LaHaye's Temperament Assessment

(Chapter written in collaboration with Michael Brock)

Michael Brock attended a WIDP Seminar given in Atlanta, GA by Dr. John Worley. He shared some thoughts about what he learned that helped him resolve quite a few conflicts, which improved both his business and home environment as well as his relationships. He implemented his WIDP training into his business and facilitated communication within his home. I requested that Michael offer a viewpoint of comparison between WIDP and another tool he had encountered, Tim LaHaye's Temperament Assessment. This chapter contains a general overview of his thoughts and observations behind both tools. It is written primarily from his perspective to capture the personal essence of his experience with these tools.

TIM LAHAYE TEMPERAMENT ASSESSMENT

<u>Transforming Your Temperament</u> by Tim LaHaye (we'll just say "the book") contains temperament information and an assessment Mr. LaHaye created. The temperament info and the assessment itself are somewhat of a contrast to WIDP, though both are temperament assessments. The test in Mr. LaHaye's book simply did not go into as much depth as WIDP. The book does enable you to examine yourself, as does the WIDP Profile, but it does not allow you to get to the core of a person.

While the test in the book shows you how to evaluate yourself, you must, however, give the test to two people that know you so that they can assess you, also. Once the evaluations have been completed you mail them to Mr. LaHaye and he sends you your profile description. His profile descriptions are like the WIDP Profile, but there are some significant differences. Mr. LaHaye's temperament descriptions imply that the four temperament descriptions that exist may overlap. He feels that a person can have more than one temperament type, they can overlap, and there could even be multiples. For example, Mr. LaHaye represents that you could have the traits of a Melancholy Choleric that are Sanguine Choleric or Phlegmatic Melancholy.

Mr. LaHaye's chart is broken down in certain parts where I could not understand them, so explaining these to others or marketing them in the business arena isn't possible, at least, not by me. Furthermore, I don't agree with this part about letting your friends examine you. There's no way to ensure they are grading you from a truthful standpoint but could simply classify you certain ways simply because they are your friends – obviously this would skew results. While I'm sure this could be considered as a tool for hiring, this would not bring quality results, as accurate results rely on too many other people.

Logically, when you are taking any test, it should be to see what you know, not to confuse you. Mr. LaHaye's profile does not get directly to the point and the profile was hard to retain. Some parts of the book I did not understand, either. Time is another significant factor as his test was lengthy, which you do not know since there is no example of how long or short the exam is until you take it. There were some areas in the book that were very good, but others needed significant improvement.

Temperament plays a significant role in our lives and lifestyle. In Mr. LaHaye's book it broke down lifestyle areas such as our eating habits. He stated that he could tell your temperament type by how and what we eat. He says that a Melancholy is a very picky eater and takes forever to make decisions. I do not believe that at all. He mentions driving skills which at times we are all crazy drivers in that area where you have much research. One point he stated was that a Melancholy always leaves home well prepared, but I am quite the opposite and love an adventure here or there on a whim. He also says a Melancholy is tough to please and I don't really see that either. While I am not a perfectionist, I do expect everyone to give their all, and then there won't be problems with me.

The book also has a standard I.Q. test that you can take. I am not sure if the accuracy rate is good, and I do not think it is an impressionable item for valuable takeaways. It has thirty different vocations, which is quite a lot to pick and choose. The vocations are ones to work within a church setting, but I'd rather operate with the intention to just take the gifts you have a use those productively no matter where you are.

In terms of weaknesses, Mr. LaHaye's book states that we have weaknesses and then he gives you suggestions on how to better control them. This is starkly different than WIDP which does not emphasize strengths or weaknesses in the traditional sense, but rather provides probable strengths and potential weaknesses, which have a very specific context. WIDP does not direct you to work on your weaknesses.

Mr. LaHaye gives good illustrations of how temperament influences the way we act. He states that Sanguine is very loud and hard to get along with, but I know some individuals that have this temperament and are entertaining, loving people. I do have to agree with him that some of them are overly expressive and that they take a little fish story and turn it into one of the largest you have ever thought of or heard.

His perspective on opposites attracting was a hard chapter to understand, but it did make me realize that willingness of both people is paramount, and adjustment is always needed when you bring two lives and hearts together.

The WIDP Profile and Mr. LaHaye's book did an outstanding job in talking about the different temperaments, in their own way. While different, they did offer ways to help you identify and understand more about yourself from a temperament perspective. For example, they both let you know how your leadership skills compare to what you think of yourself as a leader and if you are correct. Some individuals believe that they are leaders but are followers. They also give different insight into the perception of others. At times we may get self-centered and engulfed in our world. For me, it helped immensely in these areas and gave me one of the most excellent tools to use in the workplace. It changed so many things around and gave me a peace of mind to look at people and know why they do what they do.

Based on these factors, and knowing that WIDP exists, I would not recommend Mr. LaHaye's test. With that, it might be helpful to talk about how WIDP is different in more detail.

AN HONEST LOOK AT WIDP, IN COMPARISON

Before the creation of WIDP Profile, there was nothing out there that was respectable enough for me to critique as far as being good or bad in identifying the real person's intrinsic needs and desires. They all focus on personality, behavior, or character. The WIDP Profile assessment is the best resource I have seen so far focusing on your temperament.

The notable factor that separates the two profiles, for me, is that WIDP gives immediate results and Mr. LaHaye's does not. Mr. LaHaye's Profile does give you suggestions after you take the test, but the WIDP Profile breaks everything down immediately.

I do feel that getting carried away with the results of WIDP Profile could be self-destructive. I could give anyone a temperament test to see what their numbers are and just totally let that control the way I think about everything; that is how powerful this profile is. We do have to be careful who gets their hands on these tests. Someone that has low self-esteem could be taken to an all-time low after taking this test. I believe the WIDP Profile will revolutionize the way the whole world thinks because WIDP can make a believer out of you. The information is so fulfilling and validating that it helps you instantly. It will even work on those of us who like to pretend that things are all right all the time and are just outstanding actors. WIDP can penetrate the surface and make you take a good and hard look at yourself.

Anyone can take this test, which is excellent, as there are no excuses about it being too difficult. It is simple, and it takes about 10 minutes. It brought me such insight about my own temperament type, causing me to recognize little things I do that confirmed deep within me what I was reading in my temperament description. I respect people more and can understand their weak areas as well as my own.

WIDP used in the workplace brings incredible insight to assist in assessing current employees. This tool assisted me with dealing with my boss and other business associates. You can also use this tool for the hiring of new employees; all companies need help in this area. Immediately after taking the test you can see and assess the results, rather than making a bad hiring decision and realizing months later it was a mistake and a bad investment (and then starting over). Using WIDP will enable you to hire positive people, as well as people that can take you to new heights and make your business shine.

WIDP is designed to help us understand our strengths and our weak areas. Just the awareness of both gave me knowledge that I can use to benefit myself and my family. Even in friendships, it helped me appreciate how to relate with people better; we all need someone to talk with and share ideas that we have. WIDP is an essential reference tool to pull out for life situations. And when a person obtains useful information like this, it should be shared with others.

When interacting with others, some people may envy you and others may not like anything about you. Those people may not necessarily be good or healthy people and set out to harm you, so it is crucial that we understand what motivates people in healthy ways and what happens when someone is in their worst form. The WIDP Profile insight is meant for you to know yourself and others, but also to develop. We need to have compassion for each other and not criticize each other when we find out others' temperament type(s).

The WIDP Profile also helps me with communicating socially, which I don't do naturally well. My Social Numbers are 00, which means that I do not need to socialize, and I do not need affirmation from people, especially those I don't know. I realize interaction happens at times, unavoidably, like at work. Relating better to others is vital to effective communication, especially being in a management position, as I am. I must be able to talk to my employees, I don't have the luxury to go into the office first thing in the morning and not speak to anyone. Aware of this, I worked on how to break the ice and continue conversations from there. Socially, I accepted that to have friends does take being friendly.

The WIDP Profile can help you with your close relationships as well; the way you respond to things/people is the key. Personally, it enhanced the foundation of my marriage and made my wife and I take a whole different approach to the way we respond to each other and solve disagreements. It enabled us to counsel each other and hold to our common belief of not letting the sun go down before we resolve any problems we may have.

I also understand that before I have a relationship with anyone, I have first to love myself so that I can give that love to someone else. When you find out that you need help in an area, some people may not want to admit they have such problems. But humbling yourself and sitting down with your spouse and asking them if any of their needs are not met is vulnerable yet can also open the door in helping you get your needs met as well. These things are not for the faint of heart, but possible when you know what to ask and what to do with their answer. If, in these conversations, I find she isn't getting her needs met, or I'm not getting my needs met, we become aware that we are likely looking elsewhere to get them fulfilled. This knowledge is a tool that's part of our everyday life. The same is true about people not getting their needs met in the workplace, and would significantly reduce turnover, for positive short- and long-term effects.

Depression is an interesting side issue. In Mr. LaHaye's book, he talks about how to overcome your weaknesses. It is broken down into strengths, weaknesses, spiritual weaknesses, and other temperament types. It does not help you address or resolve anything in the areas of depression or esteem. I think WIDP addresses depression, but certainly indirectly. Many people do not like to face their problems and end up with a lot of self-pity. Rather than blaming how we were raised or that our environment isn't cooperative, WIDP helps look at the things that are intrinsic to empower an individual to take accountability with awareness in those areas. Consequently, we can reflect on past events and gain more of a realistic perspective of what was really going on. This can assist us in moving toward forgiveness of self or of others in those areas, just by awareness of who we truly are. The Profile helps us get beyond just ourselves all the time and see the big picture of people. We can all learn from each other and help build each other up.

The WIDP Profile is based on two scores in three main areas. The two scores are the demonstrated score and the desired score. The demonstrated score in the WIDP Profile was especially helpful to me, which indicates how I act toward other people most comfortably. If your demonstrated score is lower, which my number is, I tend protect the private environment that I have around me especially when I get off work. This privacy is very important to me.

The demonstrated (toward others) and desired (from others) is a perfectly simple concept to understand, but the gap complex could really interfere with people. A gap complex describes someone that may give more than they need or not being able to give but needing a large amount (it could be social, or it could be emotional interaction in deep relationships). This means they are really torn inside themselves, or they may be fine but have a gap with other people, which is why there is conflict between people. Mr. LaHaye's book, in contrast, does not have any of these concepts.

IN SUMMARY

My overall comparison is that the WIDP gives a lot of information about who you are and allows you to understand more in depth why you do what you do. It goes to the core of your makeup to find what God put inside of you. A personality can be formed, but temperament is who you are at your creation – your intrinsic design.

I was delighted that Dr. Worley enriched us with his teaching on the WIDP Profile at the seminar. It changed my thinking in many areas of my life. As a result, I don't walk around just picking people apart anymore. While some may take personality tests and use the information like a sword, which they could do with WIDP also, that isn't the wisest use of the information. It has been beneficial taking the WIDP to find out that my temperament is not just a smooth blend of two personality types but a trio within social, leadership, and relationship areas. Understanding that a person may have a different temperament in each of these areas would explain why we do not act the same way at work as we do at play or home. It isn't just a different face, there could be entirely different needs involved.

WIDP does not address personality type which is interesting compared to a lot of other assessments. It may be a little confusing at first when you take WIDP if you have already experienced different types of assessments, but I have found that it seems to be pretty accurate. Don't get me wrong, Mr. LaHaye's book is not entirely off the mark, it just is not quite as in-depth as WIDP, and not nearly as useful. Any tool can give you some quick lightbulb moments. The more information you can find to help understand yourself and others more accurately, the better off you are.

The overall approach of both profiles is to help people, that's clear. A person could have different impacts from the tools in their own experience and usefulness really depends on each person's desire and willingness. It is undeniable that a lot of time and research has been put into both resources. For me overall, WIDP provides more efficient and reliable information, more areas are covered, and succinctly pinpointed.

Parental/Adult vs. Peer Dependency in High School Students' Feedback, Preferences, and Agreement Relating to

Worley's ID Profile Temperament Information

RESEARCH DESIGN

Chapter 19: High School Research Project

(This project was conducted by a college Senior)

Abstract

The study was conducted to determine if freshman/sophomore and junior/senior high school students sought parental/adult feedback or peer feedback concerning the information they received from a temperament assessment instrument, as well as whether students agreed more with a parental/adult rating of assessment accuracy or with peer evaluation of assessment accuracy. Data raises questions about, and further suggests, research around issues of adolescent development including identity formation, parental vs. peer dependency, and handling of non-social information.

Introduction

Temperament as a general construct refers to a broad array of behavioral traits that are thought to be biologically rooted and first appearing (Bates, Dodge, Pettit, & Ridge, 1998). Temperamental characteristics are present early in life, are stable over time, and are related to biological factors (Capaldi & Rothbart, 1992 and Thomas & Chess, 1977, both as cited in Stice & Gonzales, 1998). Temperament is purported to be the foundation for personality (Buss & Plomin, 1984, as mentioned in Stice & Gonzales, 1998).

Worley's ID Profile, or WIDP, assesses an individual's Temperament based on an update of Hippocrates's theory while retaining his basic terminology, including Sanguine, Phlegmatic, Melancholy, Choleric, and the most recently discovered classification, Introverted Sanguine. Each Temperament type or derived blend defines a person's unique needs, desires, differences, and preferences. Dr. Worley, the developer of the WIDP, describes Temperament as an individual's inborn subjective self – his/her unique desires and needs – who one is. Personality is defined as the aspects of a person's Temperament chosen to present to society. In this model, demonstrated behavior (personality) is only one aspect of a person – desired behavior (Temperament) is the part of a person that cannot be observed – it can only be determined by testing the individual (Worley, 1998).

The Health Examination Survey (HES) (Wells, 1980, as cited in Katainen, Raikkonen, Keskivaara, & Keltikangas-Jarvinen, 1999), a questionnaire designed for use by non-professionals to screen children for potential behavioral problems. It measures behavioral components that relate conceptually to the Temperament dimensions described by Buss and Plomin (1975, as cited in Katainen et al., 1999). This instrument assesses an individual primarily through observed behavior (personality), equating personality with Temperament, even though the research on which this assessment is based asserts that Temperament is the basis for personality. Much research, utilizing the term Temperament, looks for the underlying 'nature' factors of negative behavior; (Rothbart & Ahadi, 1994; Tarter, Kabene, Escallier, Laird, & Jacob, 1990; Thomas & Chess, 1977; Watson & Clark, 1993; Kochanska, 1991; Gray, 1987; all as cited in Stice & Gonzales, 1998).

The WIDP is particularly unique in the category of Temperament assessments. WIDP distinguishes between Temperament and personality and does not represent any Temperament type as 'right' or 'wrong,' or desirable (Worley, 1998).

The developmental theory states that stable identity formation is the primary task of adolescence according to Erikson (1959/1980, as cited in Kerpelman, Pittman, & Lamke, 1997). Resolving the identity vs. identity confusion stage depends on repeated explorations and commitments in the context of an individual's emotional development, close relationships, and current societal norms (Marcia, 1966, and Kroger, 1989, both as cited in Kerpelman et al., 1997). Young adolescents indicate family having more importance than other relationships, but this family influence diminishes in older adolescents. Parents are viewed as less relevant than peers as teenagers become independent adults (Furman & Buhrmester, 1985,1992; and Cotterell, 1992, all as cited in O'Koon, 1997). A case can be made that high school juniors and seniors will seek feedback more frequently from their peers than parents/adults about their WIDP and that high school first-year students and sophomores will seek input more often from relatives/adults than peers about their WIDP. (Hypothesis 1).

Findings indicate that in issues relating to morals, values, education, occupation, and other nonsocial matters that adolescents overall are more strongly influenced by parents and other adults than by peers (Richardson, Abramowitz, Asp, & Petersen, 1986 and Sebald, 1984 and Phelan, Yu, & Davidson, 1994. All as cited in Wilson & MacGillivray, 1998). Since the WIDP assesses Temperament, a personal aspect of an individual, it's expected that high school students will be more in agreement with parents/adults than with their peers about the accuracy of their WIDP Profile results. (Hypothesis 2)

Friendship is considered a critical part of adolescent development and may even be the most significant relationship for a teen during the transition from child to adult, contributing importantly to the emergence and development of ego identity (Berndt, 1982 and Youniss, 1980 and Youniss & Smollar, 1985, all as cited in Akers, Jones, & Coyle, 1998). Many similarities between young friends have been documented including grade level, age, gender, religion, ethnicity, specific behaviors (i.e., substance use), school attitudes, college plans, and academic achievement (Kandel, 1978a, and Epstein, 1983, both as cited in Akers et al., 1998). Combining Youniss and Smollar's assertion, that it is by way of interpersonal relationship and social construction, that an adolescent develops their social sense of self, with the similarities between friends in psychological and behavioral characteristics (Kandel, 1978 a; 1978 b as cited in Akers et al., 1998). Within relationships between mental, behavioral, and identity characteristics (Bourne 1978a, and 1978b, both as cited in Akers et al., 1998), a possible conclusion is that young friends share similarities in identity development. Therefore, contrary to Hypothesis 2, a position can be taken that high school students will be more in agreement with peers than parents/adults about the accuracy of their WIDP. (Hypothesis 3).

Method (Subjects)

The subjects for this study consisted of 42 students in grades 9-12 drawn from the high school population of a private Christian school in rural New England. The sample included 28 females, 14 males, 20 first-year students/sophomores, and 22 juniors/seniors. 21 of the students lived in campus dorms, and 21 lived at home and commuted to school. After the principal permitted to conduct the research, project information with an attached permission slip was provided for distribution to the parents of each high school student.

Convenience sampling was the basis of the choice of school; this was necessary due to time constraints of the project and the difficulty of finding high schools that were willing to participate in the project. The participating school was selected based on proximity and willingness to engage. The subjects were not randomly chosen since all students were given the opportunity to participate; students without signed permission, absent, or preferring not to attend were not included. Sampling bias was evident because participants were voluntary and only recruited from one high school; therefore, they are not representative of the general high school population.

Materials

Each high school student who chose to participate and had a signed permission slip received a copy of the initial questionnaire packet, which included a cover sheet (A) and two questionnaires: a pre-assessment form (B) and the WIDP questionnaire (C), all of which were attached. The cover sheet included the title of the project, "WIDP Project," as explained in the informational sheet given to the parents. The pre-assessment form was a self-report of Temperament attributes; the WIDP a 60-item inventory relating to social, leadership, and personal relationship preferences.

Each participant's WIDP generated a personal profile, which was returned to students one week later, along with a brief explanatory note (D). One additional week later a follow-up questionnaire was administered to the subjects. Each student that participated in the first phase was given a follow-up packet. The package included a cover sheet (A) their original pre-assessment form with the results of their WIDP profile; recorded at the bottom (B) a page listing the Temperament types and characteristics for reference (E) and the Follow-Up Questionnaire relating to the perceived accuracy and usefulness of the WIDP profile (F).

Research Design

The research design of this project used attitude tests in questionnaire format. The WIDP is a 60-item inventory that generates a detailed summary of individual Temperament. The items are divided into six scales, corresponding to demonstrated and desired behaviors for social, leadership, and relationship assessment categories. However, they appear on the form as 33 questions relating to frequency and 27 questions relating to quantity. A frequency or number choice from 1 (low) to 6 (high) is chosen to answer each of the 60 items, which can be answered directly on the computer program or a printed questionnaire and entered into the computer later. The questionnaire takes approximately 10 minutes to complete. After the computer scores it, an interpretive report is generated for the individual.

A Test-Retest administration assessed the instrument's reliability with a *four*-month interval between two assessments. The Test-Retest yielded a reasonable relationship between scores on the six scales of the WIDP across the two administrations of r = .7 (Pearson Product Moment Correlation). This score compares very favorably to average scores for similar instruments, which usually fall between .7 and .8 over a *one*-month period. Also, a Measure of Internal Consistency was performed, yielding an average internal consistency score for the six scales of KR-20 = .54 (Kuder-Richardson Formula 20) comparing quite favorably to the MMPI validity score of .52.

Comparing the WIDP scores of people not in counseling with those of people diagnosed with specific psychological problems by clinical psychologists assessed the concurrent validity of the WIDP. Behavior patterns recognized by the psychological community for diagnosable issues were demonstrated by mean scale scores found on the WIDP. Problem diagnoses included: major depression, obsessive-compulsive disorder, alcohol dependence, and marital problems. While the WIDP is not to be used as a clinical diagnostic tool, the results of the comparisons indicate that the scales have concurrent validity. Also, the Rosenberg Self-Esteem Measure was administered to a sample of healthy (non-counseling, non-diagnosed) individuals who also took the WIDP. Dr. Worley's contention that healthy people can present many different scores on the six scales was supported by 5 of the scales correlating at almost zero, indicating no relationship, and only the Desired Leadership scale relating marginally to self-esteem. The lack of correlation means that the scales measure different types of efficient functioning, and that self-esteem is not tied to any of the Temperaments found on any of the scales themselves.

The Follow-Up Questionnaire (F) included nine questions. A 4-point Likert scale was used to score the first three questions; the remaining issues included two closed, two open-ended, and two modified Thurstone-type questions. Only items 2 and three were utilized in this study. Three pieces of information were gathered from these questions: how much each student agreed with their profile; who else (if anyone) the students showed their profile information to; and how much each other person agreed with the student's profile. The range of responses rated the amount of agreement from "not much" to "almost all." Due to time constraints, a pre-study administration of the questions was not conducted. Descriptive information regarding the results of questions 2 and 3, as well as the provided demographic data, was obtained. A frequency analysis was performed to compare the persons to whom first-year students/sophomore showed their profiles and the persons to whom junior/senior showed their profiles.

Further comparisons were made between dorm and town students, as accessibility to parents was an essential factor in assessing parental and peer dependency. The amount of subject agreement with the profile was measured using the Score from question 2; the sum of others' agreement with the profile was measured using the Score from question 3. An analysis of variance was completed to determine whether subjects' perception of WIDP accuracy was more in agreement with parents/adults' or peers' assessment of WIDP accuracy.

Procedure

Subjects were obtained by calling local high schools. Two granted informational interviews; one agreed to allow testing. The school set the dates for the administration of the two-wave research surveys; each wave conducted in one morning. Each grade was studied each time individually.

The researcher before the administration of the surveys did not contact individual teachers but estimates of the time required (30 minutes for the first wave, 15 for the second) were given to the principal. Participation from the entire high school (70 students) was sought; 53 permission slips were obtained. The experimental mortality was 11; 3 did not complete the first wave due to absence; 1 chose not to participate; 5 did not complete the second wave due to absence; 1 student did not receive a personal profile due to researcher oversight, and one student skipped the questions pertinent to this project. 42 subjects remained in the study.

Efforts were made to avoid response bias by standardizing the administration of the surveys to each class. After survey packets had been distributed, a brief, pre-written explanation regarding the general purpose of the research, and step-by-step instructions were read at each administration of the questionnaires to each class. Subjects were asked to respect the privacy of other students by not looking at other papers and by not talking. Participants were thanked for their participation at the end of each session.

Since this study was conducted in a naturalistic setting and without random sampling, it is believed essential to note variables that may affect the results. All subjects participated between 8 AM and 11:30 AM on each of the two days. Some were given at the beginning of class, while others were done at the end of class. While the first wave was administered on a regular mid-week school day, the second wave was administrated on the Friday after a late-night formal banquet and on the morning of the final half-day before a traditional holiday concert and dismissal for semester break. Teachers in whose classes the surveys were administered were equally gracious on each administration day.

Ethics

Informed consent obtained through parental/guardian permission forms distributed to each high school student before the surveys. The permission slip informed the parents/guardians that a Fitchburg State College student carried out the study and that the project included the WIDP and a follow-up survey about the accuracy and usefulness of the profile.

The directions read to each class before participating in the study informed them that participation was voluntary and that they could stop participating in the project at any time. The subjects were advised that some questions could potentially be upsetting. However, all questionnaires, as well as sample profile results, were reviewed by the course professor, a Ph.D. researcher, and Clinician; the practicum supervisor and developer of the WIDP, a Licensed Psychologist; the school principal; all deemed the materials appropriate for the students.

Confidentiality was established by use of a cover sheet on each survey packet, returning the profiles to students in sealed envelopes, and removing the names from questionnaires before the data was read and analyzed. Anonymity was a more complex issue. Because the research was conducted in two waves, and the second wave was dependent on the subjects referencing the questionnaires they had completed in the first wave, it was necessary to have the participants put their names on the surveys. The completed questionnaire sets were subsequently matched, numbered 1-49, moralized subjects were dropped, names removed, and only then was the raw data read and analyzed.

Some mild deception was employed. The subjects were not informed of the focus of this study: to whom they showed their results and how accurate the subjects believed their profiles were compared to how sure others thought their profiles were. We thought this was necessary so that the subjects are not overly concerned about whom they showed their profiles to or how much in agreement they agreed with the profile, and therefore tried to obtain feedback that the researcher might consider desirable or undesirable. In a general informational sheet that accompanied the results of the profile, one sentence encouraged the respondents to share their findings with people who knew them well, but this suggestion was not especially emphasized and constituted an appropriate recommendation for minors dealing with personal information.

Results

While the participants in this study were all high school students, the demographic information obtained indicates that they are not representative of all high school students specifically regarding the type of secondary school attended, residential status, and regional distribution. The high school is private and Christian; some students live at home while others live in campus dorms; most student families live in New England.

A descriptive analysis of the data obtained from the portion of question 3 relating to whom subjects showed their WIDP Profile was done using a frequency distribution in cross-tabulation form. Subjects' possible choices included 'no one,' 'mother,' 'father,' 'sibling,' 'friend,' 'adult.' (See Appendix F). ('Sibling' was dropped from analysis due to very few responses and lack of relevance to this study.) Subjects were encouraged to list additional people to whom they showed their profile if insufficient spaces were designated on the form. Table 1 compares all first-year students/sophomore students to all junior/senior students. The freshmen and sophomores showed their profiles most to their "friends only" or "parents/adults and friends". These two categories each captured 40% of the respondents. The distant third group was, "no one" at 15%, and lastly, was "parents/adults only" at 5%. Jr/Sr showed their profiles most frequently to 'no one,' at 36%; the second category was 'friends only' at 32%; third was 'parents/adults and friends,' at 18%, and last was 'parents/adults only,' at 14%.

Table 2 compares town first-year students/sophomore to town junior/senior, and Table 3 compares dorm first-year students/sophomore to dorm junior/senior. Because most dorm students did not have access to their parents between the survey dates, 'parent' and 'adult' categories were combined for all statistics, and the descriptive data was separated into dorm and town student groups to highlight any differences between the groups. The data distributions for both the town and dorm students were very similar to the combined group, the notable exception being that none of the dorm students showed their profiles exclusively to parents/adults. Table 4 compares first-year students/sophomore and junior/senior ranking of persons shown their profiles. Differences in classification and percentages were observed between subject groupings; the first-year students/sophomore ranking most closely resembled the overall classification.

A Chi-square test was done using data from the portion of question 3 relating to the people subjects showed their WIDP profile. The categories of first-year students/sophomore and junior/senior were compared to whom they showed their WIDP results to parents/adults *and* friends, friends only, and a combination cell of parents/adults just and no one, yielding a 2x3 contingency table. All cell frequencies were over 5, but the chi-square value was not significant at the .05 probability level, failing to support hypothesis 1.

TABLES

Table 1

Frequency and Percentages of Persons Shown WIDP Profile Results by High School Freshmen/Sophomores and Juniors/Seniors

Persons showed profile	Freshmen and Sophomores		Juniors and Seniors		Total	
	N	%	N	%	N	%
Parents/adults and friends	8	40	4	18	12	29
Friends only	8	40	7	32	15	36
Parents/adults only	1	5	3	14	4	10
No one	3	15	8	36	11	26
Totals	**20**	**100**	**22**	**100**	**42**	**101**

Note: Percentages may not add to exactly 100% due to rounding.

Table 2

Frequency and Percentages of Persons Shown WIDP Profile Results by High School Town Freshmen/Sophomores and Juniors/Seniors

Persons showed profile	Freshmen and Sophomores		Juniors and Seniors		Total	
	N	%	N	%	N	%
Parents/adults and friends	4	45	2	17	6	29
Friends only	3	33	3	25	6	29
Parents/adults only	1	11	3	25	4	19
No one	1	11	4	33	5	24
Totals	**9**	**100**	**12**	**100**	**21**	**101**

Note: Percentages may not add to exactly 100% due to rounding

Table 3

Frequency and Percentages of Persons Shown WIDP Profile Results by High School Dorm Freshmen/Sophomores and Juniors/Seniors

Persons showed profile	Freshmen and Sophomores		Juniors and Seniors		Total	
	N	%	N	%	N	%
Parents/adults and friends	4	36	2	20	6	29
Friends only	5	46	4	40	9	43
Parents/adults only	0	0	0	0	0	0
No one	2	18	4	40	6	29
Totals	**11**	**100**	**10**	**100**	**21**	**101**

Note: Percentages may not add to exactly 100% due to rounding.

Table 4

Ranking and Percentages of Persons Shown WIDP Profile Results by High School Freshmen/Sophomores and Juniors/Seniors

Rank	Freshmen and Sophomores		Juniors and Seniors		Total	
		%		%		%
1	Friends only *(Tie)*	40	No one	36	Friends only	36
2	Parents/adults and friends	40	Friends only	32	Parents/adults and friends	29
3	No one	15	Parents/adults and friends	18	No one	26
4	Parents/adults only	5	Parents/adults only	14	Parents/adults only	10
	Totals	**100**		**100**		**101**

Note: Percentages may not add to exactly 100% due to rounding.

A descriptive analysis of the data obtained from question 2 and the portion of question 3 that reported the amount of agreement with the WIDP profile subjects, as well as those who read their profile, was done using measures of central tendency and measures of variability (Table 5). In question 2, the three sections of the profile were each scored on a scale ranging through four options: 'not much,' 'some,' 'a lot,' to 'almost all'. The choices were each assigned a numerical value of 2, 4, 6, or 8, with the least (2) corresponding to 'not much,' up to the most (8) corresponding to 'almost all.' The numerical values chosen for the three sections were averaged, yielding one score for the overall perceived accuracy of the WIDP to the subjects themselves. In question 3, the subjects also reported the amount of agreement other people had with the subjects' profile corresponding to the same scale of equal numerical values. The three sections of the profile were not scored individually in this question. Rather, the perceived accuracy of the entire profile was rated once. Multiple scores within the parent/adult or friend categories for each profile were averaged to obtain one score for each group. There was a possible high score of 8 and a possible low score of 2. High scores indicate that the individual or group was more in agreement with the WIDP Profile results. This data was broken down into several measures of central tendency and variability analyses as follows:

All profiles:

Table 5 - Profiles rated by subjects, parents/adults, and friends
Table 6 - Profiles rated by subjects and friends
Table 7 - Profiles rated by subjects and parents/adults
Table 8 - Profiles rated by subjects only
Table 9 - Profiles rated by subjects and any other group(s)
Table 10 - Mean accuracy score for subjects was highest on the profiles that only parents/adults reviewed; the subjects' mean accuracy score was lowest on the profiles that were not shown to anyone else.

A one-way ANOVA of the data from question 2 and the portion of question 3 that reported the amount of agreement with the WIDP profile subjects as well as those who read their profiles was conducted. Profiles shown to both parents/adults and friends (Table 6) were included in this analysis. The amount of agreement with the WIDP profile as reported by the subjects, parents/adults who reviewed their profiles, and friends who examined these same profiles were analyzed for significant variation. The F ratio was not statistically significant at the .05 probability level, failing to support either hypothesis 2 or hypothesis 3.

Table 5

Measures of Central Tendency and Variability in Agreement Scores for All Profiles

Profile raters	Mean	Median	Mode	Range	SD
Subjects **N = 41**	5.1	5.3	6	6	1.6
Parents/Adults **N = 15**	5.8	6	6	6	1.9
Friends **N = 26**	4.7	4	4	6	1.7

Note: N indicates the number of PROFILES rated by rating group, NOT the number of persons who rated profiles; the exception being several in the Subjects group.

Table 6

Measures of Central Tendency and Variability in Agreement Scores for Profiles rated by Subjects, Parents/Adults, and Friends

Profile raters	Mean	Median	Mode	Range	SD
Subjects **N = 11**	5.9	6	6	4.7	1.3
Parents/Adults **N = 11**	5.5	6	6	6	2.1
Friends **N = 11**	5.1	5.3	4	6	1.6

Note: N indicates the number of PROFILES rated by rating group, NOT the number of persons who rated profiles; the exception being several in the Subjects group.

Table 7

Measures of Central Tendency Variability in Agreement Scores for Profiles rated by Subjects and Friends

Profile raters	Mean	Median	Mode	Range	SD
Subjects	4.9	5.3	2.6	5.4	1.5
N = 15			**5.3**		
			6		
Friends	4.4	4	4	6	1.7
N = 15					

Note: N indicates the number of PROFILES rated by rating group, NOT the number of persons who rated profiles; the exception being several in the Subjects group.

Table 8

Measures of Central Tendency and Variability in Agreement Scores for Profiles rated by Subjects and Parents/Adults

Profile raters	Mean	Median	Mode	Range	SD
Subjects	6	6.3	6.6	2	.8
N = 4					
Parents/Adults	6.5	6	6	2	.9
N = 4					

Note: N indicates the number of PROFILES rated by rating group, NOT the number of persons who rated profiles; the exception being several in the Subjects group.

Table 9

Measures of Central Tendency and Variability in Agreement Scores for Profiles rated by Subjects Only

Profile raters	Mean	Median	Mode	Range	SD
Subjects	4.4	4	3.3	6	1.8
N = 11			5.3		

Note: N equals number of profiles AND number of persons who rated profiles.

Table 10

Measures of Central Tendency and Variability in Agreement Scores for Subjects whose Profiles were rated by Others

Profile raters	Mean	Median	Mode	Range	SD
Subjects	5.4	6	6	5.4	1.5
N = 30					

Note: N equals number of profiles AND number of persons who rated profiles.

Summary and Discussion

The goals of this study, to determine how high school students handled the personal information generated by the WIDP Temperament assessment, specifically by noting with whom they shared that information and by measuring with whom they agreed more, were met to some extent. Having ascertained the presence of parental/adult vs. peer dependency issues, and the shifts during adolescence through referral to theory and earlier studies, this research emphasized frequencies with which parents/adults or peers were sought and measurements of agreement with parents/adults or peers. While data obtained indicated that some shifts in dependency might be present and a deal was possibly influenced by whom subjects showed their profiles to, no statistically significant relationships were found to exist.

This study was limited by several factors that need consideration when discussing the data that was obtained. Time restrictions affected the setting of the survey such that the composition of the sample; in the short time available, only included one high school that agreed to allow the research to be conducted. Time was also a factor in obtaining signed consent from parents/guardians. The school distributed and collected the slips, however, quite a few were not returned, and so some potential subjects did not participate in the study. Time was an essential factor in the scheduling of the two sessions required to complete this study. It had been hoped that the first wave could have been conducted in mid-November, which would have allowed for the profile results to be returned to the subjects before Thanksgiving vacation, giving an opportunity for dorm students to share the results with parents/adults.

Although the school contacted and permission for the study was granted in plenty of time, administrative circumstances were such that scheduling could not start until the first week of December. Because of the time required for profiles to be generated by the subjects and the need to allow them time to read and share them if desired, the second wave of the research could not be scheduled until right before semester break. Unfortunately, the only option for this second wave was the morning after a late-night school event and on the last day of classes before semester breaks. Also, this was a half-day that included a vocal concert to be given by the high school soon after the administration of the survey. Subject mortality was already evident, as several students had left for the airport; the remaining students were noticeably tired and anxious to leave school as soon as possible. While the first wave was administered to students who appeared rested and happy for a break from their regular classes, the second wave confronted students who were exhausted and less than thrilled about yet one more task to be completed before they could go home. Since the research project was mainly dependent on the responses to the second wave questionnaire, the circumstances noted on the day in question may have affected the results.

The absence of reliability and validity for the Follow-Up Questionnaire imply that the tool of measurement used may not be an accurate indicator of whom subjects showed their profiles and the perceived accuracy of the profiles. It should be noted that all responses were self-reported; it was not within the parameters of this study to obtain independent checks on perceived accuracy from the parents, adults, or friends to whom the profiles were shown. With more time, a valid and reliable tool for measurement could have been designed, but since this was a preliminary survey relating to a unique research area, with a meager budget, the information gathered should be viewed as leading to further research.

The data relating to whom the subjects showed their profile results reveals some interesting patterns. For all students and breakdowns, (Tables 1-3), the 'friends only' and 'parents/adults and friends' categories were the overwhelming first or second choices for all freshmen/sophomore. In the full sample, these options tied; in the dorm sample, 'friends only' won out slightly (by 10%) and in the town sample, 'parents/adult and friends' won out slightly (by 12%). The results are not surprising since town students had easier access to parents and other adults they would have known for a long time, while dorm students have less access to parents and long-term adult friends, accounting for the difference. These differences offset each other in the overall sample, leaving the top two categories even.

The complete sample and the dorm sample for freshmen/sophomore both rated 'no one' and 'parents/adults only' as distant third and fourth places, respectively; town students' ratings of these same categories tied as least attractive options. Again, the dorm and town students' ratings were consistent. It is notable that none of the dorm students chose 'parents/adults only'; this is not surprising considering that they had less access to parents and adults they would have known for a long time. While some of them did show results to friends and adults, none chose feedback exclusively from a group that, given the timing of the research surveys, could primarily be drawn only from adult school personnel. The research suggests that while high school students develop close friends quickly in a new setting, parents are not as easily 'replaced' by other adults.

Patterns also emerge from the junior/senior data. For all students and breakdowns

(Tables 1-3), the 'no one' and 'friends only' categories were overwhelmingly the first or second choices for all junior/senior. In the dorm sample, these options tied; in the town sample, 'no one' won out by 8%; in the complete sample, 'no one' won out by 6%. In both the complete sample and the dorm sample, 'parents/adults and friends' and 'parents/ adults only' were ranked third and fourth choices, respectively. In the town sample, 'friends only' and 'parents/adults only' tied for second and third positions; 'parents/adults and friends' was ranked last. Junior/senior town and dorm students' ranking were similar, though not as consistent as the first-year students/sophomore rankings. No junior/senior dorm subjects chose 'parents/adults only' like the freshmen/sophomore dorm subjects.

Comparisons of ranking and percentage data for each class grouping suggest differences between younger and older high school students (Table 4). Very noticeable is the difference in ranking the category 'no one' as third and 15% for freshmen/sophomore and the ranking of the same category as first and 36% for the junior/senior. 'Parents/adults and friends' went from the 1st rank and 40% for underclassmen to 3rd rank and 18% for upperclassmen. "Friends only" dropped in prominence from the 1st rank and 40% for freshmen/sophomore to 2nd rank and 32% for the junior/senior. 'Parents/adults only' was rated 4th by each both class groupings, but the freshmen/sophomore was 5% while the junior/senior was 14%. While the underclassmen's rankings were very like the complete rankings, the upperclassmen's percentages per rank were more congruent with the total percentages per class.

The drop-in percentage points in the category 'parents/adults and friends' were almost the same as the increase in percentage points in the category 'no one,' as categories are compared from underclassmen to upperclassmen. Additionally, 15% of underclassmen sought feedback only from themselves, 45% from self and one group (friends or parents/adults), 40% from all groups. In comparison, 36% (over twice the percentage) of the upperclassmen sought feedback only from themselves, 46% (the same percentage) from self and one group, 18% (less than half the percentage) from all groups. (This suggests a shift in dependency for feedback from 'everyone available' (self, friends, parents, and adults) for underclassmen towards increasing dependence on self for upperclassmen. Further research to determine if this shift from 'everyone' and towards 'no one' (self) continues into young adulthood and beyond, as well as whether the dependency on 'everyone' increases down into childhood, is needed before present data differences could be considered 'trends.'

The data relating to the agreement on WIDP accuracy between subjects and the persons who were shown the profiles raises more questions than it answers. It is important to mention that the accuracy ratings were self-reported by the subjects; no independent checks were made with the parents, adults, or friends who also looked at the profiles.

In the measures of central tendency and variability tables, subjects' means were only higher than parents/adults' means once out of three times. Parents/adults' means were higher than subjects' means for all profiles and the group of profiles rated exclusively by subjects and parents/adults. This group of profiles was unique in that the means for both subjects and parents/adults were the highest in the whole study. Also could be because the profiles for these subjects were exceptionally accurate. Also, these subjects knew themselves and were known so well by their parents/adults that the match between profiles and subjects was recognized. Alternatively, these subjects and parents/adults could have a relationship where another or both parties strongly influence one party to think similarly, or the interaction between subjects and parents/adults particularly increased subjects' accuracy perception. The evaluation with such a small group cautions against anything more than possible implications.

Another unique profile group was those subjects who did not share their results with anyone else. In contrast to the subjects' who showed their results only to parents/ adults, the 'no one' else subjects had the lowest subjects' mean for profile accuracy. Also, this could be because the profiles for these subjects were especially inaccurate. Alternatively, it could be that these subjects did not know themselves as well as other subject groups, and did not recognize the match between their profiles, or it could be that a lack of interaction with at least one other person about the profile somehow lowered accuracy perception.

The change in the subjects' means, depending on which co-raters they shared their information with, raises the possibility that there is a relationship between the subjects' perceived accuracy of their profiles and to whom they showed their profiles. The two profile groups that included parents/adults as co-raters (Tables 6 & 8) yielded the highest and virtually identical subject means for accuracy. The friends' highest mean was in the group that included parents/adults as seen in (Table 6). However, the subjects' means in each group differed by only .1 in mean value. The parents/adults' mean in Table 8 (6.5) was almost exactly as much higher than the subjects' mean that it was lower than the subjects' mean in Table 6 (5.5). Therefore, it appears that if a relationship does exist, it may be the experience of feedback (albeit positive in both cases) from parents/adults that supported the high and consistent subject means rather than the actual level of parents/ adults' profile agreement.

The two profile groups that included friends as co-raters (Tables 6 & 7) yielded the second highest subject's mean (5.9) in the group that also included parents and the next to lowest subjects' mean (4.9) in the group that included only subjects and friends. Friends' means were not only less than the subjects' means but also consistently the lowest in every group in which they appeared. While peer dependency is often considered a fact of teenage life, it is worth noting that subjects' means were always higher than friends' means. The subjects' and friends' feedback group (Table 7) did coincide with a higher subjects' mean than for subjects who sought no comments. However, the consistently higher subjects' means could indicate that friends either did not know the subjects, as well as subjects, knew themselves or that their friends did not take a firm stance on the profile information. From lowest to highest the means for subjects ranked:

4.4 - subjects only, Table 9;
4.9 - subjects and friends, Table 7;
5.1 - all profiles and raters, Table 5;
5.4 – all profiles rated by subjects and others, Table 10;
5.9 – profiles rated by subjects, parents/adults, and friends;
6 – profiles calculated by subjects and parents.

The increase in the subjects' mean for profiles rated only by subjects and at least one other person was one full mean point. Similarly, the increase in subjects' mean for profiles rated by subjects and friends and those rated by subjects, parents/adults, and friends, was also one full mean point. If a relationship does exist between the experience of feedback and increased subject means, all feedback may contribute to an increase of the means of issue and parents/adults' feedback may mainly contribute to an increase of the means an issue.

The noticeable difference in the subjects' means, invites speculation as to how they chose co-raters. Were their choices made because of their Temperaments being extroverted or introverted, self-reliant or dependent? Alternatively, because they thought the profile was very accurate and they did not want to reveal parts of themselves to others. Alternatively, maybe they were too unimpressed with the information to bother. Alternatively, perhaps their relationships with friends and parents/adults strained or friendly, or were there special personal circumstances that either discouraged or encouraged them to share information; had they just outgrown the need for a significant amount of feedback, or did they still desire as much input as possible? Subjects' choices and no doubt the results of this study would have been affected by testing at a different time of year, under different circumstances.

Conclusion

An additional study would be necessary to attempt to meet the goals of this research project. A larger and more representative sample of the high school students in this area, including sex-linked response comparisons, the development of a reliable and valid measurement tool, independent checks, and attention to ruling out confounding variable issues around consent forms and schedules might result in more accurate and well-rounded information. After a revised administration of this study, it would be essential to contrast these results with similar studies of persons older than, and younger than, high school age.

References

Akers, A.F., & Jones, R.M., & Coyl, D.D. (1998). Adolescent Friendship Pairs: Similarities in Identity Status Development, Behaviors, Attitudes, and Intentions. Journal of Adolescent Research, 13, 178-201.

Bates, J.E., Dodge, K.A., Pettit, G.S. & Ridge, B. (1998). Interaction of Temperamental Resistance to Control and Restrictive Parenting in the Development of Externalizing Behavior. Developmental Psychology, 34, 982-995.

Giordano, P.C., Cernkovich, S.A., Groat, H.T., Pugh, M.D., & Swinford, S.P. (1998). The Quality of Adolescent Friendships: Long Term Effects? Journal of Health and Social Behavior, 39, 55-71.

Greenberger, E., Chuansheng, C., Beam, M. (1998). The Role of "Very Important" Nonparental Adults in Adolescent Development. Journal of Youth and Adolescence, 27, 321-343.

Katainen, S., Raikkonen, K., Keskivaara, P.& Keltikangas-Jarvinen, L. (1999). Maternal Child-Rearing Attitudes and Role Satisfaction and Children's Temperament as Antecedents of Adolescent Depressive Tendencies: Follow-up Study of 6- to 15-year-olds. Journal of Youth and Adolescence, 28, 139-163.

Kerpelman, J.L., Pittman, J.F., Lamke, L.K. (1997). Toward a Microprocessor Perspective on Adolescent Identity Development: An Identity Control Theory Approach. Journal of Adolescent Research, 12, 325-346.

O'Koon, J., (1997). Attachment to Parents and Peers in Late Adolescence and Their Relationship with Self-Image. Adolescence, 32, 471-482.

Stice, E. & Gonzales, N. (1998). Adolescent Temperament Moderates the Relation of Parenting to Antisocial Behavior and Substance Use. Journal of Adolescent Research, 13, 5-31.

Van Beest, M., Baerveldt, C. (1999). The Relationship between Adolescents' Social Support from Parents and Peers. Adolescence, 34, 193-201.

Vondracek, F., Silbereisen, R., Reitzle, M., Wiesner, M. (1999). Vocational Preferences of Early Adolescents: Their Development in Social Context. Journal of Adolescent Research, 14, 267-288.

Wilson, J.D., & MacGillivray, M.S. (1998). Self-Perceived Influences of Family, Friends, and Media on Adolescent Clothing Choice. Family and Consumer Sciences Research Journal, 26, 425-443.

Worley, J.W. (1998). Psychometric Evaluation Results.

Appendix II

Statistical Analyses of the Survey Data

(Form A)

PROJECT PARTICIPATION SLIP

Dear Parent,

The high school students at DCA will be participating in a research project to determine the benefits of **Worley's ID Profile (WIDP)** to high school students. As part of this study, each student will be given a questionnaire as to how he/she presently assumes leadership, makes friends and interacts socially. This information will generate a personal Temperament profile for your child that he/she may keep. Also, a brief Temperament pre-assessment questionnaire and a follow-up questionnaire about the accuracy and usefulness of the profile will be given to each student. This information will be used to help determine the most beneficial time to assess students with the **WIDP**.

WHAT IS WIDP?

Worley's ID Profile provides a comprehensive assessment of needs, desires, and interpersonal behaviors in three significant Areas of life: Social, Leadership, and Relationship. This Temperament assessment is drawn from the individual's responses to the 60-item **Worley's ID Profile** questionnaire. The **Profile** is a psychometrically approved questionnaire and based on the premise that Social, Leadership and Relationship scores can assist in understanding and predict a person's behavior.

Dr. Worley defines Temperament as a person's God-given (Ps. 139:13-15) subjective self – an individual's unique desires, needs, and ways of relating to the world – and identifies five basic Temperaments: Introverted Sanguine, Sanguine, Phlegmatic, Melancholy, and Choleric. Dr. Worley believes that Temperament and personality are **not** the same – personality is the 'mask' that an individual presents to society, often including aspects of one's Temperament, but only the elements that are chosen to show. **Worley's ID Profile** gives a detailed summary of an individual's three major life Areas: Social, Leadership, and Relationship.

1. **SOCIAL PROFILE:** General social/work orientation

    The Social Profile identifies the individual's needs and desires for socialization, work/school associations, and other superficial relationships. Requirements in this Area may range from demonstrating and desiring minimal socialization, to demonstrating and desiring constant socialization. The Social Profile helps answer the question: **"Who is in or out of relationships with this individual?**

1. **LEADERSHIP PROFILE:** Independence/leadership needs

> The Leadership Profile identifies the individual's needs and desires for influencing others, making decisions and assuming responsibilities. Requirements in this Area may range from independence to dependence. The Leadership Profile helps answer the question, **"Who maintains the power and makes decisions in relationships with this individual?"**

1. **RELATIONSHIP PROFILE:** Emotional involvement in close relationships

> The Relationship Profile identifies the individual's needs and desires in close relationships with family and friends. Needs may range from emotional relationships and expressions of love with many people to isolation from loving relationships. The Relationship Profile helps answer the question, **"How emotionally open or closed to the relationship is this individual?"**

Worley's ID Profile defines these varying needs and desires, not as **"right"** or **"wrong,"** but only as individual differences and preferences. If a person's life situation differs dramatically from his/her needs and desires in one or more areas, he/she is likely to be experiencing stress, conflict, and anxiety in relationships. The **WIDP** does **not** measure intelligence, ability, maturity, or identify mental disorders. Additionally, it is not designed to 'change' people. Rather, the positive contributions of each's Temperament are emphasized, and possible limitations will be stated in a non-judgmental manner. Any of these potential barriers can be overcome, provided the person is willing and can learn the required new skills.

Worley's ID Profile assumes that any individual can use a Temperament style, introversion or extroversion, to meet the requirements of any role or situation (Eph. 2:10). Still, each person will find some behaviors easy to use and others very uncomfortable. The interpretive reports are intended to provide enough information about a person to enable him/her to make informed choices about personal and professional development.

PERMISSION SLIP

I give my child, _____, permission to be included in the WIDP project.

Parent signature _____ Date _____

(Form B)

WIDP PRE-ASSESSMENT

Name _____ Grade _____

School _____ Gender: F   M

Here is a list of some Temperament characteristics – circle as many as you think describe the 'real you':

People-oriented	Angry	Diligent	Loving	Determined
Supportive	Loyal	Dependent	Sensitive	Manipulative
Indecisive	Introverted	Enthusiastic	Responsive	Talkative
Extroverted	Creative	Sympathetic	Emotional	Disorganized
Exaggerates	Decisive	Controlling	Humorous	Fun-loving
Unemotional	Friendly	Objective	Diplomatic	Practical
Dependable	Easy going	Procrastinate	Frugal	Stubborn
Dislike change	Moody	Perfectionist	Organized	Analytical
Self-sacrificing	Negative	Critical	Independent	Productive
Inspiring	Kind	Strong Willed	Adventurous	Impulsive
Holds grudges	Calm	Sarcastic	Demanding	Gentle

_____ **Please do not write below this line** _____

Social: _____ Temperament: _____

Leadership: _____ Temperament: _____

Relationship: _____ Temperament: _____

(Form C)

WIDP QUESTIONNAIRE

(Form D)

WIDP RESULTS

Dear Student,

Thank you *very* much for taking the time to fill out the WIDP questionnaire. Dr. Worley and I hope that the information in this profile is helpful to you. We appreciate your participation in this research project and highly value your feedback about this assessment. You will have the opportunity to give your reactions and suggestions in a follow-up survey in about a week.

On occasion, a person does not agree with their profile results. Dr. Worley offers three explanations:

1. You may not have answered the questions based on your legitimate inner needs and desires. Instead, you might have responded to the questions with the viewpoint of "whom I think I should be" or "how I should answer".

2. You might be the exact Temperament the WIDP report indicates, but you may have been molded to act and respond in ways different from your Temperament.

3. You may have matured in areas so that your behavior is different in some respects from your Temperament.

Whether you agree or disagree with your profile results, getting some feedback about this report is recommended. People who know you well and care enough to be honest with you, such as parents, other relatives, and close friends are good choices for additional discussion about your profile. Remember – ALL Temperaments bring significant strengths to life; you have a unique opportunity to impact your world in an unusual and meaningful way!

(Form E)

WIDP FOLLOW-UP

Name _____ **Grade** _____

School _____ **Gender: F   M**

Please put an X in front of each answer.

1. **How well did your pre-assessment Temperament choices match your WIDP?**

   Social: ____ not much   ____ somewhat   ____ a lot   ____ most or all
   Leadership: ____ not much   ____ somewhat   ____ a lot   ____ most or all
   Relationship: ____ not much   ____ somewhat   ____ a lot   ____ most or all

2. **How much do you agree with your WIDP?**

   Social: ____ not much   ____ somewhat   ____ a lot   ____ most or all
   Leadership: ____ not much   ____ somewhat   ____ a lot   ____ most or all
   Relationship: ____ not much   ____ somewhat   ____ a lot   ____ most or all

3. **What other people did you show your WIDP results to and what did they think? Check _all_ that apply.**

   ____ No one
   ____ Mother   ____ agreed   ____ disagreed
   ____ Father   ____ agreed   ____ disagreed
   ____ Best Friend ____ agreed   ____ disagreed
   ____ Friend   ____ agreed   ____ disagreed
   ____ Sibling   ____ agreed   ____ disagreed
   ____ Relative   ____ agreed   ____ disagreed
   ____ _____   ____ agreed   ____ disagreed
   ____ _____   ____ agreed   ____ disagreed

4. **What section of the profile results were the most helpful to you? The least?**

   Most: **Least:**
   ____ Social   ____ Social
   ____ Leadership   ____ Leadership
   ____ Relationship   ____ Relationship

5. **In what ways do you think your WIDP will be helpful to you? Check _all_ that apply.**

    ____ Understanding myself
    ____ Understanding other people
    ____ Other people understanding me
    ____ Job/career choices
    ____ Choosing classes/course of study
    ____ Relationships with people at school/work/social contacts
    ____ Relationships with close friends and relatives
    ____ Leadership and decision-making style and preferences
    ____ Solving problems
    ____ Conflict resolution
    ____ Other: _____

6. **At what times do you think the WIDP would be helpful? Check _all_ that apply.**

    ____ In elementary school
    ____ Start of junior high/middle school
    ____ End of junior high/middle school
    ____ Start of high school
    ____ End of high school
    ____ Start of school after high school
    ____ Start of job/career
    ____ While engaged to be married
    ____ At no time
    ____ Other:_____

7. **What did you like about the WIDP?**

8. **What didn't you like about the WIDP?**

9. **Would you like to have a school seminar on how to use your WIDP in school, career, and relationship decisions?**

    ___ yes   ____ no

(Form F - Modified)

WIDP FOLLOW-UP

Name _____ **Gender: F   M**

School _____ **Grade** _____ **Dorm: Y   N**

Please put an X in front of each answer.

1. **How well did your pre-assessment Temperament choices match your WIDP?**

Social:	____ not much	____ somewhat	____ a lot
Leadership:	____ not much	____ somewhat	____ a lot
Relationship:	____ not much	____ somewhat	____ a lot

2. **How much do you agree with your WIDP?**

Social:	____ not much	____ somewhat	____ a lot
Leadership:	____ not much	____ somewhat	____ a lot
Relationship:	____ not much	____ somewhat	____ a lot

3. **What other people did you show your WIDP results to and how much did they agree with your WIDP? Check _all_ that apply.**

____ No one			
____ Mother	____ not much	____ somewhat	____ a lot
____ Father	____ not much	____ somewhat	____ a lot
____ Best friend	____ not much	____ somewhat	____ a lot
____ Friend	____ not much	____ somewhat	____ a lot
____ Sibling	____ not much	____ somewhat	____ a lot
____ Relative	____ not much	____ somewhat	____ a lot
_____	____ not much	____ somewhat	____ a lot
_____	____ not much	____ somewhat	____ a lot

4. **What section of the profile results were the most helpful to you? The least?**

Most:	**Least:**
____ Social	____ Social
____ Leadership	____ Leadership
____ Relationship	____ Relationship

5. **In what ways do you think your WIDP will be helpful to you? Check _all_ that apply.**

    _____ Understanding myself
    _____ Understanding other people
    _____ Other people understanding me
    _____ Job/career choices
    _____ Choosing classes/course of study
    _____ Relationships with people at school/work/social contacts
    _____ Relationships with close friends and relatives
    _____ Leadership and decision-making style and preferences
    _____ Solving problems
    _____ Conflict resolution
    _____ Other: _____

6. **At what times do you think the WIDP would be helpful? Check _all_ that apply.**

    _____ In elementary school
    _____ Start of junior high/middle school
    _____ End of junior high/middle school
    _____ Start of high school
    _____ End of high school
    _____ Start of school after high school
    _____ Start of job/career
    _____ While engaged to be married
    _____ At no time
    _____ Other:_____

7. **What did you like about the WIDP?**

8. **What didn't you like about the WIDP?**

9. **Would you like to have a school seminar on how to use your WIDP in school, career, and relationship decisions?**

    ____ yes   _____ no

Chapter 20: WIDP Testimonies

Note: These testimonies have been compiled from decades of WIDP interactions, received by personal request and random update emails that captured the experience. Enjoy reading how WIDP has positively affected people in many disciplines and situations from all over the world.

To whom it may concern:

I've had the pleasure of knowing and working with Dr. John Worley for almost nine years. During those times, Dr. Worley helped me with numerous assignments and has also helped several of my friends and business associates with their personal and business issues. He has time and again helped me to resolve crucial business and personal matters. These include discussions relating to my creating and leading three national companies to address organizational issues to personal growth issues. John's advice and support have been precious to me.

My early involvement with John included his development of several of my senior staff – from an Executive Coaching capacity. He excelled in that task. Later, he was engaged to conduct organizational development activities, spending time with each senior leader and doing the remarkable Worley ID Profile assessment system and debriefing each. That assignment challenged the company management to better understand each person's natural Temperament, which later facilitated team building and improved communications. As an HR advisor, John is a precious resource.

I have sought John's advice many times over the years to help me sort out and resolve personal, family and business challenges. I have never been disappointed with John's support, advice, or direction. Further, I find John to be quite direct and to the point. That is a refreshing change from most HR or counselor types who seem to like to create "dependent" relationships. (Those where you always need to spend more time & money before a direction is finalized).

John has my unqualified endorsement for anyone needing an executive coach or strategic advisor. On a personal level, I find John to be one of the most brilliant, insightful, and personable and compassionate people that I know.

Sincerely,

Greg Wing
President
Bedford Capital Corp.

As President of an information technology consulting company, I have found Worley's ID Profile to be a valuable Human Resource assessment tool used to identify individual strengths and providing critical input to successful team building. Worley's ID Profile combined with the expertise of working one-on-one with the company's highly trained staff has provided greater personal insight and enabled personal improvements. The results are higher productivity and improved business and personal relationships. I highly recommend engaging Worley's ID Profile for personal growth, corporate management coaching, and team building initiatives.

Stephen Engman President ITC Consulting Group, LLC

I have been an instructor on the MBTI for years. After fifteen (15) minutes of evaluating Worley's ID Profile, I recognized the superiority of WIDP over the MBTI. Corporate America will rapidly be replacing the MBTI and the DiSC and other instruments with the WIDP when they experience the validity and reliability of WIDP. Every MBTI trainer and corporate user needs to consider WIDP!

Carl Erickson
MBTI Trainer
The Beacon Group
Northbridge, MA

Time and again I've witnessed WIDP's unique power, speed, and efficacy to substantially improve business performance using WIDP coaching services. When executives adopt it as their primary focus for executive development, or as a standard for their HR Management and HR related problem solving, they will experience impressionable results. Worley's ID Profile, Inc., is true to its commitment, delivers excellent executive coaching whether one-on-one or in workshops, and I'm very happy to represent it in Brazil.

Vera Cristina Fonseca Director, Human Resoures Stratus
Rio de Janeiro, Brazil

Having spent many years working with Personality Assessment tools such as the MBTI, DiSC, & FIRO-B, I was just amazed at the powerful and all-encompassing results provided by with WIDP. Within minutes, WIDP provided me with an individual's inherent needs, desires & motivations in three key life areas. It also offered in-depth sight into the persons Desired and Demonstrated Behaviors. Having applied this Temperament Assessment tool for many years now, I find myself in awe of its essential application value during Hiring, Team Building, Conflict Resolution, Position Strengthening, Leadership Development, and Individual Enrichment. It has helped my various teams understand the true meaning of Diversity, as this tool provides a strong message of Acceptance, Inclusion, and Tolerance. Finally, for the individuals who are assessed, resounding results are achieved time and again.

Mario di Girolamo, Medical Services Operations Manager

Regardless of if one hires, manages, coaches or commands, WIDP is the ultimate tool which ensures complete Temperament assessment of potential new, or existing, personnel. WIDP allows an organization to situate people in the proper placement to insure maximum efficiency, production, and management. I know of no other tool which delivers such consistent, accurate analysis of the human psyche.

Peter Dunnington
OSP FiOS Engineer
Project Manager (ret.)

WIDP should become mandatory training for all educational counselors. They should train every high school student on WIDP! This seminar took me fifteen (15) steps beyond the average workshop in how to deal with people effectively. I will be recommending this to our school district officials and encourage them to use the program in our schools.

Naomi Drury
High School Counselor
Peterborough, NH

As a professional clinical psychologist, I have used many psychological instruments in the last forty (40) years. I have not seen such a powerful apparatus that is so quick and easy yet provides so much critical data on my clients. Worley's ID Profile is indeed the tool of the 21st Century. I will be recommending WIDP to my professional clinical associates nationwide.

Raymond Daniels, Ph.D.
President, Institute of Behavioral Sciences
Derry, NH

For the educator, the WIDP reduces the potential for classroom misbehavior. For the counselor, it pinpoints motivators that regulate psychological patterns of clients. Dr. Worley's training sessions are equally as valuable. They are casual, informative, and practical. I was most impressed by the diverse range of professionals that attended. Only by comparing the WIDP with other programs out there can one truly appreciate its value!

Karen Dude
High School Teacher
New Hampshire Public Schools

'Fantastic!' 'I cannot believe what I am hearing!' These are just a few expressions that I have had clients exclaim upon hearing their results from the WIDP. I highly endorse WIDP for its user-friendly software, profile, accuracy, and reliability. It is a very informative and educational analysis. No other pattern that I know of reports as does the WIDP. Every clinician should complete this training and purchase the software.

C.R.Lechner Ph.D.
The Family Instructional Counseling Center
Aurora, Mo.

Wow! No more worrying whom to hire! Is this the right person or is that the right person? WIDP hit the nail right on the head. It told me precisely whom the right person was to fill the job. It worked. What a cost saver. What a time saver. Never again will I go through the anguish of not being sure. WIDP has made a believer out of me.

Martin Anderholm
President, Anderholm Press, Inc.
Orange, MA

Dr. Worley's program fascinated me. It helped me to understand those around me and myself better. WIDP is a gift that has changed my thinking toward my family, the world, and myself overall. Whenever I take the time to flip through my notes and profile, I always come out with another piece of knowledge.

Jessica James, High School Junior, Derry, NH

After being unemployed 14 months, I signed up with a career coach to help me shift to new professional status, and it is a career decision that has propelled me further than I could have imagined. He has evaluated me through a unique personal discovery profile and is coaching me on how to unify my personality with my new career. If anyone wants help transitioning to a new career (or to a new job), please let me know, and I can give you more information. He is indeed a unique and gifted coach that also provides professional coaching services to all levels of executives.

Peter Thompson, Real Estate Broker

You are in our prayers. Thanks for praying for us. I'm excited about your meeting in St. Louis. I pray God will open huge doors for you and John. The Worley ID Profile is in my opinion – pure genius – share it with the world. It's fun building His kingdom together.

Jim Charron
Executive Director Sharing Way
Atlanta, GA

I have been a WIDP Representative since attending Dr. Worley's WIDP Training Seminar in 1997. I have been using WIDP in my Christian Counseling practice since that time. I consider it an indispensable tool in assisting individuals, couples, families, and congregations. It is the most effective and detailed profile I have found in over 20 years of ministry. I highly recommend WIDP!

Don C. Stevens, L.P.C.
Burton, Texas

Dr. John Wayne Worley is my friend. He lovingly helped me to go through and successfully deal with one of the worst crises in my life. The incident happened about two decades ago when I lived and worked in the U.S. in an official assignment for the Brazilian Government. I do not exaggerate when I say that his support was paramount for me and my family at that moment, and, for those who share my worldview and my faith, that coming to know him was indeed a gift from God. At center stage of his praxis was his wonderful psychological self-discovery tool, Worley's Identity Discovery Profile, which very rapidly and precisely pinpointed my temperamental traits that contributed so markedly for the condition that led me to seek for his professional counsel, as well as potential and actual aspects of my family's interpersonal dynamics that demanded improvement. I miss the long conversations we had in his beautiful office and the wisdom contained in his specific recommendations. I wish you the very best, Doc. May your book reach and dramatically improve the lives of every human needing WIDP, the same way it did for me.

Jurandyr de Souza Fonseca
M.Sc., Colonel Aviator (Retired)
Brazilian Air Force

Worley's Identity Discovery Profile was a life-changer for our family. My father assessed me when I was 12 and found out that we were both natural born leaders. He immediately knew how to speak with me in a way that saved our relationship. Several years ago, I started my own Engagement Advising business that uses the WIDP as a fundamental tool to have conversations and effectively resolve "people issues" in any environment. Knowing that organizations, churches, corporations, families, and relationships, to name a few, are all simply the people within them, WIDP allows a person to enter any conversation or situation on a common understanding and reference point of needs to begin conversations in the right context. It was this tool that allowed me to see that God's design for me is intentional and that I'm of infinite value. Pointing people to God's voice in their life is easy with WIDP. What a powerful tool to help get our needs met and meet the needs of others in love and humility!

Sam Stevens
WIDP Certified Affiliate Manager
Owner/Founder - Humble Pie Solutions

A testimony to Worley's ID Profile. Dr. Worley and I grew up in the same small town in Southeastern OH. I have known him all his life. Our families are close friends. I have had a profile done by Humm/Woodworth Profile and WIDP. Both were very thorough, WIDP being the most recent. WIDP is a straightforward profile to take. The research provides many results to us or for our employees. It covers Social, Leadership, and Relationship and includes personal needs and desires and more. I worked at an Alloy Corporation for 22 years from Furnace Department to Personnel Director of over 1,200 employees Union and Non-union. Also, took and administered the Humm/Woodworth Profile. The WIDP gives a thorough profile of who, what, and why we are who we are. May be of some help to you if considered. I was owner/operator of several family restaurants-catering for 34 years with 49 employees. Wish I had WIDP then. The profile will help you to understand yourself or an employee. A great asset to any company to realize who, what, and why we are who we are as an individual. The excellent advantage when using this profile is that you will benefit tremendously personally and professionally.

Lewis Charles Burckholter
Papa Chucks Restaurant
Owner

John W. Worley, Ph. D. introduced me to the WIDP evaluation tool many years ago to assist me in my pastoral counseling responsibilities. As a Licensed Clinical Pastoral Counselor with Advanced Certification, I am always looking to improve my evaluation tools. I started by taking the assessment myself to determine how comprehensive the WIDP would be in helping the counselee to have a better understanding of their strengths and weaknesses. I began using the WIDP with all my counselees and heard repeatedly from them, "How can this short test know so much about me?" With God's help and a willingness to work on making the changes needed to improve their lives through the insights of the WIDP and other assessments, lives were transformed into being productive.

Thank you, Dr. John W. Worley, for helping me to be a better counselor through WIDP assessment. I would recommend the WIDP evaluation tool to all who want to improve their counseling skills.

Arthur E Burke, Ph. D.

One day, my father, Dr. John W. Worley decided to give the whole family an assessment. Once all the members had taken the test, I had a chance to go over the new data Daddy had printed out about me. He embraced me in a big hug and said, "Oh honey, I wasn't aware of how different you are from the rest of the family, and I will do my best to be sensitive to your needs."

That day changed my life. Growing up in a household of strong temperaments, I learned about who I was and how it's OK to be me and to wait for the right timing to approach others in the family. Years later and now have a family of my own, we have all taken the profile and studied ourselves and each other and live in unity, acceptance, and understanding of who each of us is deep down inside.

My relationship with my husband is stable and secure, and we live daily in the knowing of who each other is and appreciate and give each separate room to breathe when necessary and how to appropriately approach delicate subjects.

I can easily see outside of our home when other people misunderstand each other based on their different temperaments, and it saddens me. Everyone should understand who they are and how they can be the best version of themselves and that can only be through the application of WIDP.

Sincerely, the third of John W. Worley's daughters,
Melaney Michelle Worley Fodera
Lynnfield, MA

So, I must share this with you. I had a conversation with the director of my program today that left me feeling unsettled and a little depreciated. I sat and thought about it for a while, and then thought about the WIDP results that talked about my tendency to let things fester rather than rely on more direct communication. So, when next we spoke, I said, hey, can we chat for a moment about our last conversation? And we had a good, honest back and forth about it. Tensions were eased, and work continued more productively. Thanks! I'm a believer.

June Peoples Mallon

I have personally known Dr. Worley, for close to 20 years... I have found him to be a man of integrity, one who is highly qualified, and one who cares genuinely for people. His expertise in counseling, coaching, and training along with his patience and a willingness to work with people, has had an extraordinary impact on my life and the life of many others that I am personally aware. I have used WIDP in a variety of settings, as a Pastor in Counseling Pre-marriage sessions and post-marriage conflicts, I have also used WIDP in professional business context, resolving Personnel issues. In addition to a host of personal development scenarios. I have found this instrument to be precise in its detail and extraordinarily useful on every occasion. I highly recommend it.

Pastor Ken Reed
Radio Host of NEW COVENANT PERSPECTIVES
Co-Pastor of NEW CREATION CHRISTIAN CHURCH
Worcester MA.

WIDP has made a profound impact on my life personally and professionally. I have used other assessment tools in psychometrics before, but none of them created as linear of a baseline and dimensional understanding of the human temperament as WIDP. On a personal level, my level of self-understanding became more in-depth, more granular, thereby helping me to be able to explain who I am to those I am in relationship with. Conversely, I can understand those closest to me better than ever before. On a professional level, my team building skillset has become more highly advanced using WIDP. Employee coaching, conflict resolution, and task assignment have all become more efficient. People can have a more accurate picture of who they were created to be and enjoy much fuller relationships through the greater understanding of the human expression that WIDP affords.

In the 25 years I have known John Worley, his personal tutelage, along with WIDP, have forever changed and enhanced my life. But not only mine but also the countless people who have been mentored using WIDP through my life professionally and in ministry. Each coaching session and seminar using WIDP have always brought the same reaction, uplift, and enlightenment. And for that, we are all forever grateful.

Richard Henry
Pastor and Entrepreneur

WIDP is such a valuable tool for a multitude of audiences. Both professional, family and social atmospheres will benefit from a device that is designed to assess the temperament of individuals. While often differences in personalities can cause disagreements and misunderstandings, knowing the causes of behaviors and reactions can eliminate these misunderstandings. For example, while we might tag an individual as being a controlling personality, the WIDP might show us that this person isn't trying to control others but merely trying to make their world function appropriately. In understanding the human psyche better, we can be at peace and more successful in our daily endeavors.

The WIDP is an asset for the family and businesses as it teaches about individual differences. Whether it's a marriage, parent/child relationship, or professional relationship, WIDP assesses needs and desires in a way that is constructive and useful to the often very dynamic functions of a family workforce. The WIDP is also the perfect length, it is fast enough to answer promptly and thorough sufficient to come up with an accurate conclusion. I highly recommend this valuable tool for anyone who wants to improve their position in life.

Charles J DiMatteo, Jr., CPA

ACTS Inc. A NON-PROFIT COMMUNITY ACTION ORGANIZATION
ELIZABETH DORRIS PRESIDENT | LIBBYDORRIS19@GMAIL.COM
Endorsement of John W. Worley, Ph.D., WIDP

To Whom It May Concern:
I have known John Worley in a personal and professional capacity for over 30 years. I have used and will continue to use his brilliantly easy yet comprehensive Temperament Identity Profile (WIDP). It offers versatility like none other on the market today. It has proven timeless in its simplicity to pinpoint personal temperament identity, and hence their strengths and weaknesses.

I have a consulting business and find it useful when dealing with organization clients and their employee's interpersonal relationships as well as bringing clarity to individual's temperaments helping them to understand themselves and their strengths and weaknesses. I found that identifying the personal temperament of employees and co-workers optimizes productivity in the work environment as co-workers begin to understand each other and work better together and the human resource department can better manage personnel placement maximizing the best and highest use of their personnel.

In conclusion, WDIP is essential in all interpersonal interactions such as pre-marital counseling, marital counseling, group training seminars. WIDP is an asset in personal identity discovery and development, employment counseling, and family counseling.

Respectfully,

Elizabeth Dorris
President, ACTS

There are lots of personality tests out there, but none compared to the accuracy and validity of WIDP. This tool has enabled me to live a more freeing lifestyle. Granting me with the ability to understand myself and others on a deeper level; thus, increasing my interpersonal relationships and connection with them.

After taking the WIDP questionnaire and reviewing my profile with the help of my loving Grandfather; John W. Worley, I have learned SO much about myself. It has given me a sense of freedom and liberation from situations that I would shy away from before. Being an Introverted Sanguine Socially it can be hard putting yourself out there. However, once I understood my emotion, I was able to finally overcome these obstacles with a sense of confidence and reason.

In my opinion, WIDP is the key to understanding people and the psychology that drives every one of us.

Thank you so much, Dr. Worley, for not only helping me understand myself and others - but learning to live 'in the jet stream.'

Joshua Fodera, Ph.D.
WIPD Certified Affiliate Manager

Being a product of a broken home, I had a hard time identifying with anyone in my family, especially since half of my family was unknown to me. Once I got into the business world and was introduced to different personality types through sales training seminars, I started to understand some but not all of who I was. These other personality profiles could not explain everything and would leave me confused in certain areas. It was not until I met Dr. John Worley and was introduced to WIDP was I able to really understand temperament and how God uniquely wired me. The Worley Identity Profile explained everything about me in detail and was able to bring clarity to my life. Over the last four years of using this tool, I have been freed to be who I was always meant to be, and it has also given me the insight to understand others around me. Things that used to befuddle me in relationships now make perfect sense. I live and walk in a newfound understanding and freedom both personally and professionally.

Dorothy Henry – WIDP Certified Affiliate Manager
Independent Associate Executive Director
LegalShield/IDShield

What an incredible opportunity it was to be a part of the inner workings of the WIDP, I can't begin to thank you enough for all of the gifts I have received from this experience!!! My brain is on fire and has kicked itself into high gear digesting all that I have learned!!!! I love this tool and the brainpower behind its creation! NOW is the time for it to shine!!!! It is truly fascinating what is happening in the business world because of COVID. Whether it is the potential of an extremely high percentage of the workforce choosing to leave for remote options, business downsizing/combing jobs, women existing to pursue other opportunities including childbearing, or the push to "level-up" what is needed now/most in all of these scenarios is a tool that can deliver a "look before you leap" opportunity for one to consider the benefits/consequences of these momentous decisions. WOW!!! How awesome is it to be the one that has the tool!!!! On the flip side of this is where the WIDP really connects with my heart. This is such a powerful tool to bring healing to those suffering emotionally. Thomas alluded to it when he and Dr. Worley were discussing how they met. He had mentioned the difficult point he was at in his life at that time. I know this personally; its insights are life-changing!!!! I am beyond excited to help get this into the church I am working with as part of their Care Ministry. I begin training with Charmel and her team tomorrow night for their program kicking off on the 24th. She is very excited too to connect with you soon to discuss the WIDP I'm greater detail!!! Thank you both for everything and for giving my brain this opportunity to play!!!!! The attendees were magical, I could have spent days just soaking in their ideas too!!! I love this tool and can feel the energy building for all the blessings it will bring to others in this new year!!!! Please pass along to Dr. Worley a GIANT thank you for his tremendous work and lifelong commitment to helping others!!! What a beautiful loving family he has too!!!!

Many blessings to you and your families as well!!!

Kimberly McKean
Houston, TX
01/16/2022

Appendix A

Frequently Asked Questions (FAQs)
About Worley's ID Profile

What are the applications that Worley's ID Profile can be applied?

> Clinical
> Corporate
> Educational
> Ministry
> Family
> Individual

Has a psychometric evaluation been done on the WIDP?

> Yes! The assessment and the results are very favorable in construct validity as well as reliability. A formal report is available upon request. Reference Chapter 13 for details within this publication.

Is there a comparison of the WIDP Temperament Profile to other similar instruments?

> Yes! Comparisons of other tools such as the MBTI, DiSC, PPS, FIRO-B, FIRO-B/C, TAP, T-JTA, and Temperament by LaHaye have been written.

Does Worley's ID Profile produce a mental diagnosis?

> No. WIDP does not diagnose mental disorders but can determine if the individual is emotionally stable enough to complete the questionnaire accurately. The interpretive report will verify whether the person competently answered the question. Through clinical interpretation, the interpretative statement used as an assessment instrument for checking and balancing the validity of the results of the profile.

Does Worley's ID Profile measure intelligence?

> No. However, WIDP assesses the individual behavior modality which does identify whether the person is analytical and/or intellectual as well as systematic and/or rational, where they would naturally have the potential to increase their intelligence.

Does Worley's ID Profile measure an individual's ability?

No. WIDP does not measure one's ability but does assess and identify their needs and desires which will complement their potential for learning new skills.

Does Worley's ID Profile measure maturity?

No. WIDP does assess one's **perception of self** and their **emotional orientation** which can determine how well they accept their Temperament composition as well as the Temperament structure of others. Therefore, WIDP does verify and identifies one's competence to be untroubled with themselves and with others.

Does Worley's ID Profile measure self-esteem?

No. WIDP does not evaluate self-esteem currently. However, there is factored data within the present questionnaire that will provide data for future research and development of a self-esteem section of the current interpretative report.

Does Worley's ID Profile measure anger?

No. WIDP does not evaluate violence currently. However, there is factored data within the present questionnaire that will provide data for future research and development of a section on anger that will be available in a later version.

Does Worley's ID Profile interface with the ICD (International Classification of Diseases) or the DSM-V (Diagnostic and Statistical Manual of Mental Disorders-Version V)?

No.

Is Worley's ID Profile like the MBTI?

No. The MBTI is a scientific behavioral instrument classifying an individual within one of sixteen categories of behavior. Worley's ID Profile is an objective and subjective Temperament instrument that reveals the individual's needs and desires in three Areas: Social, Leadership, and Relationship. It further shows how the three Areas interface with each other. There are 55,488 combinations one could have in their Temperament classification with WIDP.

Does the program build a database of individuals profiled?

Yes! The website is HIPAA-compliant and keeps a database of profiled individuals for each registered account created.

Can the profile be taken online?

Yes! Individuals can take their profile directly on the widp.org website. Additionally, a paper questionnaire is available through a Certified WIDP representative.

How long does the questionnaire take to complete?

Seven to ten (7-10) minutes!

Can you skip questions and leave them blank?

No.   Every question must be completed for the profile to generate.

How am I to answer the questions?

WIDP interpretive reports based on sixty (60) simple questions.

Individuals or groups of individuals preparing to complete WIDP questionnaires need to be instructed on the following guidelines before completing the questionnaire:

WIDP Profile Questionnaire Instructions:

- Please answer the questions carefully.
- Do not analyze or compare the items!
- Answer each question as though it were a standalone question.
- Your first response is the best response.

It should take about seven to ten (7-10) minutes to answer all sixty (60) questions.

Can it be used with an audience?

Yes!   If the individuals have the intelligence and reasoning abilities to be able to understand the questions and respond appropriately. However, there may be cultural differences in the meaning of words, and this obviously would affect the results.

Can an individual answer Worley's ID Profile questionnaire incorrectly?

Yes!   There are two possibilities should one not agree with their profile results.

1.   Learned behavior. The person is as Worley's ID Profile report indicates, but they were **"tampered with"** or **"molded"** into someone else. The negative learned behavior would create a tremendous amount of stress, anxiety, unhappiness, and even anger in the individual's life as the primary symptom/observation.

2.   The individual did not respond to the questions honestly. It is possible that they were answering the items from the premise of **"whom they think they should be"** and **"how they should answer."**

FAQ's ABOUT WIDP TRAINING

Can anyone access the Worley's ID Profile?

Yes!   The WIDP Profile is available to everyone.

Does the use of Worley's ID Program Profile require formal training to use?

Yes!   There are four different certification training programs available for those who desire an in-depth understanding of WIDP: Certified Associate, Certified Affiliate, and Certified Affiliate Manager.

- **Certified Associate.** A Certified Associate is qualified to administer the WIDP Questionnaire and interpret results. Associates buy WIDP profiles and other services or products through the website or directly through the Affiliate Manager that Certified them.

- **Certified Affiliate.** A Certified Affiliate is qualified to administer the WIDP Questionnaire and interpret results. Furthermore, they can give informational Seminars using WIDP's presentation deck. An Affiliate is one who desires to use the tool as well as teach others about WIDP but cannot certify others in WIDP. These may include school Counselors, HR Managers, Ministers, or others. Affiliates buy WIDP profiles and other services or products through the website or directly through the Affiliate Manager that Certified them.

  The Certifying Affiliate Manager is responsible for the quality of WIDP-related work conducted by their trainees (Associates or Affiliates). Each Certified Associate or Affiliate will be required to execute a Confidentiality Agreement.

- **Certified Affiliate Manager.** A Certified Affiliate Manager is qualified to administer the WIDP Questionnaire and interpret results. Furthermore, they can provide Seminar training and Certification of individuals in both Basic & Advanced Certification Training. Affiliate Managers buy WIDP profiles and other services or products through the website or directly through the Affiliate Manager that Certified them.

  Additionally:

- All Associates and Affiliates are required to pay their annual renewal fee directly to WIDP.

- Anyone trained by WIDP will be under WIDP Agreements and responsible to WIDP only.

- There are no provisions for "Geographical or Organizational Protection," just because you have a client from Wal-Mart within your geographical area does not give you exclusivity to all Wal-Mart stores unless you have a contract with Wal-Mart Headquarters to provides services to all their Wal-Mart stores.

- No WIDP Associate or Affiliate may transfer to another person's structure within WIDP.

Are there training and seminar programs available to teach the process, theory, and application of Worley's ID Program?

Yes!   WIDP, Inc. provides training depending upon the needs of the end user. There are one, two, three, and four-day workshops designed for individuals, groups or organizations. Reach out to a known Affiliate Manager or to WIDP, Inc. via the website for programs of training and financial quotes.

Are there any credentials that I am required to obtain before I can become Certified?

No!   The level of Certification will depend on how you intend to use WIDP. This can be vetted with a Certified Affiliate Manager to ensure the right level is obtained.

What is the difference between objective and subjective Temperament?

Objective Temperament   Objective behavior is the behavior one displays depending upon the environment they find themselves in which is self-selected, also known as "masking" or "personality".

Subjective Temperament: Subjective behavior, which Worley's ID Profile identifies, is the inborn or genetic Temperament one has inherited from birth. The individual will always revert to and be more comfortable when they are functioning from their Temperament style. Their Temperament style is steady, stable, and consistent regardless of the environment.

What Temperament, psychological, behavioral, or personality classifications does Worley's ID Profile use?

Worley's ID Profile uses the standard ratings of other instruments: Introverted Sanguine, Sanguine, Phlegmatic, Melancholy, and Choleric. The Blends of the five Temperaments, are Introverted Sanguine-Phlegmatic, Phlegmatic-Introverted Sanguine, Phlegmatic-Sanguine, Sanguine-Phlegmatic, Melancholy-Phlegmatic, Phlegmatic-Melancholy, Choleric-Phlegmatic, and the Phlegmatic-Choleric. It is possible to have Temperament blends in all three of your Temperament Areas of Social, Leadership, and Relationship.

Your identification in each of the three Areas of Social, Leadership, and Relationship is determined by where your Temperament falls on a continuum of zero (0) introvert to nine (9) extrovert. Each of the three Areas of Social, Leadership, and Relationship evaluate in the two Regions of Demonstrated and Desired behavior.

What are the Demonstrated Score and Desired Score?

In each of the three Areas Social, Leadership, and Relationships there is a linear bar graph representation like this:

Demonstrated

| 0 | 1 | 2 | 3 | 4 | 5 | 6 | 7 | 8 | 9 |

| 0 | 1 | 2 | 3 | 4 | 5 | 6 | 7 | 8 | 9 |

Desired

An individual's scores will be reflected twice in each of the three Areas of Social, Leadership, and Relationships, one Demonstrated Score and one Desired Score for each of the six Regions. The Demonstrated Score indicates how the individual prefers to act toward other people. The Desired Score shows the person's preferred behavior from others toward them.

Can Worley's ID Profile be used in non-English speaking countries?

Yes! If there is someone to interpret the questionnaire for them. There is a danger of losing the meaning of some words, and the results could be negatively affected, thus rendering unpredictable results.

WIDP now is presently translated into English, Spanish, and Portuguese for Adults and for Youth (ages 6 – 16).

How many profiles can I purchase at one time?

Profiles can be purchased directly online within your own account. There is no minimum or maximum.

How often is the certification training offered?

Please contact our office for the training schedule dates, locations, and fees.

Where can I contact WIDP?

Worley's ID Profile
190 Bishop Road
Fitchburg, MA 01420-2993
1(978)400-5012
jwworley@comcast.net

Appendix B

REFERENCES AND ADDITIONAL READING

BOOKS

- **An Introduction To Theories of Personality,** B.R. Hergenhahn. PrenticeHall, New Jersey, 1990.

- **An Empirical Investigation of the Jungian Typology,** by Leon Gorlow, Norman R. Simonson, and Herbert Krauss. In Theories of Personality, Primary Sources, and Research, editors: Gardner Lindzey, Calvin S. Hall, Martin Manosevitz, Robert E. Krieger Publishing Company, Florida, 1988.

- **Dichotomies of the Mind: A System Science Model of the Mind and Personality,** Walter Lowen (with Lawrence Miike). John Wiley, 1982 ISBN 0471083313. A bizarre, but intriguing attempt to "correct" the MBTI's inherently 'F' focus to a 'hyper-T' perspective.

- **Facing Your Type,** George J. Schemel and James A. Borbely. Published by Typophile Press, Church Road, Box 223, Wernersville, PA 19565.

- **From Image to Likeness A Jungian Path in the Gospel Journey,** W. Harold Grant, Magdala Thompson, and Thomas E. Clarke. Paulist Press, 545 Island Road, Ramsey, NJ 07446. ISBN: 0809125528, 1983. This book deals with people's spiritual growth vis a vis personality type.

- **Gifts Differing,** Isabel BriggsMyers (with Peter Myers). Consulting Psychologists Press, 1980 ISBN 0891060111 (PB) 0891060154 (HB).

- **LifeTypes,** by Sandra Hirsh and Jean Kummerow, ISBN 0446388238 USA and ISBN 0446388246 Canada. Warner Books, Inc., 1989.

- **Manual: A Guide to the Development and Use of the Myers-Briggs Type Indicator**, by Isabel BriggsMyers and Mary H. McCaulley. Consulting Psychologists Press, 1985.

- **Please Understand Me, An Essay on Temperament Styles,** by David Keirsey and Marilyn Bates. Prometheus Nemesis Book Company, P.O. Box 2748, Del Mar, CA 92014 (6196321575). One of the more widely known books describing the Myers-Briggs Type Indicator. It includes a self-test (many do not consider it to be as good as the "real" MBTI test).

- **People Types and Tiger Stripes,** Gordon Lawrence. Available from Center for Application of Psychological Type, Gainesville, Florida. ISBN 0935652086. This book is written primarily to help teachers counsel students but is applicable for other related uses.

- **Portraits of Temperament,** David Keirsey. Prometheus Nemesis Book Company, P.O. Box 2748, Del Mar, CA 92014 (6196321575), 1987.

- **Prayer and Temperament,** by Michael and Morrisey. Other bibliographic information not known at present.

- **Personality Types and Religious Leadership,** by Oswald and Kroeger. Available from the Alban Institute, 4125 Nebraska Ave NW, Washington, D.C., 20016. Phone 18004572674. Other bibliographic information not known at present.

- **Psychological Types,** C.G. Jung, H.G. Baynes (Translator). Bollingen Series, Princeton U.P., 1971 ISBN 0691018138 (PB) 0691097704 (HB). This book (originally written in the early 1920's) inspired Briggs & Myers to create the MBTI test. If you have only read, Please Understand Me, then you will have some trouble making the correlation.

- **The real Please Understand Me**, from the horse's mouth (i.e., the daughter in the original mother/daughter pair). A good bridge between Jung and PUM, but no self-test included.

- **Type Talk**, Otto Kroeger, and Janet M. Thuesen. Bantam Doubleday Dell Publishing Group, Inc. (Tilden Press also mentioned.) ISBN 03852982859. An easytoread a book that gives profiles for all sixteen personality types.

- **Type Talk at Work,** Otto Kroeger, and Janet M. Thuesen. ISBN 038530174X.

- **Type Watch,** Otto Kroeger, and Janet M. Thuesen.

- **The Leadership Equation,** Lee Barr, and Norma Barr. Eakin Press, Austin, Texas. 1989.

- **The Measurement of Learning Style: A Critique of Four Assessment Tools,** Timothy J. Sewall, University of Wisconsin, 1986.

- **Using the Myers-Briggs Type Indicator in Organizations,** Sandra Krebs Hirsh. Consulting Psychological Press, Inc., Palo Alto, CA. 1985.

- **Working Together,** Olaf Isachsen and Linda Berens. New World Management Press, Coronado, CA. 1988.

PERIODICAL LITERATURE

- **Journal of Psychological Type,** The official research journal of the Association for Psychological Type, 9140 Ward Parkway, Kansas City, MO 64114.

- **The Type Reporter,** Susan Scanlon, Editor. For Subscription information, mail to 524 North Paxton Street, Alexandria, VA 22304. (703) 8233730. It comes out roughly eight times a year and costs $16 for a year's subscription. Recent topics include "Mistakes When Teaching Type," "Spending and Saving," and "Making Love."

- **Mental Measurements Yearbook (MMY).** Has lists of references to articles in peer-reviewed journals in which the MBTI test is used. Anthony DeVito gives an excellent review of MBTI in the 9th MMY, and two additional studies in the 10th MMY. The recently published 11th MMY does not include these. The MMY are available in the reference section of most college and university libraries.

Appendix C

GLOSSARY OF TERMS

Character Our family of origin, culture, and the environment in which we were raised determines character. Our character is usually defined between the ages of two to middle/late teens.

Choleric

A **Choleric** is quick to receive the information and process it. They devour the facts and are swift to conclude. Their fast action must not be confused with **"jumping to conclusions"** for they have handled the data which is available. This characteristic can cause other Temperaments much agitation and frustration. If not careful, the Choleric merely overwhelm those around them.

I. Probable strengths of a Choleric

A. Very determined and strong-willed.
B. Very independent.
C. They are visionary and adventurous to the point of leaving secure positions.
D. Is practical and happiest when engaged in a worthwhile project.
E. Is productive and will usually work circles around the other Temperaments.
F. Is decisive and can quickly appraise a situation and devise/determine solutions.
G. Has strong leadership tendencies.

II. Potential weaknesses/shortcomings of a Choleric

A. Usually cold and unemotional and the least affectionate.
B. Very self-sufficient and independent.
C. Is very impetuous, tends to start projects that he later regrets.
D. Domineering.
E. Is usually unforgiving and will carry a grudge forever.
F. Can be very sarcastic, blunt and cruel.
G. Can be angry and cause pain to others and enjoy the experience.

Demonstrated

Demonstrated is the Temperament a person expresses toward others and is observable. The Demonstrated Score indicates how the individual prefers to act toward other people. This Temperament can be observed and constitutes the image presented to others. The Demonstrated Score in each Area is the level of Temperament the individual feels most comfortable using to:

Get together with others	Demonstrated Socializing
Have his/her way with others	Demonstrated Leadership
Be close to others	Demonstrated Relationship

Desired

Desired is the Temperament that a person desires from others toward them. The Desired Score indicates the individual's preferred Temperament from others toward him/her. It is an indicator of the individual's inner needs and desires, which may differ significantly from his/her public image. The Desired Temperament in each Area is Temperament the person prefers others to use in their approach to:

Get together with him/her	Desired Socializing
Have their way with him/her	Desired Leadership
Be close to him/her	Desired Relationship

Extroverts

Extroverts are outgoing, social people who enjoy being around people most of the time and have a need and desire to be with people frequently if not always.

GAP

A GAP is the theory of the distance between the Demonstrated Temperament score and the Desired Temperament score.

Always be aware of the potential conflict with a profile G-A-P of four (4) or more in any of the three profile Areas.

The wider the G-A-P, the more anxious, intolerant, insensitive/sensitive, stressful, blunt, indifferent, cold, and driven the person will be.

Not only is this concept to be understood within your graph but also consider the G-A-P between yourself and others in each of the three Areas of Social, Leadership, and Relationship.

ID

In simple terms, ID (**WIDP**) is the subjective side of human Temperament, part of the person's original design at conception that is within us from birth and will remain throughout one's life.

ID The Division of The Psyche Associated With Instinctual Impulses and The

Satisfaction of Primitive Needs And Desires

Introvert

Introverted individuals are very rational people who need very little socialization and spend most of their time thinking out issues.

Introverted Sanguine

An **Introverted Sanguine** will process the facts and then not do anything with them unless others ask them. This Temperament will also set about questioning those they trust to see if the information and situation are correct from their perspective. This inaction is entirely in line with the other aspects of the Introverted Sanguine. They are not dense in cognitive skills, just unable to initiate action.

I. Probable strengths of an Introverted Sanguine

A. Highly relational but must be personally invited.
B. The most naturally gentle and kind of all Temperaments.
C. Have a real servant's heart.
D. Is a very diligent worker if praised or recognized.

II. Potential weaknesses/shortcomings of an Introverted Sanguine

A. Appears withdrawn and downbeat like introverts; yet desires to be an extrovert.
B. They are often alone and isolated because of their own non-assertiveness.
C. Is dependent on others to take care of him/her and to tell him/her what to do.
D. Becomes severely anxious when lack of recognition causes bitterness and resentment.
E. They are often depressed and are very sensitive to rejection.
F. Can be very manipulative and will use much indirect Temperament. Will usually check out all counseling advice with someone else.

Introvert/Extrovert

These people can function well in either environment as an introvert or extrovert.

Leadership Profile

The Leadership Profile identifies the individual's needs and desires for influencing others, making decisions, and assuming responsibilities. Needs may range from independence to dependence. The Leadership Profile helps answers the question, **Who maintains the power and makes decisions in relationships with this individual?**

Leadership: The next Area of the Temperament is called the **Leadership Profile.** Leadership deals precisely with what the title implies. How we control people and situations and how we allow individuals and situations to control us is demonstrated in the Area called Leadership. It is the decision part of our Temperament, which dictates whether we will be a leader or a follower (in general) in our life. Depending on which Temperament we are, leadership will dictate how we make decisions and who will be dominant in the relationship. The Temperament needs in leadership can range from total dominance of a relationship to being dominated by the other party in the relationship.

Melancholy

A **Melancholy** needs time to detail the incoming facts. They will retreat into their private world and analyze the situation. After this assimilation time, they are ready to make up their mind and usually have a clear understanding of the situation.

I. Probable strengths of a Melancholy

A. Usually very gifted --- more so than any other Temperament.
B. Is very analytical and is a hound for detail.
C. Is self-sacrificing and will work hard to meet deadlines will work around the clock.
D. Extremely self-disciplined.
E. A faithful friend and the most dependable of all the Temperaments?
F. They have strong perfectionist tendencies.
G. Is the most sensitive of all the Temperaments?

II. Potential weaknesses/shortcomings of a Melancholy

A. Tends to be moody, gloomy, and depressed.
B. Are naturally the most self-centered of all the Temperaments.
C. Is prone to be pessimistic, causing indecisiveness, for fear of being wrong.
D. Melancholy is the most critical of all Temperments.
E. They are touchy and thin-skinned; usually, need to be handled with kid gloves, and expects to be appreciated.
F. Is generally unsociable and needs time to warm up to people.
G. Is a very negative person.

Phlegmatic

A **Phlegmatic** will take their time and weigh it all out, dissect it and ponder the situation. After they scrutinize it, they will make the necessary decisions and be quite capable of doing so. This process will be less lengthy than that required for a Melancholy.

I. Probable strengths of a Phlegmatic

A.   Is usually calm and quiet, almost never becomes agitated.

B.   Is easy going --- most likable of the Temperaments.

C.   Phlegmatic are very consistent and dependable; is not prone to sudden change.

D.   Are usually objective, kindhearted, and sympathetic. Seldom conveys real feelings.

E.   Is usually humorous and enjoys a good joke.

F.   Efficient, organized, practical, and pragmatic.

G.   Is a born diplomat.

II. Potential weaknesses/shortcomings of Phlegmatic

A.   Phlegmatic often appears to be unmotivated.

B.   Tends to procrastinate more than the other Temperaments.

C.   Has a strong tendency to be selfish, and few people know it without the ability to recognize the trait in self.

D.   Usually the stingiest of the Temperaments.

E.   Tends to be the most stubborn of all Temperaments cannot change own mind (when unblended).

F.   Is indecisive in many areas because of not wanting to become involved.

G.   Has a fearful heart that keeps them from confrontation and decisions.

Sanguine

A **Sanguine** will not bother processing the information unless it is in simplified form. They cannot be bothered with that sort of activity no will their short attention span allow them the opportunity. They will be off to other people and situations quite quickly.

I. Probable Strengths of a Sanguine

A.   Is outgoing and is a super extrovert.

B.   Is responsive and likes to give hugs and handshakes.

C.   Is warm and friendly and is **a people person.**

D.   Is talkative and is a good conversationalist.

E.   Is enthusiastic and has no problems starting projects.

F.   Is compassionate and cries easily.

II. Potential weaknesses /shortcomings of a Sanguine.

A.   Tends to be disciplined to a fault.

B.   More emotional than everyone else except a Melancholy.
C.   Can be very impractical and disorganized.
D.   Can become obnoxious by dominating conversations.
E.   Tends to exaggerate, Sånguine invented fish stories.

Social Profile

The Social Profile identifies the individual's needs and desires for socialization, work, school, and other superficial relationships. The Social Profile helps answer the question, **Who is in or out of relationships with this individual?**
Social Profile: The first Area of Temperament is called Social, or perhaps it would be easier to think of it as socialization. The Social Profile is the Area, which dictates how you will interact with the world in general, in those situations such as parties, career, neighbors, and other circumstances, which bring you into contact with people. The Area of the Social Profile does not involve the deep, intense emotions of intimate relationships (these are in the Area called Relationship). The Social Profile deals with the surface relationships we encounter in our daily social situations. The Temperament needs of the social profile can range from involvement with many people to relationship with only a few selected individuals.

Another aspect of the Social Profile is the cognitive or intellectual functions of the Temperament. Why do we process the information we receive the way we do? Our Temperament in the Social Profile is the answer to this question. Each Temperament treats information in different ways. These are consistent with other aspects of each Temperament.

Password

An online password is generated when your account is initially created on the website. You will login initially with this password and then have the option to change it. Due to HIPAA regulations, the site will time-out after a certain amount of idle time and your password will be required again. There is a fee for needing to reset your password, so do keep it in a safe place.

Personality

Personality is the self-selected mask that people present to others. The mask is what they want you to see and is not who they are. The personality changes with each environment. The circumstances and who the audience is will determine what personality the person wants to present.

Profile: Corporations/Businesses

Corporations/Business Organizations: Worley's ID Profile Software is today's forerunner in human resource ingenuity. The state-of-the-art software gives organizations the tools to bring the psychological Temperament of its corporate members into harmony with organizational missions, goals and corporate visions. WIDP has **_unlimited_** applications in a corporate setting. Corporations can realize the return on their investment within days. Corporate executives, human resource directors, training consultants, corporate advisors, and business management consultants are profiting from the breakthrough benefits of WIDP Software.

Profile: Professional Counselors

Worley's ID Profile Software enables the counselors to quickly assess the individual's strengths and weaknesses, target potential conflicts, and develop sound therapeutic strategies for future counseling sessions. WIDP can help people achieve new levels of self-awareness, maximize their potential for fulfilled and balanced lives, and enjoy greater success in their interpersonal relationships.

Profile: Educational Institutions

Educational Institutions: Worley's ID Profile Software brings new meaning and perspective to all relationships founded in an educational setting. Immediate tangible strategies can be assessed (or available) for addressing dynamics of Temperament differences. WIDP provides highly effective approaches for even serious Temperament problems. Training is available for audiences ranging from one student to several hundred principals and school counselors.

By providing clarity and understanding of emotional and psychological needs and desires, WIDP brings together the evaluation process for teacher-teacher and teacher-student relationships.

Profile: Ministries/Clergy

Worley's ID Profile will assist pastors, youth leaders, elders, lay counselors, Sunday schools, superintendents, and teachers to effectively counsel members of their congregation. WIDP, after identifying and an individual's inner needs and desires, provides new revelation and understanding of oneself. WIDP will enable the individual, as well as the congregation, to capitalize on Temperament strengths and strengthen areas of weaknesses. Although WIDP is not a spiritual or religious evaluation, overall improvement of life will occur from understanding the results of this profile.

Profile: Family Insights Relationships

Worley's ID Profile is designed for families interested in improving their understanding. Family members use WIDP for adding insight to their knowledge of themselves and their loved ones, and for further developing people awareness skills. These skills contribute significantly to improved marriages, enhanced communication, and heightened awareness of the needs and desires of others, conflict resolution, relationship restoration, bridging generational gaps, and many other interpersonal situations.

Profile: Personal Insights

Worley's ID Profile is designed for individuals who want to improve their understanding of self and to maximize their potential for a fulfilled and balanced life.

With increased insight and self-awareness, these people enjoy greater success in interpersonal relationships.

Relationship Profile

The Relationship Profile identifies the individual's needs and desires in close relationships with family and friends. Needs may range from emotional intimacy with expressions of love with many people to isolation. The Relationship Profile answers the question, *How emotionally open or closed to relationship is this individual?*

Relationship: The third Area is called the Relationship Profile. Again, this is very clear by the title given. This Area of the Temperament determines how we want to love and receive affection from others and how we will provide love and devotion to others. The Relationship Profile is the area of the Temperament where the focus is one-on-one. The relationship is not a group function as are the Social Profile and the Leadership Profile. This Area deals with the more in-depth relationships, which we have in our life as opposed to the general social situations covered by the social profile.

In a nutshell, the Social Profile determines who is in or out of the relationship, Leadership Profile determines who maintains the power and makes the decisions in the relationship, and the Relationship Profile defines how emotionally close or distant the relationship is.

Temperament

Temperament is the inborn genetic makeup of who we are from birth and does not change like one's character and personality.

Temperament Blends

Temperament blends occur when some person's Temperament response renders any score that has a four or five in the combination of their profile numbers. See the examples below, which lists ALL the blends. There is only one Temperament that blends with other Temperaments, and that Temperament is the Phlegmatic.

WIDP　　　　　　　**Worley's Identity Discovery Profile (W I D P)**

W	Worley's	
I	Identify	Identify Your Inner Needs and Desires
D	Discovery	Dare to Become All You Can Be!
P	Profile	

WIDP Profile

A Temperament assessment report (5-11 pages) generated by the online WIDP Program from the 60 questionnaire responses of an individual.

WIDP User

WIDP User is the person who has registered for an online account and been Certified in one of the three Certification levels.

3,449 Combined Spreadsheet										
	Social		%	Leadership		%	Relationship			%
C/Cc	50	/ 0	1.45	415	/ 175	17.11	16			0.46
C/P	39		1.13	36		1.04	41			1.19
IS/Isc	202	/ 13	6.23	82	/ 26	3.13	243			7.05
IS/P	91		2.64	64		1.86	334			9.68
M/Mc	1355	/ 303	48.07	1084	/ 839	55.76	800	/	22	23.83
M/P	164		4.76	142		4.12	482			13.98
P	133		3.86	65		1.88	318			9.22
P/C	94		2.73	194		5.62	27			0.78
P/IS	120		3.48	17		0.49	223			6.47
P/M	274		7.94	249		7.22	265			7.68
P/S	152		4.41	12		0.35	176			5.10
S/Sc	345	/ 55	11.60	26	/ 4	0.87	362	/	71	12.55
S/P	59		1.71	19		0.55	69			2.00

APPENDIX D
REFERENCES & ADDITIONAL READING

An Introduction To Theories of Personality, B.R. Hergenhahn. PrenticeHall, New Jersey, 1990.

An Empirical Investigation of the Jungian Typology, by Leon Gorlow, Norman R. Simonson, and Herbert Krauss. In Theories of Personality, Primary Sources, and Research, editors: Gardner Lindzey, Calvin S. Hall, Martin Manosevitz, Robert E. Krieger Publishing Company, Florida, 1988.

Dichotomies of the Mind: A System Science Model of the Mind and Personality, Walter Lowen (with Lawrence Miike). John Wiley, 1982 ISBN 0471083313. A bizarre, but intriguing attempt to "correct" the MBTI's inherently 'F' focus to a 'hyper-T' perspective.

Facing Your Type, George J. Schemel and James A. Borbely. Published by Typophile Press, Church Road, Box 223, Wernersville, PA 19565.

From Image to Likeness A Jungian Path in the Gospel Journey, W. Harold Grant, Magdala Thompson, and Thomas E. Clarke. Paulist Press, 545 Island Road, Ramsey, NJ 07446. ISBN: 0809125528, 1983. This book deals with people's spiritual growth vis a vis personality type.

Gifts Differing, Isabel BriggsMyers (with Peter Myers). Consulting Psychologists Press, 1980 ISBN 0891060111 (PB) 0891060154 (HB).

LifeTypes, by Sandra Hirsh and Jean Kummerow, ISBN 0446388238 USA and ISBN 0446388246 Canada. Warner Books, Inc., 1989.

Manual: A Guide to the Development and Use of the Myers-Briggs Type Indicator, by Isabel BriggsMyers and Mary H. McCaulley. Consulting Psychologists Press, 1985.

Please Understand Me, An Essay on Temperament Styles, by David Keirsey and Marilyn Bates. Prometheus Nemesis Book Company, P.O. Box 2748, Del Mar, CA 92014 (6196321575). One of the more widely known books describing the Myers-Briggs Type Indicator. It includes a self-test (many do not consider it to be as good as the "real" MBTI test).

People Types and Tiger Stripes, Gordon Lawrence. Available from Center for Application of Psychological Type, Gainesville, Florida. ISBN 0935652086. This book is written primarily to help teachers counsel students but is applicable for other related uses.

Portraits of Temperament, David Keirsey. Prometheus Nemesis Book Company, P.O. Box 2748, Del Mar, CA 92014 (6196321575), 1987.

Prayer and Temperament, by Michael and Morrisey. Other bibliographic information not known at present.

Personality Types and Religious Leadership, by Oswald and Kroeger.

Available from the Alban Institute, 4125 Nebraska Ave NW, Washington, D.C., 20016. Phone 18004572674. Other bibliographic information not known at present.

Psychological Types, C.G. Jung, H.G. Baynes (Translator). Bollingen Series, Princeton U.P., 1971 ISBN 0691018138 (PB) 0691097704 (HB). This book
(originally written in the early 1920's) inspired Briggs & Myers to create the MBTI test. If you have only read, Please Understand Me, then you will have some trouble making the correlation.

The real Please Understand Me, from the horse's mouth (i.e., the daughter in the original mother/daughter pair). A good bridge between Jung and PUM, but no self-test included.

Type Talk, Otto Kroeger, and Janet M. Thuesen. Bantam Doubleday Dell Publishing Group, Inc. (Tilden Press also mentioned.) ISBN 03852982859. An easytoread a book that gives profiles for all sixteen personality types.

Type Talk at Work, Otto Kroeger, and Janet M. Thuesen. ISBN 038530174X.

Type Watch, Otto Kroeger, and Janet M. Thuesen.

The Leadership Equation, Lee Barr, and Norma Barr. Eakin Press, Austin, Texas. 1989.

The Measurement of Learning Style: A Critique of Four Assessment Tools, Timothy J. Sewall, University of Wisconsin, 1986.

Using the Myers-Briggs Type Indicator in Organizations, Sandra Krebs Hirsh.
Consulting Psychological Press, Inc., Palo Alto, CA. 1985.

Working Together, Olaf Isachsen and Linda Berens. New World Management Press, Coronado, CA. 1988.

PERIODICAL LITERATURE

Journal of Psychological Type, The official research journal of the Association for Psychological Type, 9140 Ward Parkway, Kansas City, MO 64114.

The Type Reporter, Susan Scanlon, Editor. For Subscription information, mail to 524 North Paxton Street, Alexandria, VA 22304. (703) 8233730. It comes out roughly eight times a year and costs $16 for a year's subscription. Recent topics include "Mistakes When Teaching Type," "Spending and Saving," and "Making Love."

Mental Measurements Yearbook (MMY). Has lists of references to articles in peer-reviewed journals in which the MBTI test is used. Anthony DeVito gives an excellent review of MBTI in the 9th MMY, and two additional studies in the 10th MMY. The recently published 11th MMY does not include these. The MMY are available in the reference section of most college and university libraries.

Made in the USA
Coppell, TX
20 June 2023